SAFE HARBOR

A WORLD WAR II NOVEL BY

GERHARDT ROBERTS

ALSO BY GERHARDT ROBERTS

The Wall Between Us

ACKNOWLEGMENTS

I would like to thank my wife, Sheila Roberts, as well as Jan, Elizabeth and Ruth for the many hours they invested reading and editing this novel.

CHAPTER ONE

B erlin. October, 1935.

ON A THURSDAY AFTERNOON Erich Reinhold discovered he was a Jew. At least according to the German government. Only moments earlier he'd been a carefree seventeen-year-old, in love for the first time. Up until that day, the miasma of racial hatred spreading across Germany hadn't touched him. Now it had and it didn't feel good.

ERICH AND HIS SWEETHEART, Nessa Baumgartner, strolled along a remote path in Berlin's Tiergarten, the popular urban park in the center of the city, on their way home from school for *Mittagessen*, the German midday meal. The labyrinth of peaceful tree-lined trails provided a welcome escape from the hectic pace of the German capital.

"I've always loved coming here," Nessa said. She smiled at Erich as they moved hand-in-hand past one of the many arms of the

Neuer See, a placid lake on which a bevy of swans circled. "Isn't it beautiful today?"

Yes, it was. From the canopy of trees above them, hundreds of multi-colored autumn leaves pirouetted down, some coming to rest on the water, where they bobbed about like miniature sailboats. But Erich was much more interested in Nessa than he was in taking in Mother Nature's display.

The path looped to the left, a secluded romantic detour for lovers, and Erich pulled Nessa behind an oak tree and kissed her. Then he kissed her again. And again.

Every kiss tasted like more, and he could have gone on indefinitely, enjoying the thrill of it all. Life in Berlin in 1935 was wonderful if you were young and in love. The disturbing events that sometimes took place in and around the city – those things were for older heads to worry about.

After a few minutes Nessa pulled away and slipped back onto the path, straightening her hair and adjusting her headscarf. "We need to pick up those groceries for your mother." She held out her hand to Erich. "Our parents will wonder what's taking us so long to get home."

"I suspect they'll guess," Erich said with a grin, "but you're right, we should get going."

Still he wished he could take as long as he wanted getting home, wished he could stay all day in the solitude of the park with the pretty, dark-eyed girl who'd come into his life. With a sigh he took her hand and let her lead him back onto the path.

They left the park, turned onto Lichtensteinallee, and did their shopping at a small open-air market halfway down the block – some cheese for *Abendessen*, an onion, some carrots. And apples for strudel. He kept one out for them to share and took a bite. Apples were his favorite fruit. And autumn with its crisp air and vibrant colors was his favorite time of the year.

They were about to move on when he noticed a large group of people standing around a public bulletin board. A banner across the top of the board declared: "The Jews are Our Misfortune."

At almost the same moment that his brows creased in puzzlement and his intuition warned him to look away, to move on, something else urged him to go over and look. He gave in to the urge. "Let's see what's going on over there," he suggested. He led Nessa across the street, and they pressed up against the crowd.

A poster entitled, "Who is a Jew?" seemed to be the center of attention.

Erich, peering through the sea of heads, skimmed the placard, which was full of small charts resembling family trees.

"What's all the commotion?" he asked a large man with dark hair and eyes.

The man, dressed in a brown, wool suit and hat, wrinkled his forehead. "The government has just posted a summary of the new Nuremberg Laws on Race and Marriage," he said, his breath sending a puff of mist into the cool air.

"I don't understand."

"Nobody does," the man said, shaking his head. "But I can tell you that this is not good." He raised a pudgy finger and pointed to a chart on the left side of the placard. "See those small white figures in that family tree?"

Erich nodded. The figures had been drawn to look like people.

"Aryans – the racially pure members of the Volk."

Erich looked at the man with a mixture of confusion and irritation. Ever since Hitler had taken power two years earlier, the adult world had wasted a lot of breath trying to convince Erich's generation that Germans were the master race and Jews were subhuman. But he didn't believe a word of it. To him all people were of equal value in God's eyes.

The man directed the couple's attention to the right side of the poster. "Now look at the black figures under that column entitled *Jews*."

Nessa scowled. "Black, evil. White, good."

"Exactly." The man glanced over his shoulder, then lowered his voice. "The black figures represent the non-Aryans – Gypsies and Jews and other undesirables."

Confusion flooded Nessa's face. "My grandparents were Jewish, and now they're considered undesirables?" she whispered. "They can't do that!"

"They can and they have." The stranger reached past the man in front of him and put his finger on one of the charts. "Here's your family tree, young lady. Since you have four Jewish grandparents, your parents are Jewish, which means you are Jewish."

Nessa scowled at the poster, her expression still puzzled.

"I didn't mean to upset you, dear," the man said. "My dear, departed wife always said I was entirely too blunt." He tipped his hat and bowed. "Allow me to introduce myself. Jakob Nussbaum, attorney at law." He winked at them and smiled. "Actually, I should have said, 'Jewish attorney-at-law,' although I don't advertise my Semitic roots. Not good for business these days, you know."

After introducing himself and Nessa, Erich returned his attention to the poster. The people in front of them had moved on, allowing them an unobstructed view. Eric ran his finger down the right side of the placard, and then turned to Nessa. "Here's my family tree. Three of my grandparents are Jewish. I'm a '*Mischling ersten Grades*.'" His hands closed into fists. "Mongrel of the first degree?" He knew exactly what a mongrel was, but thought the term only applied to dogs.

"Shocking isn't it?" said the attorney. "The Nazis consider you a Jewish mongrel, my young friend."

"No!" Erich spat, shaking his head as if denial could invalidate the new Nazi laws. "My family's Lutheran and so is Nessa's," he insisted. How did that make them suddenly Jewish?

"Well, according to the law," Nussbaum said, "we three are now members of the club of the unworthy. No membership card required."

Unworthy? The degrading word made Erich's stomach roil.

Suddenly, because he and Nessa had Jewish blood, they were worthless in the eyes of the government? He didn't care what the new race laws said. Their Jewish heritage didn't make them inferior, just more interesting than the bigots who had come up with the laws.

Erich's eyes fell upon the words: *Which Types of Marriages are Forbidden?* "Look at this," he said, pointing to the bottom of the poster. "A *Mischling* isn't allowed to marry an Aryan and two *Mischlings* can't even marry one another."

"And Jews can no longer marry one another or anyone else," said the attorney. "A sad time for you young people."

Nessa turned at Erich, tears working their way down her cheeks.

He hammered the fist of his right hand into the palm of his left. "I don't care what the government says, we're still going to get married when we're older," Erich insisted, taking her hand. When two people loved one other the way he and Nessa did, nothing could keep them apart.

"The way things are going? Only in your dreams, young man," Nussbaum said. He crossed his arms in front of his generous chest. "I used to raise purebred Rottweilers, you know. If some mongrel got into my kennels and impregnated one of my bitches, it would ruin her bloodlines. I'd have her put down."

"So, we're the mongrels who can't be allowed to reproduce and defile the Aryan bloodlines," Erich said bitterly, arriving at an epiphany.

"Precisely," whispered the attorney. "That would be *Blutschande*. Blood desecration is a serious offense in the eyes of the government."

Erich had had enough. He turned his back on the poster and led Nessa away, turning their steps toward home. As they passed along the narrow, uneven cobblestone streets his heart pounded so violently in his chest that it hurt. Yesterday he and Nessa were members of the German Volk and today they were mongrels, no longer worthy of sharing in the life of the German Nation. And yet he looked more Aryan than Jew – tall, with blond hair and pale blue eyes. A friend had once told him that his eyes were as blue and hypnotic as the Führer's.

A sign in a shop window they passed boasted, *"Deutscher Kaufmann"* – German Merchant. It was bordered by swastikas. But the larger sign next to it, Eric and Nessa now discovered, applied to them and their families: *"Juden nicht erwünscht!"*

Erich, the newly classified Jew, was indignant. "Jews not welcome!" he muttered through gritted teeth. "This is wrong."

"Stop clenching your teeth," Nessa teased. "Someone might think you're some sort of rabid mongrel."

He didn't laugh. Neither did she.

Only an hour earlier, Erich's life had consisted of going to school and playing soccer. His greatest challenge had been to see how many kisses he could steal from his pretty girlfriend. Now something cruelly ugly had descended upon them like a giant bird of prey, snatching them up and dropping them into the adult world of darkness they had been trying to ignore.

HE DROPPED Nessa at her home with a kiss goodbye and then doubled back toward his house, pulling his coat collar tighter around his neck to seal out the cold wind blowing in his face. Before long he reached the three-story brick house that had been home to three generations of Reinholds.

Two large linden trees dominated the front yard, their branches stretching out over the roof. Flower boxes in the windows sat empty, waiting for spring, when his mother would make sure they spilled over with color.

Erich shared the home with his parents and his paternal grandfather, Opa Gottlieb, whose wife, Hannah, had died right after he had returned from the Great War. Erich's maternal grandparents had emigrated to America, to the state of Ohio, in 1925. In 1933 his older brother, Karl, had gone to study in America and was living with them.

The family rarely used the front door, reserving it for guests. Erich circled around and entered through the back door, which opened into a small foyer. From there one could access both the kitchen and a narrow staircase, which led to the upper bedrooms.

Opening the door to the kitchen, he found his father, mother and grandfather sitting at the table. Their faces seemed somber. Had they been discussing the new race laws?

Erich put the groceries on the counter and kissed his mother on the cheek before taking a seat next to her. "The Nazis have hung posters all over town," he said. "According to the law we're Jewish now."

His mother, Greta, was a small, quiet woman. Today she was more so. She studied the floor tiles as if searching for a response to her son's announcement.

"I read about the Nuremberg Laws in the paper today," his Opa said. "There's really nothing to worry about. The Nazis bluster about getting rid of the Jews, but they'll eventually blow themselves out and everything will return to normal again."

"Papa, the Nazis sacked you two years ago because of your Jewish heritage," Erich's father, Franz, pointed out.

"I never liked being a government attorney, anyway," Gottlieb replied. "The job was stressful and thankless."

"I think we should seriously consider going to America," Greta said. "My parents would be glad to take us in."

A few months earlier Erich would have been intrigued by the thought of living in America with his grandparents, seeing his brother again. But not now, not when he had Nessa.

"Out of the question!" Gottlieb snarled. He smacked the thick oak table with his big hand, making Greta jump.

"Papa," Franz said, "according to the new laws everyone in this room has enough Jewish blood to make him an undesirable. The government no longer considers us Germans. It's dangerous and foolish for us to stay in Germany."

"The civilization that gave the world the genius of Beethoven and Bach would never turn on its own people," Gottlieb insisted, sounding like a defense attorney.

Franz gripped the arm of his chair so hard his knuckles turned white. "Papa, you're not listening!" He took a deep breath before continuing. "We're now aliens in our own country."

"Bah," Gottlieb scoffed. "Just ignore Hitler and his tirades. People will soon tire of his wild ideas. Leaders are like streetcars. If you don't want the one that just stopped, just wait a while – another one will be along soon."

The look Franz and Greta exchanged showed exactly what they thought of that remark.

"We're citizens of the Reich," Gottlieb continued. "I fought in the Great War – as did the Führer – and I have the crippled hand and the limp to prove it. I'm not leaving Germany because a pack of thugs has reclassified us."

"I think we should eat." Greta rose from the table and began dishing up the midday meal – her unspoken signal that the subject was closed. If only they could stop what was happening as easily as they could stop talking about it.

In the evening, as the sun set, all was peaceful in the house. Franz and Greta had gone out for the evening and Erich was where he spent most of his time: with Nessa. Gottlieb had the house to himself.

He loved this time of day. He could sit in the soft light of sunset and drink in the tranquility. It was his time to be alone with memories of his Hannah.

But tonight, he couldn't seem to connect with her. The discussion that afternoon in the kitchen had unsettled him, and his thoughts insisted on traveling back to the day he had been dismissed from his position as a civil attorney.

It was the last day of March, 1933. A Friday. Hitler had been in power only two months. As usual, Gottlieb had left home early to make his way to the courthouse on Alexander Square. The air was chilled, but the sun had broken through the morning fog and somewhere a robin was singing. All in all, it promised to be a pleasant spring day in Berlin.

Once at the office, he shed his hat and coat and changed into his judicial robe. For a moment he stood before the mirror on his wardrobe, adjusting his vestments. Then he combed back his thick grey hair and twirled the ends of his Nietzsche-mustache with his fingertips. From the mirror a pair of intense brown eyes scrutinized him from head to foot. Yes, he looked the part. He was ready to seize the day.

A few of his scheduled clients had already been in the waiting area when he had arrived, and he had quickly summoned the first one.

Shortly after ten – he had just finished his third consultation – he heard a commotion in the hallway outside his office door.

Then someone shouted, "All Jews report to the courtyard!" Gottlieb felt a nauseous panic, the kind of panic he had not felt since that day in 1917 in Verdun when French soldiers suddenly breached the German lines and began flooding into the German trenches.

He went to his office door and poked his head into the corridor. He spotted several stormtroopers escorting a group of judges, attorneys and office workers down the marble staircase.

"All Jews to the courtyard!" This time the voice was harsh and insistent.

Gottlieb stepped out into the hallway, approaching a stormtrooper holding a clipboard. "What's the trouble?" he asked.

The man pointed at him with his clipboard. "Sir, if you are Jewish it would behoove you to report to the courtyard at once."

"Jewish?" Gottlieb stammered. "I'm not Jewish." His parents had been Jewish, but had become Lutheran before the Great War.

The soldier stepped closer. "What's your name, please?"

"Gottlieb Reinhold."

The trooper ran his finger down the length of the piece of paper on his clipboard, his hand stopping halfway down the page. He looked up at Gottlieb. "Report to the courtyard."

Gottlieb was stunned, but decided it best to comply. He locked his office door and then headed down the stairs to the courtyard.

The scene that greeted him there was unlike anything he had ever experienced. Stormtroopers stood at the perimeters of the courtyard. Judges and attorneys in black robes, office workers clustered in small groups – all stood whispering nervously with one another. *Are all these people Jews?* Gottlieb thought. Many of them could have traded uniforms with the stormtroopers and passed for Aryans.

The troopers began circulating through the crowd, relieving judges, and attorneys of their robes. Gottlieb turned to speak with Amran Rosenthal, one of his colleagues, but before he could form the words, the same soldier who had ordered him to the courtyard was at his elbow.

"Sir," he said politely, "your office door is locked. May I please have the key?"

Gottlieb fished the key out of his pocket and handed it over.

The man gave a curt bow, clicked the heels of his highly polished jackboots, and disappeared.

"Do you have any idea what's going on?" Gottlieb asked his colleague.

Rosenthal scowled. "We are obviously being sacked."

"Sacked? Whatever for?"

"A few days ago Hitler fired all Jewish doctors from Berlin's hospitals. It looks like he's continuing the process with the legal profession." A wry smile crossed his face. "At least they're throwing us out with Prussian precision and propriety."

"But I'm Lutheran, not Jewish," Gottlieb protested.

"Yes," replied Rosenthal, "but Hitler's agenda has nothing to do with religion and everything to do with race. You once told me that both of your parents were Jewish, right?"

Gottlieb nodded slowly, sensing the onset of a migraine. "Which means I qualify as Jewish in the eyes of the government," he said, grabbing his forehead. "I never dreamed Hitler would go this far."

Rosenthal laid his hand on Gottlieb's shoulder. "Nor did I, my friend," he said.

A few minutes later the trooper returned with the contents of Gottlieb's wardrobe.

"Sir, may I help you out of your robe?" he asked.

"No, you may <u>not</u>!" Gottlieb shot back.

The soldier dropped the polite façade and declared in a voice that left no room for misunderstanding, "Sir, I must have your robe." Without waiting for a reply, he relieved Gottlieb of the garment, ripping the fabric in the process. He then handed him his coat, hat, and briefcase, which Gottlieb later discovered had been emptied of his case files. Then the trooper nodded curtly, clicked his heels and went through the same process with Rosenthal.

After every judge and attorney in the courtyard had been stripped of his vestments, after every non-Aryan had received his or her personal property, a stormtrooper mounted the courthouse steps. "Ladies and gentlemen," he said, "a word to the wise. If you leave now quietly and never again set foot on these premises, you have nothing to fear."

They had received their "*Hausverbot*" and could never again enter the courthouse voluntarily.

~

GOTTLIEB SHOOK his head in disgust. Sacked for having Jewish heritage! In the presence of his family he had tried to pretend that losing his job didn't bother him. But in reality, he felt violated.

Gottlieb took Hannah's picture from the table next to him. "Oh Hannah," he sighed, "how I wish I could have done something to prevent that war." How different things had been before the Great War. Life had been easy; they had been wealthy. Germany had been wealthy. Now, under Hitler's leadership, the future seemed uncertain.

"Maybe we *should* ..." His voice echoed in the darkness. He stopped himself before saying the word "emigrate." Doing that was out of the question – no matter what, they couldn't leave their homeland. Things would get better. They had to.

CHAPTER TWO

Berlin. Summer, 1936.

The streets of Berlin were awash in sunshine and swastikas. Hitler's Olympics were in full swing, and every magazine and newspaper in Germany was already celebrating the inevitable triumph of the German athletes at the Games.

The hustle and bustle of the New Germany was evident everywhere. Cars, trucks, buses, bicycles, electric streetcars, and motorbikes clogged Berlin's motorways, interspersed with foolhardy jaywalkers cutting through traffic. Open-air tour buses swarmed the city, each with a uniformed tour guide standing among the tourists, yelling into a megaphone to make himself heard.

Sightseers flocked the streets, eager to enjoy the Games and spend money. Good for shop owners, maybe even good for a pair of young German undesirables taking it all in.

Erich and Nessa had finished high school and now worked as apprentices at Morgenstern's Department Store, but today was their day off and they had taken the subway into the heart of the city to do a little window shopping.

The linden trees in Alexander Square, swaying in a warming breeze, had shed their canary-colored spring blossoms and now tilted their dark green leaves toward the sun. In the shadow of the trees, an old man sat on a bench playing the violin while a pigeon meandered about at his feet, both fiddler and fowl hoping for a handout.

Erich and Nessa strolled arm-in-arm through the square, past a clothing store and a hat shop, but it was the jewelry store that caught Nessa's eye. "Didn't that store used to have a 'No Jews' sign in the window?" she asked. Most shops had, before Hitler ordered them removed before the Olympics to create the façade of a tolerant and free Germany.

"I don't see the sign now," Erich said, leading her over to the shop's display window.

Nessa tapped on the glass with her finger. "I love that heart-shaped locket," she said.

"And I love you," Erich whispered. He pressed her against the window and kissed her, slipping his fingers into her thick, dark hair. She smelled of roses and the scent was more intoxicating than the port wine his family drank at Christmas. Nessa was the first girl he'd ever kissed – the only girl he ever wanted to. How lucky they were to have found one another.

She sighed. "Oh, Erich, I do love you. I wish we could go someplace where there's no hate and just forget what's happening in Germany."

He cupped her face in his hands and kissed her again. "Things will get better," he promised. "Don't worry. We'll get through this."

He stepped back and slipped his arm around her waist. "Come on. Your birthday's next week. I'll buy you that locket."

She shot a nervous glance through the glass door. "I don't think that's a good idea."

"Sure it is."

He opened the door and pulled her in behind him.

At the counter, a middle-aged couple, speaking in strong French accents, haggled with the shop owner over the price of a ring.

"Moment," the Frenchman said after a while, leading the woman to the end of the counter for a tête-à-tête.

Erich coaxed Nessa up to the counter. Behind it, leaning against the wall, he spotted the "No Jews" sign, which was patiently waiting to be re-hung once the Games were over. Well, the sign wasn't in the window now. "I'd like to see the heart-shaped locket in your display window," he told the shopkeeper, a haggard little man with a thick, black Hitler-mustache.

The man ignored his request, scowling at Nessa instead. He took in her olive skin, dark hair, and brown eyes, before jabbing a finger in her direction. "I don't sell to Jews," he spat, as if the young woman were leprous.

Nessa's face flushed. She took a step forward, returning the man's glare. "It might interest you to know that I'm Lutheran," she scolded.

"And I'm the King of Prussia," the man shot back.

Erich resisted the urge to reach out and grab the shopkeeper by his mustache, instead leaning into the man's face. "We're Germans and we're customers and we want to see that locket," he insisted.

The French couple had interrupted their discussion to watch the escalating altercation.

"And you ..." the shopkeeper hissed, the stench of beer and sausage on his breath, "I saw you through the window kissing this ... this Jew! Why on earth would an Aryan kiss a Jew?" he spat.

The French couple inched closer, straining to grasp the essence of the confrontation.

"We'll take that locket in the window," Erich demanded, slapping his wallet on the counter.

"Out!" the shop owner snarled, pointing to the door, his face a mask of rage. "Get out of my shop, now!"

"You can't do that," Erich protested.

"Oh, yes I can," the man insisted, his finger still leveled at the door.

Nessa tugged at Erich's arm. "Come on," she begged. "Let's go."

"Fine," he seethed. "We'll take our business elsewhere." He took Nessa's hand and marched to the door, flinging it open with a bang, somewhat disappointed that the glass didn't shatter from the impact.

The French couple left the shop right behind them, the woman flashing Erich a sympathetic smile as she passed. He smiled back, taking some satisfaction in the fact that his outburst had cost the shopkeeper a sale.

"Erich, you shouldn't have created such a scene," Nessa lamented.

"Well, it's wrong," Erich sputtered, his face still burning with humiliation. "Our money is as good as anyone else's."

"Not anymore, I'm afraid," The voice was succinct, like that of a lawyer's. Erich turned to see the same attorney they had met the previous fall. He wore the same brown suit and matching hat, which he doffed, revealing a head with only a few strands of dark hair.

"Herr Nussbaum," Nessa said. "It's nice to see you again."

"The pleasure's entirely mine," the attorney said, before furrowing his brow. "It would appear you had a less than satisfying shopping experience. I believe I can guess why."

Erich gave the shop window an angry slap, sending ripples through the glass. "I don't care what the Nazis say," he said, putting his arm around Nessa. "We're people, not animals." No law the government could ever pass would convince him that people with Jewish blood were less than human.

Nussbaum raised an eyebrow, before placing his hand on Erich's shoulder. "This is the New Germany, where bloodlines matter, my young friend."

Erich didn't reply. He was too busy glaring at the shop owner through the window, who returned his dirty look and shook his fist.

Nussbaum cleared his throat nervously and glanced at his watch. "Well, I've got to get to the office. The Nazis haven't shut down my practice yet, and I intend to earn as much money as I can before they decide I'm no longer worthy to work." He stepped closer and lowered his voice. "I would advise you to keep a low profile, my young friend," he told Erich. "There are more effective ways to deal with the Nazis than public outbursts, you know." He pointed down the street. "My office is just around the corner. Kirsch Strasse, number 21. I offer more than just legal advice," he added with a wink.

"What other kinds of advice do you offer?" Nessa asked.

Nussbaum shrugged. "You'd be surprised," he said cryptically. He gave a curt bow, turned on his heel and was gone.

"What on earth was that all about?" Nessa wondered.

"I have no idea," Erich said, shaking his head and steering her in the opposite direction. He was in no mood for riddles. "Come on, let's get out of the hot sun."

They moved along under the shadow of a row of sycamore trees before stopping in front of a secondhand shop. In the window hung a painting of a little boat harbored in a lagoon. Palm trees lined the shore, laughing children ran along the sandy beach. A small, rectangular brass sign attached to the bottom of the picture frame bore the words, "Safe Harbor."

Nessa sighed. "I'd love to climb into that picture and escape all this. Do you think we'll ever reach our safe harbor?"

"Of course," Erich assured her, leading her away from the shop. One of his father's uncles, an old sailor had once told Erich that a ship in harbor was safe. "But that's not what ships are built for," his uncle had added, "they're meant to carry us to adventure." He'd shaken a gnarled finger at Erich, before continuing. "Never be afraid to put out to sea and face danger," he advised. "God will always guide your ship." *This is probably not the moment to share that advice with Nessa,* Erich thought.

A few meters down the street, a red balloon on a string bobbed toward them at eye level. It was covered with swastikas and attached to a young boy, who was attached to his mother's hand. As they pushed past Nessa and Erich, the boy chanted, "Everything changes, everything passes, even Hitler and his masses." The mother yanked the boy's arm, hissing "hush!" before hurrying the child away.

Erich watched as mother and son disappeared into the crowd. *If only we could wish the Führer away as easily as that.*

Two days later Erich was back at Alexander Square, hoping to find a jeweler more interested in his money than his heritage. It was evening, almost closing time for most shops. The people he passed looked content, purposeful and liberated. A woman hurried past, carrying a treat from the bakery. A mother and her grown daughter walked arm-in-arm, window shopping, their voices full of exuberance and hope. A man left the tobacconist, calling a cheerful "see you next week" over his shoulder. Everywhere Erich looked he saw smiles. Even he was smiling until he saw two men raise their right arms, greeting one another with an energetic "Heil Hitler," before stopping to chat.

The Führer was Germany's hero. He had saved the nation from the hopelessness and unemployment of the previous decade. The Fatherland was enjoying a fresh start. Everything was in order, everything was under control, and if a few Jews had to suffer so that Germany could take her place in the new world order, so what? Germany was strong again and the Volk were confident that their new Reich would last for centuries.

Maybe it would. If it did, what would this new Germany look like for people such as Erich and his family, people who had been pushed to the edges of society?

Well, we haven't been completely pushed out yet. Berlin has plenty of jewelry stores, Erich assured himself. He'd try that one across the square.

He found it empty except for the shopkeeper. Above the counter a ceiling fan churned sluggishly. From the wall behind the counter a portrait of the Führer glowered at Erich. *Hitler,* Erich surmised, *had probably never smiled in his life – not even as a baby.*

The shop owner seemed to recognize his young customer as a kindred Aryan. His arm shot up. "Heil Hitler!"

Erich raised his hand a few centimeters and nodded, all the while feeling guilty for even acknowledging the offensive greeting. What had been wrong with just saying "*Guten Tag*"?

He leaned over the counter and studied the jewelry on display. "I'm looking for a locket for my girlfriend. Silver. Heart-shaped."

"We have several she might like," the man said, reaching into the display case and then laying three lockets on the counter. "These are on sale during the Olympics." He placed a nicotine-stained forefinger on the locket in the middle, which was embossed with a swastika. "Your sweetheart might especially like this one. Every Aryan girl should have one. He handed it to Erich. "Look inside."

Erich opened the locket and frowned.

"A color picture of the Führer on one side," the shop keeper continued, "and on the other side a space to put your picture. Every time your sweetheart opens it, she'll see the two men she loves most."

Erich laid the swastika locket face down on the counter and picked up one of the others.

The man drew closer, his breath reeking of nicotine. "I'll even give you my Aryan discount," he said in a low voice, as if inviting Erich to participate in a conspiracy.

"Thank you," he managed, smiling vaguely.

"We Germans have to stick together, you know," said the shop-keeper. You wouldn't believe how many Jews have tried to sneak into my shop since I took down my 'No Jews' sign."

"I can only imagine."

"I can smell Jewish blood a kilometer away. Do those parasites really think they can come in here and put one over on me?"

How would you like a 'Mischling' to bust that sign over your bigoted

Aryan head? Erich forced himself to tamp down his ire and picked up the third locket. "I'll take this one. With a silver chain."

"You have exquisite taste, my young friend. Your girlfriend will be very pleased."

The shopkeeper placed the locket in a small box, wrapped it, and handed the package to Erich.

He paid and thanked the man. "*Wiedersehen,*" he said, turning to go.

"Heil Hitler."

Never!

~

The next afternoon, Erich and Nessa strolled along a remote path through the Tiergarten, as they so often did.

"It's so peaceful and romantic here," Nessa said.

Erich smiled to himself. Nearly every time they came to the park Nessa repeated the same words. He led her to a bench under an oak tree and took a small package from his pocket after they sat down. "This is to prove that I'll love you always. Happy Birthday."

She tore open the wrapping and opened the small box to reveal the locket. "Oh, Erich. It's beautiful."

"Just like you," he whispered, making her blush. "I wish I could afford a ring."

"Don't worry about that," she said, putting a hand to his cheek. "This is perfect. But how were you able ...?"

"I found a way. Open it."

She opened the locket to find Erich's picture inside. She smiled and threw her arms around his neck. "I'll wear it next to my heart forever! Here, help me put it on." She gave him the necklace and turned her head, lifting her hair from her neck.

He draped it around her, secured the clasp, then kissed her neck, catching a whiff of her perfume. She let her hair fall back down and looked up at him, fingering the locket. "Thank you."

How he loved those eyes. Brown with small greenish flecks. And those lips. They were beautiful, but it was kissing them that intoxicated him. "If you really want to thank me, you can give me a kiss," he teased.

She smiled and leaned in toward him and he stroked her lips lightly before kissing them, their softness intensifying his passion.

Suddenly, a shriek shattered the tranquility. "Kill the Jew! Kill the *Stinkjude!*"

Nessa's gave a start, her smile crumbling, and Erich put a protective arm around her.

A group of boys in *Deutsches Jungvolk* uniforms crashed out of the bushes. Waving sticks shaped like swords, they stormed past, chasing a boy wearing a black shirt. They circled a tree and then scampered back past them in the other direction, lashing out at the boy in black with their make-believe weapons. When their prey darted back into the bushes, his pursuers laughed and bent over, putting their hands on their knees to catch their breath.

"What in the world are you boys doing?" Erich demanded.

"We're playing a game," one of them informed him, still panting. "It's called 'Kill the Jew.' We made it up ourselves."

The look Nessa shot Erich revealed what she thought of their game.

Erich was also disturbed, yet a little intrigued. "How does the game work?"

"One of us puts on the black shirt," said another boy, the only dark-haired one in the group. "He's the Jew. Then the rest of us chase him." He pointed with his sword into the bushes where their quarry hid. "That boy in the bushes is the Jew. Once we corner him, we beat him with our swords until he yells, 'Stop, stop, I'm a *Stinkjude.*' It's great fun."

"Unless you're the one being beaten," Nessa scolded. "Why on earth would you want to play a game like that?"

"Because we want to make Germany *judenrein*. Only when we

have cleansed the Fatherland and the world of Jews can we live in peace. Getting rid of the Jews is what the Führer wants."

"How old are you boys?" Erich asked.

"Eleven," said the first boy, pretending to run someone through with his sword. "We're in the German Youth. In three years' time we can join the Hitler Youth," he added proudly.

The "Jew" darted out from his hiding place and fled for his life. "Get him!" his tormenters screamed. "Kill him! Kill him! *Stinkjude! Stinkjude!*" They stormed off after their prey and were soon out of sight and out of earshot.

"There go the perpetuators of Hitler's Thousand Year Reich," Erich lamented. "If they knew you're Jewish and I'm a *Mischling*, they'd take their sticks to us."

Nessa shook her head. "Hitler keeps saying that Germany needs more living space. If he has his way, those boys will soon be dying for him on some battlefield."

"Did you have any friends in the League of German Girls?" Erich said, steering the conversation away from talk of death.

"My best friend, Irmgard," Nessa said. "She had hair the color of honey and pretty blue eyes. She got to go to summer camp where they sang songs around campfires and hiked in the woods. When we were alone in Irmgard's room, she'd let me try on her uniform. I'd admire myself in the mirror and then close my eyes and imagine myself joining her and the other girls on their adventures."

Erich shook his head. "All so innocent sounding."

"Even if I could have joined the League, my parents would have never allowed it. They hate everything Hitler stands for." Nessa smiled sadly as if recalling a cherished memory that had forever slipped out of reach. "When I wore Irmgard's uniform, I didn't think I looked any different than any other German girl. Of course, these days the government doesn't even consider me a German girl – just some kind of untouchable."

Erich knew the feeling. He gave her hand a comforting squeeze, then smiled and began nibbling on her ear. "I hope I don't contract some horrible disease doing this."

She pulled away and held up a scolding finger. "I was trying to be serious, Herr Reinhold."

He drew her back to him and slipped an arm around her waist. "So, in all seriousness, do you still see your old friend, Irmgard, Fräulein Baumgartner?"

Nessa's shoulders sagged and she shook her head. "No. One day I stopped by her house to return a book she'd lent me. Her mother answered the door and snatched it out of my hand. 'The Führer doesn't want my daughter associating with Jews,' she said, and slammed the door in my face. A lot of people hated my family because of our Jewish heritage long before the Nuremberg Laws were enacted."

"I'm sure Irmgard still wanted to see you anyway."

"She did. When I walked down the front steps after her mother yelled at me, I saw Irmgard in an upstairs window waving to me. She was crying." Worry flooded Nessa's face. She leaned her head on Erich's shoulder. "Erich, what's going to become of us?"

"Whatever happens, I'll always be here to protect you, I promise." He hoped he'd be able to keep that vow.

CHAPTER THREE

September, 1938.

The elevator ascended toward the sixth floor of Morgenstern's Department Store, lurching and rattling as it went. The lift-boy announced the floors: "Second floor, furniture, third floor, linens and sundries, fourth floor, women's and children's apparel, fifth floor, men's wear, sixth floor, administrative offices."

When Erich and Nessa got out on the sixth floor, silence greeted them. Fräulein Braun, the chatty receptionist, murmured a quick *Guten Morgen* and then lowered her eyes to her telephone console. They passed half a dozen other employees. Curt nods. Blank stares.

"Something's wrong," Erich said to Nessa. "I'm going to find out what's going on." He gave her a quick kiss on the cheek. "I'll see you after work."

On the way to his desk in Accounts Payable, he stopped to talk to Hilda, one of the secretaries, who was typing furiously and scowling. "Why's everyone so glum?"

"A few minutes ago, the Gestapo took Herr Morgenstern away again."

For a moment Erich struggled to inhale. "What?"

"They said he *might* be back. It's not right what they're doing to that poor man."

Erich continued on to his desk and took a seat. He drew a deep breath and then called Nessa at her desk. "Herr Morgenstern's been picked up by the Gestapo again."

"Oh, no," she gasped. This was the fourth time in the past year that the owner of the store had been taken to Gestapo Headquarters.

"When I know more, I'll call you back," Erich promised.

It was close to noon when Herr Morgenstern returned. His mouth was bleeding and his business suit rumpled and torn. Twenty minutes later the office intercom crackled. "Attention. Staff meeting in the conference room at two p.m. Attendance is mandatory."

For Nessa the wait was nearly unbearable. It seemed like days had passed before it was time to head to the meeting.

The double doors to the conference room had been propped open and as Nessa entered, the din of concerned voices greeted her. She spotted Erich near the back and slipped into the seat he'd saved for her.

Herr Morgenstern was in front at a desk conferring with his department heads. He had changed into a clean suit, but his lower lip was swollen and one eye blackened.

Nessa turned to Erich. "You didn't call me back. Have you heard anything?"

He shook his head. "Nothing concrete. I didn't want to worry you with rumors."

"What kind of rumors?" she asked, searching his face for an answer.

"Everything from closing the store to selling it to Aryans."

Nessa's body stiffened at the word "Aryan." It didn't trouble her in the least that she and Erich had been excluded from that group of racists, she just wanted them to stop deciding who was worthy to be a German citizen and who wasn't. Where would all of this end?

She sighed and shot a glance at the clock on the wall. Exactly two o'clock.

With German efficiency the double doors in the back of the room swung closed and Herr Morgenstern rose. "Ladies and gentlemen," he said, "thank you all for coming this afternoon. We have some serious matters to deal with this afternoon."

It was as quiet as a tomb as Morgenstern continued. "As you know, the government has been pressuring Jewish businesses into selling to Aryans. During the past year I've managed to hold the administration at bay, but now it's clear that our grace period has run out."

Bad news was coming. Nessa bit her lip in an effort not to cry.

Morgenstern went on. "As you know, the Gestapo has taken me to their headquarters on a number of occasions because of my unwillingness to cooperate with government demands. Today they gave me a non-negotiable deadline for selling the store."

It wasn't hard to guess what kind of encouragement they'd used. How had the poor man managed to resist for this long?

Morgenstern surveyed the room. "My dear employees, here at Morgenstern's we are family and it is always tragic when a family breaks up." His voice cracked and he cleared his throat, trying to regain his composure. "Unfortunately, I must announce that effective next Friday, September 30th, our store will be Aryanized."

Surely everyone there had known this moment would eventually come. Still the announcement sent a shock wave through the room. Hilda, who was sitting on the other side of Erich, threw her hands over her face and began sobbing.

"We do have some reserve funds," Morgenstern continued, "and we will be paying each of you through next Friday. Thank you for your years of loyal service. You have truly been a blessing." He surveyed the room again, forcing himself to smile. "This meeting is adjourned."

"What will I tell my parents?" Nessa asked Erich as they filed out. "We need the extra money."

"The new owners won't be retaining any of us," Erich said. "We're tainted goods. They would never hire Jews or anyone who has been working for Jews. The way things are going, we'll be reduced to robbing Aryans in back alleys." Erich's dark smile disturbed Nessa more than losing her job.

Erich glanced at his watch. Two minutes past five. It had been three hours since Herr Morgenstein had announced the sale of the store. He slid his ledger into the top drawer of his desk and locked it.

Moments later he was standing in front of Nessa's desk. "Are you ready to head home?" he asked.

She nodded and rose from her chair.

They stood in silence while they waited with a few other employees for the lift to arrive. Soon the bell sounded, and the elevator boy slid the door open. As they descended, the only sound inside the elevator was the voice of the lift-boy announcing the floors.

They exited the store onto Alexander Square. The late summer sun was making its way toward the western horizon and shadows were beginning to move across the plaza. The cobblestones were still warm, but as usual the square was breezy, and Nessa pulled her scarf tighter around her neck.

A group of stormtroopers had stationed themselves outside the store and were passing out flyers. One was Gerhardt Schmutze. Erich knew this man. He'd been a bully as a boy. Now he'd found the perfect outlet to occupy his primitive brain.

One of the troopers shoved a leaflet into Erich's hands. A glance at it confirmed his suspicions:

"Do Not Buy From Jews! Jewish Treachery Will Not Go Unpunished!"

Erich's first impulse was to crumple the flyer and throw it in the trooper's face, but that could expose Nessa to harm.

Schmutze had spotted him, his expression darkening the way black clouds hiding the sun spoil a pleasant day. "Reinhold," he said, his face a mask of hate. "I should have known you'd be here, giving your money to Jews. You might look Aryan, but from what I hear you have more Jewish blood running through your veins than King Solomon."

Eric refused to dignify Schmutze's remarks with an answer.

"Don't you know that this department store is a monopoly?" Schmutze continued. "It has put hundreds of honest German merchants out of business." His litany sounded rehearsed.

"We're not shopping," Erich said, his heartbeat accelerating. "We work here."

Schmutze scowled at him, and then at Nessa. "You're working for Jews?" he said with undisguised disdain.

Erich wasn't about to give the hateful man the satisfaction of knowing the store would soon be taken over by Aryans. He would discover that fact soon enough. "That's right," he replied. "Herr Morgenstern hires people based on their qualifications, not their ancestry."

Schmutze ignored the remark. He turned his attention to Nessa, looking at her the way a spider scrutinizes the insect caught in its web, just before pouncing on it. "Is she Jewish?" he demanded.

Erich felt sweat trickling down his back. He opened his mouth to speak, but his enemy cut him off.

"She *is* Jewish, isn't she?" Schmutze said triumphantly, pleased with his revelation.

"And what if she is?" Erich snapped. He felt his throat tightening with rage.

Schmutze thrust his forefinger toward his adversary, stopping just short of Erich's face. "You and Morgenstern and that Jewish slut with you are what's wrong with Germany today," he spat. He punched his forefinger onto one of his flyers. "And like it says here, your sins will not go unpunished."

Nessa took a step toward Schmutze. "Sir, we have no quarrel with you," she said, attempting to defuse the confrontation.

Schmutze motioned to the other stormtroopers lurking behind him. "Well, we have a quarrel with your kind," he said. He turned back to Erich. "Reinhold," he barked, "clear out and take your Jewish slut with you before my friends and I forget that we're German gentlemen."

Erich's hands curled into fists. How easy it would be to punch that hateful face.

Nessa tugged at his arm. "Erich," she pleaded, "let's go. This can't end well."

She was right, of course, he reminded himself. He put his arm around her and led her across the square, the stormtroopers' taunts pursuing them all the way to the stairs that led down to the subway station.

Once they reached the platform, Nessa looked over her shoulder as if expecting to see the stormtroopers following them. "Who was that horrible man?" she asked.

"Gerhardt Schmutze. We used to be friends."

"He certainly doesn't seem very friendly these days."

The train lumbered into the station and they joined the throng of commuters squeezing onto it, finding two seats together in the back of the last car.

"Gerhardt and I had a falling out three years before I met you," Erich told her.

"Go on," she urged.

"One day I saw him stealing some rolls from the bakery and reported him to the owner. Of course, he got in trouble and blamed me. A few weeks later his father's business failed, and he blamed it on Jewish competition. So did Gerhardt. My family's Jewish heritage gave him even more reason to hate me, of course." Erich looked out of the train window into the darkness, clenching his jaw. "It's always nice to have a scapegoat to blame your problems on."

"I'm just glad no scapegoats were harmed today."

Erich smiled at her. "You were very brave back there."

She smiled back. "I can't always be a timid mouse."

"I like mice." He snuggled his face into her neck and kissed it.

"I didn't want to see them hurt you."

"I wouldn't have wanted that either," he joked. "I rather like my face arranged the way it is."

She kissed him. "So do I."

The train slowed and jogged to the left. "Here's our stop," Nessa announced. "Time to tell our parents we're unemployed."

Poor Nessa. After high school she'd been denied entry into nursing school because of her race – the school had been conveniently full – no room for one more student – and now this.

Of course, it was no better for him. His future was looking equally bleak. He'd been so proud of being able to contribute to the family income. Now he felt like a failure, even though losing his job wasn't his fault.

At home he found his family in the living room, his mother finishing up some mending, before making *Abendessen,* his father and grandfather reading the paper.

"How was work?" his mother greeted him.

"Nessa and I lost our jobs today," he said and sank onto a nearby easy chair. "Morgenstern's is closing next Friday."

"Oh, dear," Greta moaned, her face drawn.

Gottlieb lowered his paper. "Well, we knew it was coming. The authorities have been pestering Morgenstern to Aryanize the store for over a year now. I'm surprised he held out this long."

"Business has pretty much dried up anyway," Erich said. "The newspapers won't accept our ads anymore and most of the store catalogues we mailed out were sent back to us." Almost every returned catalogue had the words "Return to the Jew" written on it.

"That makes sense," Franz said sadly. "No Aryan would be caught dead with a catalogue from a Jewish department store in his home."

"And today the Gestapo took Herr Morgenstern away and beat him," Erich said.

Greta shook her head. "I'm sure they've threatened his family too."

"All is not lost," Gottlieb told Erich. "We always need help at the bookstore. You can have your old job back."

"Until they make us Aryanize our store, too," Franz conceded. "I'm expecting visitors any day."

"Well, life is change and we must change with the times," Gottlieb asserted, trying to put a positive spin on a desperate situation. "If we have to sell, we'll get jobs at an Aryan bookstore."

And who did his grandfather think was going to hire them? Erich felt short of breath, suddenly overcome by a nearly paralyzing fear that the country he loved was hurtling toward a disastrous fate from which there was no return.

CHAPTER FOUR

Paris. November 6, 1938.

The young man studied the cinema posters at 17 Boulevard de Strasbourg. American gangster films with men waving .45-caliber pistols. "Dead End." "Each Dawn I Die." Titles which seemed to describe his life.

To his left, a stairway led up to l'Hôtel de Suez, one floor above the cinema. He turned away from the posters and climbed the steps to the front desk of the hotel.

"A room, please," he said, his French tainted with a German accent.

The woman behind the counter looked him over. "Identification papers," she said, no expression in her voice. She did not turn him away when he shrugged and told her he had no papers – in Paris there was always room for any German illegal who had managed to escape Hitler's Germany.

The man scrawled a fictitious name in the hotel register: Heinrich Halter.

In his room he threw his few belongings, including his expired Polish passport, onto the bed. Taking a seat at the table by the window, he lit a cigarette and watched the Parisians moving past, some strolling, some hurrying. He studied their faces. How would they react when they heard of the bloodshed for which he would soon be responsible?

He took out his wallet and removed the postcard he had just received from his family near Hanover. Hastily scribbled words: "Deported from Germany to Poland. We have no money." Had the Nazis beaten them, abused them? Was his family starving, reduced to begging? The words on the postcard had begotten a sense of helplessness, which had given birth to rage. And his rage demanded retaliation.

Heinrich slept poorly that night, tortured by thoughts of what had befallen his family and obsessed by what he planned to do once the sun rose the next day.

Slowly the night drained away and at half past seven in the morning he got up to prepare himself for his mission. But how did one prepare oneself for the unthinkable?

His wallet contained another postcard, imprinted with a photograph of himself, a purchase from an itinerant photographer at a street fair. The handsome, dark-haired man in the picture had sad eyes and wore a three-piece suit and a tie; a cigarette dangled from his left hand.

On the back of the postcard he scribbled a desperate message. "With God's help," he wrote in Hebrew, and then continued in German. "My dear parents...I must protest in a way that causes the world to listen...I beg your forgiveness." But how would going through with his plan possibly benefit his family?

He addressed the card to his Uncle Grynszpan in Paris and placed it back in his wallet.

Heinrich gathered his belongings and slipped into his overcoat before descending the short staircase to the street. The weather was unusually mild. As he walked along, he realized that his overcoat would be unnecessary, even uncomfortable, but it would be convenient to conceal what he planned to purchase at the gun shop.

Around half past eight, barely an hour after waking, he entered the shop.

The shopkeeper at the counter looked up at him from some paperwork without speaking.

"I need a gun," Heinrich announced.

"And why do you need a gun?"

"For protection. I often transport large sums of money to the bank for my father," he lied.

"What kind of gun?"

Heinrich recalled the weapons the American gangsters had brandished on the cinema posters. "A .45." In his mind he saw his intended victim collapse to the floor after the first shot. Then he saw himself fire into the man until the gun was empty.

The voice of the shop owner interrupted Heinrich's musings. "A .45 is much too large and unwieldy," the man said. He laid a small five-shot revolver on the counter. "This one is lightweight and perfect as a concealed weapon."

Heinrich picked up the gun, commanding his hand not to shake.

The shopkeeper took the weapon from Heinrich and then grabbed some bullets from under the counter. "It's easy to load." He demonstrated. "Just slide in the bullets like this. Then aim and fire." He removed the bullets and returned the gun to Heinrich. "I'll just need your identity papers and 235 francs for the gun and the bullets."

Heinrich held his breath, then handed the man the money and his Polish passport.

The foreign passport didn't surprise the proprietor. His face remained expressionless while he filled out the registration form. "You'll need to take the weapon and this form to the police station to complete the registration." He pointed toward the door. "Go left and then take the first right. It's just a few blocks down."

Heinrich left the shop and turned dutifully in the direction of the police station. He stopped at a restaurant where he ducked into the restroom to load the gun. He pointed it at himself in the mirror, pretending to dispatch his prey.

The Metro station was not far from the restaurant and the German Embassy was only a short ride.

Near the embassy he passed a newsstand. Headlines told of thousands of Polish Jews in northeastern Germany deported to Poland. In his mind's eye he saw his family beaten and then dumped over the border like so much rubbish. He clenched his fist around the gun in his pocket. *Being a Jew is not a crime. We are not dogs. We have the right to exist on this earth.*

Next to the newsstand a young couple shared breakfast at a sidewalk café. They smiled into each other's eyes, more interested in one another than in their food. *Would they still be smiling when they heard about the Jewish Avenger?*

Getting into the embassy was not difficult. "I wish to deliver a very important document," he lied to a guard.

The guard held out his hand without looking at Heinrich. "Identification papers?" Heinrich handed him his Polish passport and the guard gave it a cursory examination. Then he returned it and pointed to his right. "Through that door."

Inside, Heinrich repeated his lie to another staff member.

"You will need to speak to our envoy Ernst vom Rath. Please have a seat. I will see if he is available."

Heinrich waited. He lit a cigarette. American gangsters always had cigarettes dangling from their lips. Cigarettes settled their nerves and gave them courage. He fingered the gun in his pocket. His hand was sweaty and trembling. *What am I doing here? This is insane.* He glanced toward the exit. *I should leave.*

He put out his cigarette and began to push himself to his feet.

Footsteps. The staff member had returned. "Secretary vom Rath will see you now."

Heinrich was ushered into vom Rath's office. The German diplomat sat behind a desk in the corner of the room. He gestured toward an overstuffed leather chair. Heinrich sat down on the edge of it.

Vom Rath leaned forward and held out his hand. "So, let's see this document."

Heinrich jumped to his feet, gun leveled at the German. "You filthy kraut, here's the document."

The diplomat lifted both hands, palms facing his assailant. He rose from his chair, eyes wide in disbelief. "Was? Nein!"

Bang!

The first bullet whisked past vom Rath and smashed into the wall, the concussion effect causing the German to reel and stumble back onto his chair. "Bitte..."

Bang!

The second bullet also missed its target.

A third bullet strafed vom Rath's shoulder, sending blood spatter and shreds of flesh onto the wall behind him. He yelped and grabbed the wound, blood oozing between his fingers. He tried to stand.

Bang! Bang!

The fourth bullet sailed past vom Rath, but the fifth slug penetrated the German's gut. He convulsed and listed to his left, his shirt dripping blood. Groaning, he staggered to his feet and stumbled out the door into the corridor, both hands clutching his abdomen, blood pulsating onto the floor.

Heinrich, ears ringing, once again leveled the gun at his enemy through the open door and squeezed the trigger several more times. *Click! Click! Click!* He looked quizzically at the weapon and then at the serpentine trail of blood that led from the diplomat's desk and into the hallway, where two embassy officials held the wounded man.

Heinrich dropped the gun, the price tag still dangling from the trigger guard. He fell back onto the easy chair, making no attempt to flee.

"I did this to avenge my parents," seventeen-year-old Herschel Grynszpan, alias Heinrich Halter, later told French police. The postcards in his wallet explained the rest.

CHAPTER FIVE

November 8, 1938.

The melancholy strains of Beethoven's *Sonata Pathétique* filled the Reinhold's living room. Nessa and Erich nestled together on the sofa, holding hands; him thinking ahead to walking her home, and wondering how many kisses she'd let him steal. Erich's parents, Franz and Greta, sat in chairs near the window, and grandfather Gottlieb relaxed next to them in an easy chair.

As the last tones of the sonata faded, Franz smiled. "It was nice to listen to Radio Berlin for once without all the political ranting."

But the reprieve was short-lived. Beethoven's despondency yielded to the angry voice of the announcer. "Yesterday, Herschel Grynszpan, a Jew, shot German diplomat Ernst vom Rath in the German Embassy in Paris. Our attaché's condition is grave. Terrorist attacks by Jews will not be tolerated. There will be consequences."

Franz switched off the radio. "That's terrible."

"It sounds like they're blaming every Jew for one man's crime," Nessa said in disgust.

"The Nazis can't blame this on Jews," Gottlieb insisted, picking up a newspaper. "The Jewish community had nothing to do with what happened. Anyway, it sounds like they've apprehended the shooter. Case closed."

Franz shook his head. "The radio announcer said there would be consequences for the shooting. That can only mean that more German Jews will suffer."

Nessa's hands began to tremble, and Eric took them and cupped them in his.

"Relax, Franz," Gottlieb said. "If we keep a low profile, we'll be fine. Don't make waves and you won't end up on the government's radar, that's my motto."

"We're already on the government's radar, Papa," Franz said. "A couple of 'gentlemen' stopped by the bookstore today. They ordered me to do a complete inventory. We're being forced to sell."

"Oh, no! What will we do now?" Greta said, searching her husband's face for an answer.

Franz shook his head in resignation. "Without the income from the bookstore, we'll have to live off our savings. Once that money is gone, we'll be penniless. We really should think about leaving Germany before we have no money left to finance the trip."

Nessa and Erich exchanged terrified looks. Even with all the horrible things that were going on, Erich didn't want to leave. If he did, he'd never see Nessa again. "God will protect us, won't he, Opa?" he asked hopefully.

"Of course. And when this madness ends, we'll buy back the bookstore," Gottlieb said. "This can't go on much longer."

But what if it did? Erich wondered. He also wondered if his Opa was beginning to lose his mind. Sometimes the things he said didn't make sense. How could they possibly buy back the bookstore if they ended up penniless?

～

At dusk the next day, Gottlieb sat in the living room in his favorite chair, relishing the idea of a quiet, peaceful evening alone. Franz and Greta were visiting their friend Frau Sturm, who lived next door to Nessa and her parents. Erich had volunteered to complete the inventory of the bookstore in preparation for the sale. Gottlieb had no illusions about how much work Erich would get done, since Nessa had volunteered to help. No doubt there would be a bit of inventory and a lot of canoodling going on, but Gottlieb could hardly blame the boy for being in love.

The old man sat in the dim light in his blazer, listening to Radio Berlin, arms akimbo directing the music of Mozart's *Requiem*. The sun dipped below the horizon and soon a streak of moonlight began working its way across the living room. He reached through the moonbeam and took his wife's photograph from the table next to him. A vibrant middle-aged woman with intense, mysterious eyes smiled at him, eyes that seemed privy to a wondrous secret which only she knew.

"Oh Hannah," he sighed, "how beautiful you were." His mind went back to the day he had returned from the Great War. Food shortages had ravaged Germany during his absence and Hannah had wasted away to a shadow, but she had made sure that their son, Franz, had gotten enough to eat.

And then she had contracted influenza, her body burning with fever and convulsing with chills. Their physician had prescribed medication, but it hadn't helped. Gottlieb had nursed her for weeks, not caring whether the disease would also do violence to him.

After that she had come down with pneumonia: labored breathing, delirium, her lungs filling with fluid. Gottlieb was holding her, kissing her, bathing her in his tears at the moment she had left him – snatched out of this world forever. The doctor had called her pneumonia an act of mercy. It had ended her suffering, he had said.

Halfway through the requiem, the caustic voice of the announcer intruded.

"The Volk mourn the death of German diplomat, Erich vom

Rath, who was taken from us today. He was shot two days ago by a Jew at our embassy in Paris. Dr. Goebbels has called this terrorist act 'cowardly.' He and our Führer share the outrage and indignation of the German people in the face of this inexcusable act of violence. The murder of our diplomat will not go unavenged."

There was further talk of a Jewish conspiracy to overthrow the German government – such rubbish! Just as Gottlieb was about to turn the radio off in disgust, the station returned to the requiem. He relaxed, closed his eyes, and soon dozed off.

The mantel clock was striking seven when a commotion in the front yard startled Gottlieb out of his dreams. He got up and spotted a group of men coming up the front walk. They rushed up the front steps and began pounding and kicking on the door. "*Sofort aufmachen!*" they screamed.

No, he wasn't about to open the door!

Propelled by fear, he rushed to the phone and called the police station. "*Herr Wachtmeister*, a gang of men is trying to break into my home!"

A bored voice asked, "Are you Aryan?"

"I'm a German citizen who..." The voice on the other end of the line was gone, leaving only a dial tone.

Before Gottlieb could hang up, the front door burst open and sailed into the foyer, crashing onto the floor with an ear-splitting bang. The intruders spilled into the living room brandishing hammers and lead pipes. Most of them were stormtroopers, drunk and swilling from beer bottles.

"Get out of my home," Gottlieb commanded. "I've called the police! They're on the way!"

No one believed his lie. An inebriated, sweaty stormtrooper approached him. "Are there any Jews here?" he demanded.

Gottlieb stared at him, speechless.

"Are you deaf, old man? Answer me! Do any Jews live here?"

Gottlieb glared at the man. "I'm a German citizen and a citizen of the Reich. Leave my home at once."

Another trooper stepped up and hurled the old man against the wall. "You're neither a German nor a citizen of the Reich, you impudent Jew swine!" Spittle exploded from his mouth as he spoke.

"Gerhardt? Gerhardt Schmutze?" Gottlieb stammered. "Son, you remember me, don't you? You went to school with my grandson, Erich. Your father and I used to meet at the pub to play cards. We were good friends."

"Jews and Aryans can't be friends, you swine," Schmutze seethed. "You Jews are the reason my father lost his business. We're here tonight to settle that score."

"I had nothing to do with that!"

"Don't play the innocent! You know exactly what I'm talking about." Schmutze spat on the floor. "My father was barely able to earn enough money to feed us. Then that Jew Morgenstern opened his department store down the street. Father's shop lasted two weeks before he had to shut it down. All because of Jews like you and Morgenstern undercutting honest Aryan merchants and bankrupting them."

"But I was an attorney, not a merchant."

"Shut your mouth!" Schmutze punched him hard in the stomach. Gottlieb dropped to his knees, then crumpled onto his face.

The men began smashing the living room to rubble, while Radio Berlin played Beethoven's *Pastoral Symphony*. Schmutze yanked the radio cord from the wall and hurled the radio through a window, sending shards of glass flying into the front yard. The vandals threw down the china cabinet, which crashed into a bookcase, sending books and china spilling onto the floor. Other men toppled lamps and vases, dashing them to pieces underfoot.

Gottlieb, clutching at consciousness, rolled over onto his back. His eyelids fluttered as he watched the men race upstairs like an army of poltergeists. He heard them ransacking the upstairs rooms. The grandfather clock Hannah had given him for his thirtieth birthday sailed down the staircase like an out-of-control toboggan and exploded into kindling.

After the demonic horde ran out of things to destroy upstairs, they stormed back down to the first floor. For a moment they stood panting and sweating in the living room, laughing and congratulating one another. One of them pulled Gottlieb to his feet. He reeled, barely able to support his own weight. *God in heaven, this can't be happening.*

Schmutze took two photographs from the mantel that had somehow escaped destruction and shoved them into the old man's face. "This looks like Erich and his father. Where are they?"

"I have no idea," Gottlieb lied.

Schmutze jabbed his forefinger into Gottlieb's chest, making the old man wince. "You Jews always lie, don't you? You can't help it. It's part of your nature. Rest assured, old man, we'll find them. In the meantime, you're going on a little excursion to the police station at Alexander Square. We've reserved a luxury suite there just for you."

Gottlieb was dizzy, nauseous, and afraid, but his pride wasn't done resisting. "I'm going no such place. I'm a citizen of..."

Schmutze cut him off with a hard clout in the face, making the old man's ears ring. The taste of blood began to fill his mouth.

The intruders dragged and prodded Gottlieb through the frame that once held his front door, and out to the sidewalk.

"What are you people doing?" a man on the sidewalk said. It was Gottlieb's childhood friend and next-door neighbor, Josef Mühlberger.

"We're taking out the trash, old man," Schmutze snarled. "If you know what's good for you, you'll go home."

"Josef, my friend, do go home," Gottlieb pleaded.

"Better take your friend's advice," Schmutze said.

Josef stepped back and Schmutze hurled Gottlieb into the back of a flatbed truck parked at the curb. Several other bruised and disheveled men already sat on the truck bed. Two of them were neighbors.

"Welcome to the party," one said around a swollen lip.

This was no party Gottlieb wanted any part of. He could only pray his captors didn't track down the rest of his family.

Gottlieb had been right in surmising that a young man's fancy would concentrate more on love than on business. Taking inventory could never compete with nibbling on Nessa's neck.

"Erich, we have work to do," she scolded, pushing him gently away.

"I am working," he said, pulling her to him and biting gently at her ear.

"What about the books?"

"I'm busy, I don't feel like reading right now." His lips moved toward hers.

"Erich, we need to finish the inventory. It's already dark and I'd like to get home before it gets too late."

"We've been counting books all afternoon," he mumbled against her mouth. "I need a little rest and relaxation."

A kiss stifled any response Nessa might have given.

The sound of shattering glass from outside the store made Erich jump and he pulled away from Nessa. "What was that?" He gave her a quick kiss. "Stay right there," he said. "We'll resume where we left off when I get back."

He ventured out onto the cobblestoned street. A large group of swaggering stormtroopers wielding crowbars rushed along Hirsch Strasse in his direction. He stepped back to let them pass, somewhat surprised that they completely ignored him.

Near the end of the street one of them yelled, "Here's one!" They smashed the display windows of Rosenblatt's Appliance Shop, then kicked in the front door and continued their destruction inside. Whoops of excitement mixed with the harsh sound of appliances crashing onto the street as the men launched radios, vacuum cleaners, even a stove through the broken windows onto the street.

A sick panic stabbed at Eric's insides. A moment later Nessa stepped out onto the street next to him. "What in the world is going on?" she gasped, her face taut with terror.

"Those men are demolishing Rosenblatt's shop," he replied, trying to comprehend why.

A minute later the vandals slowed their pace and then stopped. They returned to the sidewalk to stand in groups, smoking and laughing. One of them had tucked a radio under one arm and a toaster under the other. "That takes care of my Christmas shopping for this year," he bragged. The rest of the men roared their approval.

Then, for a few minutes they played soccer in the street with a mop bucket they had found in the store, before tiring of their fun and moving on, their laughter ringing through the streets.

In the distance Erich heard more glass shattering and then even more. "Something terrible is happening," he said to Nessa. "We need to get home!"

He locked up and they hurried down the street toward the subway station at Alexander Square. When they entered the plaza, they saw gangs of stormtroopers demolishing almost every store on the square.

"Good Lord," Erich whispered. "Has all of Berlin gone mad?" *Are they going to destroy the entire city?*

"They're ignoring some of the stores," said Nessa.

She was right. "They're only going after Jewish businesses!" Erich realized. He whirled around. Morgenstern's was still intact. From where they stood, he could read a large sign in a well-lit display window that boasted: "Morgenstern's Department Store is Now Weinlig's. Now Under Aryan Ownership."

"Of course," said Nessa. "Morgenstern's is no longer a Jewish business. They're going to leave it alone."

"Which means our bookstore is safe, since it will soon be Aryanized," Erich said. But part of him wished the stormtroopers would destroy it. That would be fitting retribution for the Aryans who had offered his family next to nothing for their business.

"Why aren't the police trying to stop this?" Nessa asked, pointing to the police station. Several policemen, arms folded across their chests, leaned against the station house, watching the mayhem.

"I'm guessing they've been ordered not to interfere."

He looked across the square at one of the demolished Jewish businesses. A crude banner had been draped across the front of the building. It read: *"Revenge for the murder of vom Rath. Death to international Jewry."*

"Erich, let's go," Nessa whispered. "I'm scared."

So was he. He pulled her closer and folded her into his coat. They crossed the square quickly and descended into the subway station. It was practically deserted, of course. Nearly everyone else was above ground, either creating mayhem – or watching it happen.

They were relieved when the subway arrived and whisked them away from the devastation and madness. But the relief was short-lived. They arrived in their suburb to find the streets and sidewalks strewn with their neighbor's heirlooms and memories. In the light of the street lamps they steered around furniture, china, pictures, a baby bassinet. Shards of glass from shattered mirrors reflected a thousand-fold the agony of ransacked lives. Disheveled men slumped on their front steps, faces in their hands. Mothers wept; babies wailed. Two keening women attempted to revive a man lying outstretched in a yard, blood pouring through his beard and onto his black velvet evening coat.

Suddenly a look of terror distorted Nessa's face. "I've got to get home." She broke into a dead run.

Worried for what she might find, Erich took off after her. His concern increased as he saw that vandals had plundered nearly every house they passed – except those belonging to Aryans.

As Nessa raced ahead of Erich, almost out of her mind with fear, she tripped half a dozen times over the clutter that littered the sidewalks. Arriving at her home, she stopped, letting out a scream of horror. Erich soon stood next to her, gaping at what had, only hours earlier, been a clean, orderly residence. Most of the windows had been smashed and almost all of the living room furniture lay in the front yard.

Frau Sturm, a friend of both the Reinhold and Baumgartner families, stood at Nessa's front door sweeping a path through the rubble.

"Frau Sturm," Nessa wailed, unable to take another step. She dug her fingers into her hair and gaped at the carnage. "My parents! Where are my parents!"

Frau Sturm hurried down the front steps and slipped her arm around the young woman's waist. "Come over here and sit down, dear." She motioned to a chair that had landed intact on the sidewalk. She took a deep breath and took Nessa's hands. "I can't make this easy, so I'll tell you outright. They've taken your father away."

Nessa jumped up. "Taken him away! Why? Where?"

"To the police station on Alexander Square."

Nessa grabbed Erich's arm, squeezing it so hard that he winced. "We have to go there!" she screamed. "We have to go right now!"

Before he could speak, Frau Sturm caught Nessa's arm. "Nessa, sit down." Nessa sank back onto the chair, her lips quivering as Frau Sturm continued. "Child, your mother is gone."

"Gone? Gone where? The police took her as well? Why?"

Frau Sturm pointed to the house and took another deep breath. "The stormtroopers who did this...they hit your mother. She fell and hit her head. She's dead."

"Mama!" Nessa screamed, jumping up and running into the house.

Erich sprinted in after her. Nessa's mother lay on the floor. Frau Sturm had shrouded the body in a white linen sheet. A large red stain had spread across the linen, outlining Ruth Baumgartner's facial features in shimmering crimson. Nessa fell onto the body and began to wail. She probably would have stayed there indefinitely if Frau Sturm and Erich hadn't coaxed her to her feet after a while and led her into her bedroom.

Erich cleared a path through the rubble to her bed and settled Nessa under the covers. He sat on the bed, stroking her hair until she fell asleep.

In the meantime, Frau Sturm phoned a funeral home. The funeral director was sympathetic and promised to come by that evening to take away the body.

All the while Erich kept wondering what had happened back at his house. What horror would he find there? He called home. After his mother spoke a timid "Hello," he explained what had happened at Nessa's.

He could hear tears in his mother's voice. "Oh, Erich, tell Nessa we're so sorry. How is she doing?"

"She's sleeping now. I want to stay here with her."

"Yes, you must. Best not be wandering the streets tonight."

"Is everything all right there?"

"They've been here also. They've taken your grandfather away," she finished, her voice catching on a sob.

"Taken him? Where?"

"We think he's at the police station at Alexander Square."

"I really should come home."

"No, no, stay with Nessa."

"But Opa ..."

"There's nothing to be done tonight with madness everywhere. Papa will fetch him tomorrow and bring him home."

"Then Papa's okay?"

"Yes, but our home is in ruins."

Just like their lives.

CHAPTER SIX

Gottlieb and his partners in misfortune cowered in the back of the truck as it roared through the dark Berlin streets. The vehicle lurched at break-neck speed around narrow corners and the two-dozen prisoners on the truck bed clung to the sides of the vehicle and to one another to avoid being catapulted out onto the street. *What's the rush?* Gottlieb thought. *Will they give our jail cells away to someone else if we show up late?*

Their hosts, a handful of stormtroopers, bellowed out "Germany Awake," forcing their captives to join in. When the prisoners' enthusiasm for singing waned, the truck screeched to a halt and the soldiers employed their rifle butts and riding crops to restore their captives' zest for vocalizing. "Sing, you Jewish swine!"

"Germany awake from your nightmare.
Jews have no place in your Empire.
Jews have made our land impure.
Aryan blood will e'er endure."

As they sang, Gottlieb studied the faces of his fellow prisoners. *How many of us with Jewish heritage bled for our Fatherland in the Great War? And now we're the enemy! Surely this is a demons' chorus.*

Once they arrived at the police station at Alexander Square, the soldiers pushed, pulled, and prodded their victims off the truck, barking orders with voices hoarse from singing. Their tormentors then shoved them across the courtyard and into a narrow passageway lined with iron doors.

Halfway down the corridor a guard yelled, "Halt." Another guard forced his way through the crowd of captives to cell 137, the jangling of his key ring echoing in the passageway. Once the cell door was open, the guards bullied their prisoners inside, banging the door shut and locking it. In the dim light Gottlieb stumbled against a small cot, and nearly fell.

The new arrivals took a few moments to introduce themselves, "Since we may be cellmates for a while," one said.

Several of the men squatted on the cot and others on the floor. For the rest of them it was standing room only. Gottlieb leaned against a dank wall and took inventory of the amenities. "A cot with no blankets, one stool, and a chamber pot. One chamber pot is hardly adequate for this many of us."

"This isn't exactly the Hotel Excelsior, in case you hadn't noticed," a man called Aaronsohn scoffed.

Gottlieb lit a match. Scrawled on the walls, in French, German, and Russian, were the tirades and confessions of generations of former prisoners. "It's good to be home," Gottlieb read aloud. He shook his head. "That poor soul must have spent a lot of time here."

"Dear mother, forgive me," another inmate read.

"What does this say?" asked Aaronsohn.

They assembled in front of two lines written in Russian. None of them could decipher the message, and after a few moments they gave up and drifted into the corners of the cell.

"I'm still trying to figure out why we've been arrested," Gottlieb complained, standing on tiptoes and peering out the barred window into the dark night. "We're German citizens, not a bunch of criminals!"

"Haven't you been paying attention?" Aaronsohn said. "They beat us and insulted us all the way here. It's obvious. We're no longer welcome in Germany."

"I pay no attention to insults spat by crude, sweaty, unwashed halfwits," Gottlieb retorted.

"Well, those halfwits are the people in charge now, my friend," Aaronsohn sneered. "Welcome to the New Germany."

At that remark Gottlieb's stomach shifted uncomfortably. He closed his eyes and pressed his fingertips against his throbbing temples. This couldn't be happening. Were Germans really turning against other Germans?

He heard the guards screaming at a group of new arrivals as they prodded them down the corridor and past his cell to their accommodations. Had Aaronsohn been right? In the New Germany were the lunatics in charge of the asylum?

Gottlieb and his cellmates decided to try to get some rest. Most of the men lay down on the cold, damp floor, but the younger men insisted that Gottlieb and three other older men sleep on the cot. They squeezed onto it like so many sardines. The cot was lumpy and smelled of urine, but Gottlieb was too exhausted to care. He snuggled into the mass of bodies and closed his eyes, thankful for the body heat of his bedmates, but all the while wondering how his family was. What had befallen them?

∾

What took place all over Germany that night, November 9th, 1938, was a deadly turning point for German Jews and, ultimately, for multitudes of European Jews. After the fact, the Nazis called it *Kristallnacht*, The Night of Broken Glass.

∾

The next morning Erich brought Nessa home to his house, where his mother took over, comforting her with coffee and a listening ear.

After a breakfast of *Brötchen*, cheese and sliced ham and a quick change of clothes, Erich was ready to go with his father in search of Opa and Nessa's father. "I know it's hard to believe right now, but we'll get through this," he told Nessa. "Mother will stay with you while Papa and I fetch your father and my grandfather. Will you be all right?"

Nessa gave a weak nod. He kissed her, then he and his father left the house.

On their way downtown the crunch of broken glass accompanied their every step. The possessions and memories of so many Jewish families lay shattered and discarded on Berlin's streets and sidewalks. "Aryan Shoppers" looted half-demolished homes and shops. Other Germans stood by, stunned, watching the thieves. Still others hurried past, eyes cast to the ground, faces somber.

The Alexander Square Police Station loomed above them as Erich and his father climbed the steps leading out of the subway station. The noise of traffic assaulted them. Streetcars, trucks and cars rumbled past, interspersed with bicycles and men pushing carts. The clock on the police station's tower read ten past nine. Debris and glass still littered the sidewalks; pedestrians steered carefully around the rubble strewn across the plaza.

A large crowd of people, whose relatives had apparently been dragged away the previous night, milled about the entrance of the police station.

"Let's see if that policeman over there can tell us anything," said Franz.

Erich followed his father across the street to where an overwrought officer paced nervously in front of the station, removing his hat frequently and raking his fingers through his hair.

"*Herr Wachtmeister*," Franz said, "we're hoping to visit two gentlemen who were arrested last night. We..."

The policeman cut him off. "No visitors at this time. *Hat keinen Sinn*. It's senseless for you to wait. The people you want to see have already been transferred to Sachsenhausen. Or soon will be."

Erich's body stiffened. "Sachsenhausen?" he said. "The concentration camp? Whatever for? What laws have they broken? Last night a bunch of criminals hauled away my grandfather and my fiancée's father." His voice was approaching a scream. "I demand to know why they're being detained!"

The officer was in no mood to elaborate. "Young man, I've told you all I know." He pointed to the door behind him. "Now move along unless you want to end up in a jail cell."

Bewildered, Franz and Erich moved away and started across the square.

Two well-dressed women passed them. "It serves those stinking Jews right," one of them said. "*Rache ist doch süss, nicht wahr?*"

Revenge is sweet? Revenge for what?

"Well, young man, we meet again," a voice behind Erich said. "And obviously, once more under not so pleasant circumstances."

Erich turned to see a familiar looking heavy-set man. "The attorney!" he said, astonished.

"Today I'm merely a fellow sufferer." The man held out his hand to Franz. "Jacob Nussbaum, attorney-at-law. Glad to meet you."

"Franz Reinhold, Erich's father."

Nussbaum reached out and shook Erich's hand. "I saw you talking to the policeman over there at the station." He smiled. "I asked myself, 'Where have I seen that angry young man before?' Then I remembered – it was two years ago during the Olympics. A shopkeeper had just thrown you out of his jewelry store."

Erich reddened. "You have a good memory."

"A valuable asset when one's an attorney," Nussbaum said. He pointed across the square at the police station. "Did they scoop up your family members as well last night?"

"My grandfather, Gottlieb," Erich said. "And my fiancée's father."

"Sorry for your loss."

"They're not dead yet," Erich protested, although he secretly feared the worst.

"One of your relatives was taken, too?" Franz asked the attorney. Nussbaum's brows dipped. "Yes, my brother, Jeremiah. The worst part is not knowing what they've done with him. What kind of a country allows thugs to destroy your place of business and abduct your family members?"

Germany. Erich pointed toward the police station. "I suppose you tried talking to that policeman by the door."

"He was no help," Nussbaum said. "When I asked him a question, he didn't say a word – just looked at me as if I had two heads. I would have gotten more information out of a fish. Did he tell you anything?"

"Yes. The detainees are probably on their way to Sachsenhausen," Franz said.

"Then Jeremiah is lost," Nussbaum said, almost under his breath.

"Your brother and my father might come back," Franz insisted. "We can't give up hope."

"Clinging to hope is good," Nussbaum replied. "Taking action is better." He looked over his shoulder and then lowered his voice. "There are those of us ..." He stopped and looked around again. Then he reached into his pocket and pulled out some business cards, giving one each to Erich and Franz. "My office address and phone number are on those cards. If you want to do more than stand by and hope that the Nazi cancer goes away, if you want to fight it, contact me."

"Fight it, how?" Erich asked.

"I have connections in the underground. I can arrange for you to disappear under the surface of everyday life. Many Germans, especially Jews, have already taken me up on my offer. From the shadows we stand against the Nazis."

Franz stared at the man in disbelief. "Fighting against the Nazis is insanity, unless you have a death wish."

"You have to die of something," Nussbaum said, with a fatalistic shrug. "One might as well die doing something worthwhile." He gave them a grim smile and tipped his hat. "Now, if you'll excuse me, I have work to do." He took a step in the opposite direction, then turned around. "Oh, and by the way, I also give legal advice if the need arises."

Franz watched the attorney disappear around a corner. "You've met that man before?"

"A couple of years ago."

"He's a dreamer," Franz said. "His schemes won't amount to much. Trying to combat what's happening in Germany is madness. Or suicide."

As Erich and his father moved on, crunching through the rubble, they encountered an old man surveying the ruins of a leather goods shop. The man shook his head and said to them, "This is no longer Germany. The people who did these things are not Germans."

Expressing such contempt publicly was dangerous. Members of the Volk had disappeared for less. "Lower your voice," Franz cautioned. "You never know who might be listening."

The man spat on the ground. "Did you know they burned the synagogues last night? Would you think that Germans would ever desecrate holy places?"

"Only mad men would do that," Franz murmured, as the three of them watched a group of men laden with clothing emerge from a partially demolished shop.

How do you know about the synagogues?" Erich asked.

Surely this man had to be mistaken.

The man grunted. "I spent the night with a friend over on Fasanen Strasse. Around midnight we heard a terrible row in the street. We scrambled out of bed to the window and saw the synagogue on fire. People in the streets were shouting and dancing around like a bunch of druids." He spread his arms out. "And what did the police do about the arson? Nothing! They just stood there like statues, watching. Dozens of firemen stood with their backs to the flames, hosing down the buildings around the synagogue."

"Probably to keep the fire from spreading to Aryan property," Franz said a frown.

The man spat again. "Animals, that's what they are."

Erich heaved a sigh. "Let's go home, Papa."

They picked their way through the sea of debris and shattered glass, Franz kicking at a broken bottle on the sidewalk. *"Scherben bringen Glück."* he said cynically.

"Tell me the story again about how broken glass brings good luck, Papa."

"It's an old superstition. Who knows how old? The day before we got married your mother and I announced a 'Polterabend.' It's a wedding tradition that involves making as much noise as possible on your last day of freedom. Our friends showed up at your mother's house with glasses, flowerpots, even old toilet bowls, and smashed them all on the doorstep. The noise was supposed to frighten away evil spirits. Then your mother and I went outside and swept up the shards together. That was supposed to bring us luck and teach us that we'd have to work together to manage the challenges of life."

Erich looked at the millions of pieces of broken glass littering the sidewalk. They didn't seem to portend good fortune for Germany.

~

That same morning, a guard shoved a tray with pieces of stale bread and containers of bitter coffee into the cell Gottlieb shared with two dozen other men. For lunch and supper, the same guard delivered a soup consisting of water and potato peelings. Then followed another long, cold night.

The next morning Gottlieb stood near the cell door rubbing his hands on his arms to stay warm, trying to ignore the fact that he could see his breath. Somewhere, far away, he heard hysterical voices sobbing. Then came the jangling of keys in their cell's lock. The door banged open and crashed against the wall.

"It's time for registration," a guard barked, strutting into the cell. He grabbed Aaronsohn and shoved him through the cell door into the hallway. "You're first, Jew-swine. Now march!"

Ten minutes later the guard returned with Aaronsohn, bullied him back into the cell, then leveled his rifle at Gottlieb. "You're next, old man."

The guard marched him down the damp hallway and then shoved him into a small reception room. The room was warm and cozy, almost welcoming.

A diminutive, sinewy stormtrooper with rimless glasses hunched behind a battered wooden desk. He resembled a rat: bald except for a few wiry hairs on his scalp, small round ears and a pointed nose.

The rat glanced up from his paperwork. "Name?" he demanded, with extreme disinterest.

"Gottlieb Reinhold, citizen of the Reich."

The rat peered over his glasses at Gottlieb as if the old man were something nasty he had just stepped in. He snorted, then smiled. "You're a funny one, Gottlieb Reinhold, citizen of the Reich. Do you think what is happening here is amusing?"

Gottlieb remained silent, staring at the man's carefully manicured nails.

"Occupation?" the rat said.

"I used to be a government attorney."

"Oh, a big man, eh?" The trooper leaned back in his chair. "It doesn't matter what you once were," he snapped. "I was a chicken farmer before the Führer came to power." He pretended to dust off his dung-colored uniform. "And now look at me."

Your mother must be very proud.

The rat continued his lecture. "As a former attorney, you surely know that the man who holds his tongue has very little chance of incriminating himself."

Gottlieb said nothing, but maintained eye contact, as if the little rodent in uniform really did have something to teach him about the legal system.

"Let's get one thing straight – no, two things," the man said. "The first is this: what you once were no longer matters. The Reich doesn't employ parasites like you any longer. You are a drain on society, like every other Jew throughout history. My second point is this: I am a patient man. But do not test my patience by spouting droll answers. Is that clear?"

Gottlieb nodded, remaining silent. The clout in the face from Schmutze two nights previously had dislodged two of his molars. There was no sense jeopardizing any more of his teeth by saying something else that might further antagonize the little bully.

"Now, empty the contents of your pockets onto the desk. We'll take an inventory of your belongings, including any money you have."

Another stormtrooper stepped up to record what Gottlieb placed on the desk. "Look over this list and sign at the bottom," the man commanded, after he had finished writing.

Gottlieb complied.

"Fortunately for you, you are in possession of nothing illegal, such as weapons," the little man went on. "Put everything back in your pockets. Did you notice that we're allowing you to keep your possessions?"

Gottlieb nodded.

"Never let it be said that Germans rob Jews the way you've been robbing us for centuries." The rat turned to the guard. "Get this Jew out of my sight."

Later Gottlieb sat on the cot in the half-dark cell, trying to ignore the nauseating stench coming from the chamber pot. He rose to his feet and spread his arms. "Did you know today is the 11th of November?" he asked. "The Great War ended exactly twenty years ago today."

"I served my Fatherland for four years during the war," said a man on the cot.

"I was wounded three times and received the Iron Cross," another man said. "I had three brothers. None of them came home from the war. They're all buried somewhere in France."

"And this is how we are rewarded for serving our fatherland," Aaronsohn snorted.

That appeared to be the case. More and more arrestees arrived. Gottlieb heard voices in the corridors, the jangling of keys. Someone yelled, "Remove your hands from me, *blöder Hund!*"

The guard did not take the insult in good grace. "Who are you calling a stupid dog?" he bellowed. Gottlieb heard a sick thud followed by the sound of a body collapsing onto the floor. After that came the sound of the body being dragged away.

Day turned into night. Gottlieb woke to the sound of two men talking outside the cell door. One spoke in a low, rough voice; the other's speech was nasal, toneless. A clock tower in the distance struck midnight as a shimmering sliver of moonlight worked its way across the floor of the cell.

Then the door crashed open. "Out, out, out, you swine!" shouted a guard.

Gottlieb jumped to his feet with a groan and risked a question. "Where are you taking us?" The guard rewarded his curiosity with a blow to the head, knocking him to the ground.

"We're taking you into 'protective custody,'" the guard snarled with an amused smirk. He pointed to the cell door. "Now get up and get moving."

Dizzy and confused, Gottlieb obeyed. Outside, flatbed trucks filled the courtyard. A stormtrooper the size of a Zeppelin beat and pushed the prisoners onto the trucks with the butt of his rifle, ordering them to sit on the truck bed.

The Zeppelin climbed into the back of Gottlieb's truck after the prisoners had been loaded. "Put your faces on your knees," he commanded, holding up a bayonet. "If I catch anyone lifting his head during our little excursion, I'll remove it from his neck."

The truck engine roared to life, backfired, then lurched forward as the driver let out the clutch.

Gottlieb felt the vehicle lumber out of the prison courtyard and into traffic. After a few minutes he risked looking out of the corner of his eye. The Zeppelin was hunched over, hands cupped around his mouth, trying to light a cigarette. On the crest of the hill up ahead, Gottlieb saw a sign for the town of Oranienburg.

They were heading northeast. *Isn't Sachsenhausen just outside of Oranienburg? Why would they be taking us to a concentration camp?* Gottlieb shot another quick glance toward the front of the truck.

Ahead of them a car lurched into the intersection from a side street, blocking their path.

Their truck braked quickly and fishtailed, sending the prisoners sprawling across the truck bed with the Zeppelin tumbling over them like a huge brown yo-yo. "*Verfixt und zugenäht*," he sputtered. He struggled to his feet and banged on the window that separated the back of the truck from the cab. "Becker, you idiot, where did you learn to drive?"

The Zeppelin kicked the men on whom he had landed. "Come on, you lazy swine, sit up. You'll have plenty of time to sleep when you reach your new accommodations."

As the prisoners returned to a sitting position, one of them leapt over the side of the truck and fell with a thud onto the street. Gottlieb watched him groan to his feet, then hobble off into the shadows.

The Zeppelin squinted into the glare from the headlights of the truck behind them. "One of my prisoners just jumped off my truck," he screamed, pointing into the night with his rifle. "After him!" He leveled his weapon and fired into the shadows, then screamed at his driver. "Becker, get back here and watch these prisoners until I get back."

The driver turned off the engine, climbed out of the cab and shuffled to the back of the truck. The Zeppelin rolled his huge body over the side of the truck, then turned to Becker. "If any one of these swine gives you any trouble, shoot him."

Becker nodded and watched his colleague lumber away. He leaned against the truck and lit a cigarette.

Gottlieb looked the driver over. No weapon. Their eyes met. *I wonder...*

Becker spoke, interrupting Gottlieb's thoughts. "You're right, sir, I have no gun. I'm just a driver."

What's wrong with this man? He calls me "sir" instead of "Jewish swine."

Becker looked into the eyes of the captives. "Look, men, please don't try to escape. That would only make trouble for me, not to mention the fact that it would not go well for you once they caught you." He shook his head and stared at the ground. "What they're doing to you is shameful." He looked back into the truck. "On behalf of all decent Germans, I ask your forgiveness."

"Where are you taking us?" Gottlieb asked.

"To ..." Gunfire interrupted Becker.

The escapee was back, staggering past the truck and into some bushes. Becker watched him disappear without sounding the alarm.

Shouts in the night. More gunfire. "There he is. Get him. Corner him."

In the surrounding apartment houses lights flashed on in the windows, framing faces, some curious, some terrified. A man threw open his window and leaned out. "*Hey da, was machen Sie bloss?*"

"Never mind what we're doing," yelled the Zeppelin from out of the darkness. "Shut your window and shut your mouth and go back to bed."

"You're shooting in the streets and I'm supposed to just go back to bed? I'm calling the police."

"Yes, call the police you moron," the Zeppelin barked. "And tell them that the Führer's stormtroopers are disturbing your sleep."

The man's countenance changed from anger to terror. He slammed the window shut, let down the shade and extinguished his light.

Then another man's voice called out. "Don't shoot. Please don't …"

Two shots rang out, echoing like thunder in the canyon formed by the surrounding apartment buildings. Bile rose in Gottlieb's throat, choking him.

A moment later he heard something being dragged along the street. Then the Zeppelin, bathed in sweat, emerged from the night. He and another man towed the escapee behind them by his feet. They let down the tailgate, groaned as they lifted the man, and hurled him face up onto the truck bed.

The Zeppelin heaved his body back onto the truck and Becker slammed the tailgate shut. Gottlieb could see some of the victim's blood, black as tar in the dim light, clinging to the front of the Zeppelin's coat. "That's one less Jew we'll have to feed," he spat.

He aimed his weapon at his prisoners. "Anyone else in the mood for a game of hide and seek?" He got no answer. "Good. Now get your heads down before I blow them off your shoulders."

Back behind the wheel, Becker started the engine, let out the clutch and stomped on the gas pedal, sending the vehicle jerking into motion.

The escapee's head had landed at Gottlieb's feet. *Dear Lord, have mercy on this poor soul.* Light from passing street lamps flashed across the man's body. A wound in his stomach gushed like a waterfall, but he was still alive. The blood trail shone in the moonlight as it worked its way along the truck bed, flowing past the captive's feet before disappearing under the tailgate.

The wounded man raised a feeble hand. His eyes pleaded with Gottlieb and he mouthed the words, "*hilf mir.*"

I suspect you are beyond help, my friend. Gottlieb took the man's hand and clasped it, not caring how the Zeppelin would react. The dying man smiled weakly and squeezed back. Then his eyes flew open; he wheezed, struggling to breathe. A few seconds later the wheezing stopped, the hand went limp, and the man stared lifelessly into the night sky.

"A quick death," whispered one of the men next to Gottlieb. "He's the lucky one."

The truck raced up hills, through valleys, and around curves. The wind whipped around Gottlieb, freezing him to the bone. He peeked up again. The Zeppelin had clamped his rifle barrel between his enormous thighs and was lighting another cigarette. The cold didn't seem to bother him. Of course, why should it? He wore a thick winter coat.

Up ahead, lit by the glare of their truck's headlights, Gottlieb saw a sign announcing their arrival in Oranienburg. They passed through the town and traveled another two or three kilometers and just when Gottlieb thought he was going to succumb to frostbite, the truck lurched around a corner and raced through an archway, coming to a sudden stop in a cobblestoned courtyard. Several other trucks that had been in their convoy screeched to a halt next to theirs. Gottlieb nearly gave a sigh of relief.

Half a dozen spotlights, each brighter than the sun, illuminated the courtyard. For a moment Gottlieb basked in the imagined warmth of the light. Then the guards closed the gates between the courtyard and the outside world. A sign near the gates announced the name of the prisoners' new home: Sachsenhausen.

Then a cacophony of shrill voices screamed, "Out, out, out, you pond scum! You have three seconds to get off those trucks, and two of them are already gone!"

Gottlieb, slow to climb down, was yanked by the hair from the truck bed to the ground and then kicked along.

The guards assembled their prey in the courtyard. *"Stillges-tanden! Augen geradeaus!"* The men froze in place and stared straight ahead as commanded. It looked to Gottlieb as if thousands of other prisoners stood with him in the frigid air.

"Hats off!"

For what seemed an eternity, Gottlieb watched the moon drag itself across the sky as guards moved slowly through the ranks, recording names, addresses and dates of birth. He shivered and clenched his fists in frustration. *Can't they write any faster?*

A dog howled in the distance. Gottlieb looked up at the moon again. When was it going to set? How long before the sun took its place in the sky and bathed them in warmth and light? *It's November, so the sun probably won't provide too much warmth,* he reminded himself.

A prisoner two rows up wavered like a drunk, then dropped to his knees before falling with a sickening smack, face first onto the cobblestones. He lay bleeding from the mouth, a pool of blood forming on the pavement like wine from an overturned bottle.

The fallen man gurgled for a minute, then choked, before finally turning silent and lifeless. The guards who had been recording names turned and looked at the dead man for a few seconds, then continued their work.

Gottlieb heard groaning and whining all around him, then one thud after another. By the time the moon had worked its way most of the way to the western horizon, he had counted eighteen fallen men. The guards finally yanked a few prisoners from the ranks to haul away the dead and dying men who littered the courtyard.

Now Gottlieb's legs were screaming in agony. The old bullet wound in his calf felt as if it were on fire. *Dear God, let this torture end. Lord, if I could only sit down, lie down, for just a moment.* But his greatest agony was the torturous uncertainty of his fate.

"Weggetreten!" a guard finally commanded. They were finally dismissed! It was as if God had heard his prayer.

Guards appeared from every corner of the courtyard to herd the prisoners into the barracks. The floors and walls of the barracks were unfinished wood. No beds, no mattresses, no blankets.

The guards extinguished the lights and the men settled down next to one another on the floor. For some sleep came instantly, but Gottlieb lay there cold, shivering, and exhausted, listening to the snoring and whimpering of a hundred other men. He folded his arms tightly around his chest, trying to insulate himself against the frigid air. *At least you're off your feet. That in itself is an answer to your prayer in the courtyard.* Perhaps next time he should add some specifics to his prayer, like requesting a warm bed as well.

~

Ruth Baumgartner remained in the funeral home while Nessa and Erich searched for a place to lay her to rest.

"Your mother was Jewish, Fräulein Baumgartner," Pastor Schultheiss told Nessa, without looking up from his paperwork. His office was musty and dank. The smoke from his cigarette danced in the faint winter light coming through the window. "This is a Lutheran church. I cannot allow Jews to be buried in our church yard. That would defile hallowed ground."

"But my mother was *Lutheran!*" Nessa protested. "And she was a member of your congregation, pastor. You know that."

Schultheiss laid down his pen and frowned at Nessa and then at Erich. He turned and stared through the window for a long moment, as if there were something outside that intrigued him. Erich followed his gaze. At the edge of the graveyard a group of cedar trees, vibrant and strong, stood in a straight line, rustling in the breeze. Beyond them a bank of dark clouds brooded on the horizon.

The pastor leaned back in his chair and folded his arms across his chest. "Fräulein Baumgartner," he said, looking at her again, "were you in coma when the Nuremberg Laws were passed? All four of your grandparents were Jewish. That makes your parents

Jewish – which, by the way, means that you are also Jewish," he added, as if arriving at some great epiphany. "German law states that you and your family are Jews, not Christians. As I attempted to explain to you a few moments ago, I will allow only Christians to be interred in my church yard. I'm sorry."

Erich could see no hint of sorrow or compassion in the minister's eyes. "You value Nazi law over God's law, don't you, pastor?" he scolded. "Isn't a Christian supposed to love his neighbor as himself? Love doesn't distinguish between Jews and Christians. A pastor is supposed to be moved with compassion when someone else is in need and suffering and feel moved to relieve their suffering." He placed his hand on Nessa's shoulder. "This young woman is suffering because she needs a place to bury her mother and you refuse to help her."

Schultheiss furrowed his brow and puckered his lips as if Erich's plea had perhaps penetrated to that part of his heart that still contained a measure of compassion. But in the end, he simply shook his head. "I'm sorry, my hands are tied – I can't help you," he said, returning his attention to his paperwork.

"Then what are we to do, pastor?" Nessa asked.

The pastor shook his head again without making eye contact. "I don't know. These are hard times. Now, if you will excuse me, I have a sermon to prepare."

"I don't know what I'm going to do," Nessa lamented as they walked past the graveyard that bordered the pastor's office. Her mother and father, the two people she had cherished and depended on all her life, and whom she had never appreciated as intensely as she should have, had suddenly vanished into thin air. And she would never be able to cry hard enough to bring them back.

"We'll go to see Herr Nussbaum," Erich said.

"Who?" Nessa said, dabbing a handkerchief at the corners of her eyes.

"You remember him," Erich said, putting a comforting arm around her waist. "He's the attorney we met on the street the day we got thrown out of the jewelry store."

"That was two years ago. He won't remember us."

"He'll remember me. I never told you that Papa and I ran into him the day after Kristallnacht. He told us to look him up if we ever needed legal advice. I'd like to find out if this Pastor Schultheiss can legally deny us the right to bury your mother in his church yard. There must be a way around it."

He fumbled in his wallet. "I have his business card here somewhere. Here it is. His office is on Kirsch Strasse, number 21."

Nussbaum shook his head, his heavy jowls quivering. "Finding a cemetery willing to accept a deceased loved one reclassified as Jewish is almost impossible. This Pastor Schultheiss is more a victim than a cold-hearted racist. If he allowed Ruth Baumgartner to be buried in his church yard, he'd be arrested by the Nazis and probably executed."

"He valued his own skin more than doing what was right in God's eyes," Nessa said bitterly. But she could hardly blame him. The man was as terrified of dying as anyone else.

"I'm so sorry for your loss, Nessa," the attorney said. "My advice is to find a relative outside of Berlin who would allow you to lay your mother to rest on his property."

Nessa's lower lip began to tremble, and Nussbaum put his arms around both of them. "I know these are dark times, young ones. The Nazis are making good on their threats to go after the Jews. They've imprisoned hundreds and robbed many more of their businesses, forcing them to live as vagrants on the streets. But darkness cannot prevail forever, not when there are people willing to do battle against it."

Nessa gave him a confused look.

"Nessa," Nussbaum said, "I help Jews in need – those who end up on the streets and those who just want to disappear." He squeezed her even tighter, nearly lifting her off the ground. "But enough of that for the moment. Right now, you need to find a place to lay your mother to rest and mourn her loss."

The family did, indeed, lay Ruth Baumgartner to rest outside of the city, in a plot next to her brother, Stefan Bacharach, who had lived and died on the fringes of Berlin in a cottage near the banks of the Schlachtensee. The property and the cottage now belonged to Nessa's cousin, who had given her permission to bury Ruth there.

For November, it was a surprisingly balmy day. The horse-drawn carriage carrying Nessa, her great-aunt Helen, and the Reinholds rattled and creaked along the forest path that led to the lakeside cottage. The stale air in the carriage smelled of wet hay. Outside, a light mist hung in the trees and the fallen autumn leaves rustled and crunched beneath the carriage wheels. Ahead of them the hearse carrying Ruth Baumgartner led the way.

Memories of her childhood washed over Nessa as they moved deeper into the forest. Not much had changed since she'd played in these woods so many years before. The same labyrinth of paths and trails crisscrossed the forest floor. The same trees lined the route, although by now they had grown much larger.

What was left of her uncle's cottage came into view. An oak tree, apparently uprooted by a windstorm, had crashed onto the moss-covered roof. The impact had burst the door open and shattered the windows.

Nessa saw two men standing a few feet from the edge of the lake, smoking and leaning on shovels. The one standing on a wooden leg had a red, swollen face. The other, with his pointed nose and small mouth, resembled a weasel.

When the hearse came to a stop near the cottage, the men dropped their shovels and sauntered slowly over to it as if they had much better things to do. They unloaded the casket, a small white wooden cross with Ruth's name, and a wreath, placing them next to an open pit.

The mourners' carriage stopped, and the family climbed out, Franz helping Nessa's great-aunt Helen, an elderly, frail woman, to the ground. Then they walked to the gravesite. Erich slipped his arm around Nessa as she stood stiffly, unable to look into the pit that would soon swallow up her mother forever. Instead she studied Stefan's gravestone. 1871 – 1932. Lucky man – he had died just in time to miss Hitler's rise to power.

Her uncle, as well as her mother, had been born in the cottage; Stefan had lived and died there, rarely venturing out of the forest. He hunted and fished, kept a garden and had no real need to throw himself into the frenetic city swarming around the Spree River, not many kilometers away.

From a distance, somewhere beyond the lake, Nessa heard a shrill whistle as a train thundered toward Berlin. Stefan had never even ridden a train. He had often threatened to hitch up his horse and drive his buggy into Berlin to see the city, to ride a train. But nothing ever came of that. His cottage would always remain both his home and his self-imposed place of exile – or perhaps his place of refuge.

Nessa leaned her head on Erich's shoulder, glad of his support. With her father missing and her mother dead, he was all she had left. Behind her came the impatient murmurs of the gravediggers, evidently anxious to lower the casket into the pit, fill in the hole and be on their way. To them this was a routine occurrence. To her it was the end of the world as she had known it.

"We have gathered here today," Franz said, "to mourn the loss of Ruth Baumgartner, whom death has removed from our midst. But we know we will see her again at the resurrection and we take comfort in that knowledge. Until then, Ruth, may you rest in peace."

They sang a hymn and then the gravediggers lowered the coffin into the hole. Nessa squeezed her eyes shut, unable to watch.

Then Erich took her hand and placed something soft and moist and cold into it. She looked down to see a clump of earth in her palm. *How Mama loved to work in the garden.* The thought brought fresh tears.

Nessa forced herself to step to the edge of the grave and drop the dirt into the hole, which caused a gentle thud as it hit the coffin. Then, one by one the family members released their handfuls of soil into the grave.

The ritual complete, the gravediggers set to finishing their grisly work.

Both of Nessa's parents were gone now – her mother dead – her father who knew where? The impact left her emotionally reeling. So often they'd all sat at the dining table sharing the details of the day, discussing the books they were reading, laughing. She'd never hear her mother laugh again, never again see her smile. They'd never again work together in the kitchen, never again bake cookies for Christmas day. Her confidante and advisor was gone.

After the gravediggers finished filling in the hole, they pounded the earth firm with their shovels until nothing was left but a small, rounded mound. One of the men used the head of his shovel to drive in the cross at the head of the grave; his partner placed the wreath on the mound. Then they clasped their hands in front of them, looking expectantly at Franz, who reached into his pocket and handed them some money. They bowed, took their shovels, and walked to a horse-drawn wagon parked under some trees. Then they drove away, disappearing into the forest.

As a child Nessa had really thought she knew what death was all about. When her grandma died, Mama had told her that Oma was just "away" for a while, lying underground, awaiting the resurrection. But now, standing at the place where her mother would forever lie, Nessa was doubtful and afraid. Perhaps everything she had been taught was just a delusion. Maybe death was the end of everything. Maybe there was nothing after death but an eternity of darkness in a rotting coffin.

She shook her head and moaned, "No, no."

An embrace interrupted her thoughts and Erich kissed her on the cheek. It was almost as though he had read her mind, felt her fear. "Don't be afraid, Nessa. You *will* see her again."

She and Erich stayed behind for a few minutes, while Franz and Greta and Helen returned to the carriage. She knelt by the grave and placed a hand on it. With her other hand she touched the cross, running her fingers over the coarse wood. "See you at the resurrection, Mama."

CHAPTER SEVEN

Long before sunrise, an ear-piercing siren jolted the prisoners out of their sleep. The lights in the barracks flashed on and guards stormed into the building. "Get up, you vermin!" they screamed. "Everyone to the courtyard."

Gottlieb groaned to his feet, limped out of the building and lined up outside with the rest of the prisoners. After roll call, they stood in the cold for two hours while stormtroopers ushered a few dozen prisoners at a time to the latrine.

Finally, the column in which Gottlieb stood was pulled out of the formation. "Come on, you *Stinkjuden*," a guard barked, "it's your turn."

The soldiers marched them to the latrine, a long wooden building they could smell before it came into view. While Gottlieb and several others did their business, their captors stood outside screaming at them to be quick. In a corner of the latrine Gottlieb saw perhaps twenty corpses stacked like cordwood in a neat pile. *The men who collapsed in the courtyard last night.*

By the time his column returned from the latrines, the first few rays of sunlight had crept over the horizon. Gottlieb noted that a stone wall, half again as tall as a man, enclosed the camp. Inside that ran a barbed wire fence. In front of the fence, at regular intervals, stood warning signs: "If you go beyond this point, you will be shot." A number of guard towers stood sentry around the perimeter of the compound. There appeared to be no possibility of escape.

Breakfast consisted of cold coffee and stale bread. After that it was off to the barber, who shaved off the prisoners' hair and beards. Gottlieb suspected his new look was far from charming.

Next came a march to the nearby brick factory, where the prisoners received basic training in brick-making. Gottlieb found the process fascinating but exhausting. They loaded shale into a grinder which ground it to powder. The powder was combined with water in large troughs and that mixture was shoveled into brick molds to dry before being fired in a huge kiln to give the bricks their final hardness. All the while guards wielding clubs and ox-whips made sure the prisoners worked at a break-neck pace.

Lunchtime arrived and their captors allowed the men to sit on the ground to eat. The soup of the day was something that resembled goulash, but the contents were unidentifiable. Then came more brick-making and after work a brisk march back to camp, followed by more standing in formation in the courtyard.

After another hour, the guards pulled three prisoners from the ranks and stood them in front of the formations, commanding them to face the rest of the prisoners. The guards then gave each of the three a large sign.

A trooper leveled his rifle at a man in the first row. "You are our spokesman," he barked. "When I give the signal, you will shout out what you see written on these signs." The trooper then turned his attention to the ranks. "I want the rest of you to repeat what your spokesman says. I expect you to impress me with your gusto." He turned back to the spokesman. "Now read each sign, one at a time."

The man began to read. "We are..."

"*Lauter, du Stinkjude!*" the guard bellowed. He smacked the prisoner on the side of the head with a riding crop, making him yelp.

The spokesman began again, this time somewhat louder.

The guard hit him again. "Shout out the words like you mean it, you little rodent!"

"We are to blame for the murder of Herr vom Rath!" shouted the spokesman. The crowd of detainees yelled back the words.

"We are the destroyers of German culture!"

The prisoners shouted out these words. The guards whipped and kicked those lacking in enthusiasm.

"We are Germany's misfortune!"

The process was repeated over and over and after an hour of yelling, Gottlieb's throat was screaming in pain and he understood how one could admit to anything, sign any confession, just to end the torture. Still, forcing him to repeat lies and making him believe them was another matter entirely.

Then a young stormtrooper marched out of one of the buildings and planted himself before the group. His appearance and demeanor evoked authority and demanded obedience: highly polished jackboots, impeccably tailored uniform, angry, dispassionate eyes that seemed to miss nothing. He stretched out his arms and began to address the men as if delivering a sermon.

"I am Commandant Weber. If you learn nothing else here at Sachsenhausen," he preached, "you will learn the meaning of discipline. You have had a taste of life in a concentration camp. Now you need to know what will be expected of you." He took a step toward them and lifted his hands higher. "Before you stands the messenger who will reveal these things to you." He leveled his riding crop at his congregation. "My message today consists of three parts."

A good sermon always has three main points.

"First," the young man continued, "while you are here, we expect you to work diligently. Our motto is *Arbeit macht frei*, work makes you free. We expect every guest here to embrace this motto. Failing to do so is punishable by death." He looked up and down the ranks, then began striding back and forth, hands clasped behind his back.

"Second, do what you are told without hesitation. Make it easy on yourself – obey. Obedience is a virtue." He stopped in his tracks and surveyed his flock. "My last point is this. Always be generous. In a moment we will afford you the privilege of contributing to the Winter Relief Program."

"Every sermon ends with an offering," Gottlieb whispered to the man next to him and they exchanged smiles. He now knew why the Germans had allowed their captives to keep their money.

"Your contributions will benefit individuals less fortunate than yourselves," the preacher said.

Gottlieb bit his tongue to keep from laughing. *Anyone not imprisoned within these walls is infinitely more fortunate than we are.*

"The Winter Relief Program, as you may know, is a benevolence fund for the German Volk. We help those who are experiencing hard times. We will now circulate through your ranks and we expect your generosity."

Everyone was generous.

The evening after Gottlieb's arrest, while picking up rubble in the front yard, Erich came across the family radio under a laurel bush. He took it into the house, cleaned it off and plugged it in. It sputtered for a few seconds, then sprang to life, filling the living room with a beautiful sonata by Schubert. The radio was something the intruders had failed to destroy. The thought made Erich smile, at least a little.

After dinner his family, along with Nessa, gathered around the radio to listen to Mozart's Ninth Symphony.

Nessa clung to Erich, her head on his shoulder. He thought she was done shedding tears, but now her eyes were welling up again. He leaned his head against hers, wishing he could take away her pain.

"I wish I knew what happened to Papa," Nessa lamented.

"I know, *Liebling*," Erich soothed. But he didn't. She had lost both parents in the space of an evening. What would that be like? He couldn't imagine.

"Not knowing makes the pain worse," she said, then bit her lip. "But you've lost someone, too."

After a few minutes, the symphony ended, replaced by the mordant voice of the announcer. "The Jews must bear full responsibility for the murder of Erich vom Rath," he seethed. "On November 9th, the Volk responded to the assassination with spontaneous reprisals against the Jewish criminals in our midst."

"I heard that the attacks began all over Germany at exactly the same time," Erich said. "The reprisals sound more orchestrated than spontaneous."

"I think the Nazis had been planning attacks on Jews for some time," Franz said. "The assassination gave them the perfect excuse for implementing their agenda."

"I said it two years ago. We need to leave Germany before it's too late," Greta reminded them.

"I'll pick up the emigration applications tomorrow," Franz said to Greta. "Let's pray that Opa and Nessa's father return soon, so we can take them with us. In the meantime, we'll write your parents in Ohio and ask them to sponsor us."

The next morning, after roll call, Commandant Weber strode out of his office to address his prisoners.

"I'm a patience man," he began. "I have to be." He gestured toward his guards. "I have to please my staff members." He swept his other arm toward the prisoners, "And I have to please you, our guests. That puts a lot of pressure on me."

He motioned to a pair of guards near the barracks who stood next to a man lying motionless in the dirt. They hauled the prisoner to his feet and dragged him across the courtyard, dumping him like a sack of potatoes onto the cobblestones near the commandant.

The prisoner writhed on the ground, blood oozing from his mouth and both ears. Even though the temperature in the court-yard was near freezing, Gottlieb felt sweat forming between his shoulder blades and moving down his back. They were probably going to watch a man die.

"You people are here to work," the commandant continued, "not to waste our time and yours trying to escape. In a few moments you will witness what happens after a failed escape attempt." Weber motioned to the guards again, then stepped back and clasped his hands behind his back.

The two guards picked up the prisoner again and dragged him to the middle of the courtyard to where a four-meter-tall wooden post stood with a half-meter long horizontal bar attached to the top. They lifted the man up and looped a noose around his neck while a third guard threw the other end of the rope over the bar.

If they're going to hang him, why don't they tie his hands together behind his back?

Then all three guards used the rope to hoist the prisoner a few meters in the air until he wriggled like a fish at the end of a fishing line.

Almost immediately the man reached out and grabbed the pole, clinging to it with both hands and both legs. When he tried to remove the noose from his neck, a guard shot him in the right arm.

The prisoner screamed and threw both hands up, clutching his left hand to the wound while once again dangling in the air.

Once more he managed to clamp his body around the pole, only to be shot in his left arm. He screamed once more and released his grip, swaying again by his neck.

A group of guards by the front gate stood watching the specta-cle, laughing and smoking. *This is not only an execution, but also a game,* Gottlieb thought.

The prisoner struggled in the air for another thirty seconds before managing to get his legs and his wounded arms around the pole again.

The next shot hit him in the leg. He let go of the pole and swayed back and forth, blood pulsating from his wounds, dripping down to form a pool on the ground.

The guard with the rifle allowed the condemned man a few seconds reprieve before shooting him in the head. Gottlieb bent over and threw up his breakfast. He wasn't the only one.

The three guards holding the dead man aloft released the rope, letting him plummet to the ground where he hit the cobblestones with a sickening smack.

The commandant stepped forward again, pointing at the iron gates at the front of the camp. "The sign on those gates says that work makes you free. While you are our guests, I suggest that you take those words to heart." He gestured toward the lifeless body in the middle of the courtyard. "Escape attempts just add to my stress. You are here under protective custody." He pointed at the walls surrounding the camp. "Stay put, don't try to breach these fortifications. Many of the Germans living outside of this sanctuary don't care for Jews. The walls enclosing you are there to protect you from those people."

But who was going to protect them from the people in here?

Later that day at the brickworks, Gottlieb tossed another shovelful of shale into his wheelbarrow, while the shadow from the factory chimney slowly worked its way across the courtyard like the shadow of death.

Once he had filled the wheelbarrow, he rolled it inside the factory and transferred the load onto a conveyor belt, which transported the material to the grinder. Then he went back outside to get another load.

"They were quite nice to me on Kristallnacht," a man working nearby said. "'You served in the Great War?' they said to me, 'Nothing much will happen to you. We'll take you to the police station for a few minutes tonight and before long you'll be back home again, snuggling next to your wife in bed.'"

Gottlieb stabbed his shovel into the pile of shale. "And you believed them?"

"Until they started beating us. Is all that violence really necessary?"

"That's how one treats animals," Gottlieb said facetiously, tossing more shale into his wheelbarrow.

"Do you know who Caspar David Friedrich was?" the other man asked.

"The German painter?"

"The same. He painted peaceful landscapes drenched in fog and light. Can you believe a Volk capable of producing such sublime beauty could also be capable of clubbing people to death simply because they're Jewish?"

Gottlieb shook his head but didn't answer. And to avoid a clubbing, he didn't stop working either. *Making bricks like the Jews in Egypt.*

He had to muster all of his strength just to overcome the daily routine: an early wakeup, roll call, the march to the brick factory, working like a slave for twelve hours. Then came the march back to the camp and another roll call, followed by trying to sleep on the barracks floor while a hundred other men coughed and wheezed and wept all night long.

He had to find a way to escape this hell. If they caught him, they would execute him, but he was willing to take the risk. He had to warn his family. Tell them he had been wrong. Tell them to leave Germany at once. Why hadn't he seen the truth sooner?

~

Four weeks after his arrest Gottlieb discovered a possible way out of the camp. If his plan worked he would make his way back to Berlin on foot, or, if he were fortunate, hitch a ride there.

He had noticed that the camp's central office building had rooms that were neither occupied nor guarded most of the time. Through one of the windows he had spotted some uniform coats and hats hanging on a coat rack.

One evening after lights out he slipped to the back entrance of his barracks. He peered through the windows near the door. All seemed quiet. The guards had already locked the barracks for the night, but that would not be a problem. From his pocket he removed the small crowbar he had stolen that morning from the brickworks. He jimmied the door lock for thirty seconds and the door sprang open. Getting past the guards was easy. In the bitter cold they huddled around a fire barrel, obvious to everything but the warmth coming from the flames.

Gottlieb sneaked through the shadows to the back door of the central office building. After a long minute, the lock yielded to his crowbar and he slipped inside, ducking down below the level of the windows. The lights from the front gate illuminated the room. Hugging the wall, he scooted and crawled along until he found the office in which he'd seen the uniforms. He picked out a shirt, a pair of pants, a hat, and a colonel's winter coat.

In another office he located a pair of winter boots and a flashlight. He took his new wardrobe to the restroom, and there, using the razor and shaving cream he found on the sink, he shaved and washed up. Once he donned his new attire, he admired his murky reflection in the mirror. He looked the part. *I could fool even the Führer in this outfit.*

He tied his old clothes into a bundle and stashed them and the crowbar behind a cabinet. Next, he crawled through the offices in search of food, finally finding half a ham sandwich and a nibbled-at apple in a waste basket. He sat against a wall and enjoyed the best meal he'd eaten since his arrival at the camp.

Then came the moment of truth. He turned up his coat collar to obscure the sides of his face and pulled the brim of his cap deep over his forehead. He slipped out of the office building, and, with the confidence of a stormtrooper, he began marching toward the main gate.

As he approached the guards, his arm shot up as if it were spring-loaded and he bellowed a "Heil Hitler" loud enough to wake the dead.

The two guards, who had been smoking and chatting, spun around, throwing their cigarettes to the ground. They returned the Hitler greeting and stood at attention.

"Corporal," Gottlieb commanded, looking at one of them, "open the gates. I need to inspect the perimeter wall."

"*Zu Befehl, Herr Oberst*," the guard barked and swung the gates open.

Gottlieb liked being called a colonel, a *Herr Oberst*. He especially liked ordering Aryans around. "I'll be back in one hour," he said. "Lock the gates behind me. We wouldn't want any of our guests slipping past you and disappearing into the night."

Then, with a final "Heil Hitler," he marched off into the dark.

CHAPTER EIGHT

Gottlieb walked for a few minutes, using his flashlight to light the way, before coming to a sign at the side of the road. "Oranienburg. Three kilometers," he mumbled to himself. Surely, he could make that distance in about forty minutes. Then he'd look for a pub. Maybe he could find someone there to give him a lift to Berlin.

He had no idea what he would do once he got to Berlin. He couldn't go home – that was the first place they'd come looking. Perhaps his old friend and next-door neighbor, Josef Mühlberger, would hide him.

He turned down a wooded road, passing farmhouses and residences. Through the windows he saw families gathered around their dining room tables, sharing their evening meal. Oh, how he'd missed that simple pleasure.

Soon he came to a house that was dark except for a porch light at the back door. He stopped and looked around. No one in sight. A shed stood in back of the house. Maybe he could find some other clothes in there.

He slipped through the gate, closing it behind him. He tried the door to the shed, found it unlocked, and went inside. He stood at the shed window for a few moments and watched the street, the house and the yard. No movement anywhere. Then he turned his attention to the contents of the shed.

He was in luck. Along with the usual array of garden tools, he found a worn out pair of pants and a work shirt hanging on a nail. *Is it all right to break the commandment about not stealing in order to save your life?*

He changed quickly, then sneaked out of the shed and back onto the street. He peered into the darkness in every direction. Nothing. No sounds, no headlights. He tied his uniform clothes into a bundle, drew back his arm and hurled it into the woods as far as he could. It was cold without a coat, but the unheated barracks at Sachsenhausen had acclimated him to such discomforts.

Arriving in Oranienburg, Gottlieb took a right onto Bernauer Strasse and soon found himself standing in front of the *Gasthof zur Eiche*. Two huge oak trees drooped over the roof of the building. Light blazed out of every window and laughter and music blasted out of the first-floor pub. He examined the cars in the parking lot. Three of them had Berlin license plates. He might be in luck. He inhaled for courage, mounted the stairs to the pub, and stepped inside.

The strong smell of beer and cigarette smoke assaulted his senses. He closed the door behind him. A few patrons turned their heads, looked in his direction and then returned to their drinks, their conversations, and their cigarettes.

In the kitchen a cook stood smoking while preparing food, his face gleaming with sweat. A long snake of ash fell from his cigarette into the scrambled eggs he was cooking. He continued stirring the eggs as if nothing had happened.

Gottlieb took a seat at the bar next to a man about his age who was busy draining a glass of beer.

The bartender appeared. "Do you have a phone I can use?" Gottlieb asked him. Perhaps he could call his family, ask Franz to come and fetch him.

"We have a phone, but it's not for customers."

"Is there a pay phone in town?"

"At the post office," the man said, "but it's closed this time of night." He leaned his hands on the bar. "Are you going to order something?" he asked impatiently.

Gottlieb ordered a beer. He didn't have any money, but it would look suspicious if he sat at the bar without ordering anything. He'd just nurse his beer and, in the meantime, figure out what to do when it came time to pay.

He turned to the man sitting next to him. "*Guten Abend*." The man returned his greeting in an unmistakable Berlin accent. His face was round and red, his nose riddled with spider veins.

Surely God was smiling on him. "Oh, you're also from Berlin."

"Yes, I drove up to visit my sister. What brings you here?"

"I took the train up yesterday to visit my brother. He's a guard at Sachsenhausen."

The man didn't question his story and they fell into lengthy conversation. Gottlieb soon learned that his new friend, Ludwig, had also served in the Great War. It wasn't long before the two veterans were reminiscing about their battle experiences and pulling up their pant legs and rolling up their shirtsleeves to compare bullet wounds. It turned out that both had been corporals.

"You know," Ludwig said, "the Führer was only a corporal in the war and look at him now."

Yes, look at what horror that mad man is bringing on our country. "That's true," Gottlieb said. "Speaking of the Führer, what do you think of this business of rounding up Jews and destroying their businesses and homes?" He bit his lip, wishing he'd kept his mouth shut. His heart began to drum.

Ludwig's forehead furrowed. He shot a dubious glance at Gottlieb, as if trying to surmise whether he was being drawn into a trap. Gottlieb met the man's gaze, forcing himself to look innocent.

Ludwig's countenance relaxed. He leaned over in Gottlieb's direction. "Just between you and me, I think the Party has gone a bit too far. Yes, we need to find a solution to the Jewish problem.

They should be removed from the Reich to Palestine or to America, but I'm not sure persecuting them is the right approach."

The bartender set a beer in front of Gottlieb. "Maybe the Führer is finally making good on his threats to get rid of the Jews, starting with the ones in Germany."

"I certainly hope he's not behind the violence." Ludwig shook his head. "If that were the case, I'd be very disappointed." Then his expression brightened. "You won't believe this, but my son, Mathias, is a colonel in the SS. He's quite important."

Gottlieb cringed. Sweat beaded on his forehead. Why had he let this conversation drift into such dangerous waters?

"He had the privilege of meeting the Führer in Bavaria at the Eagle's Nest. Eighteen hundred meters up, high above the rest of the world. Mathias has told me his story about meeting Hitler at least a hundred times.

"What was the Führer like in person?" Gottlieb asked. Not that he wanted to know, but it would look suspicious to show no interest.

"My son says he's rather short and reserved. Ah, but what a great man he is."

What a great monster he's turning out to be. "He's certainly making his mark on history." And a very black mark it was. "So, you have a son. Do you have any more children?" Gottlieb asked, moving the conversation into safer and more mundane territory.

"Ah, yes, a daughter and three fine grandchildren," Ludwig beamed, launching into a detailed description of the exploits of each grandchild.

They talked and joked for a few more minutes, the Aryan and the Jew, as if they had been close friends for years. Then Gottlieb ventured, "I don't suppose you could give me a lift back to Berlin. My brother was going to take me, but he couldn't get his car started. I could take the train, but..."

"Say no more. You're coming with me," Ludwig insisted.

They finished their drinks and Gottlieb fumbled in his pockets for money he knew he didn't have.

"I'll buy this time," his new friend said.

Ludwig paid, and they headed for the door. To not have a coat would look odd, so Gottlieb casually took one of several hanging on a coat tree by the front door, draping it over his arm.

"This is my car," Ludwig said once they were outside, reaching for the rusty handle on the driver's door of a dilapidated Opel. The door refused to budge for a moment, then squealed open under protest. "It's not much, but it won't stop running," he laughed.

To Gottlieb this decrepit wreck was his ride to freedom, a vehicle far more precious than even the Führer's Mercedes-Benz Touring Limousine. He reached for the door handle. *What would my new friend say if he knew he was helping an escapee from a concentration camp?*

Then Gottlieb heard it. The roar of a car engine coming from the direction of Sachsenhausen. He looked to see a military truck screech to a halt behind Ludwig's Opel. Three men jumped out, two of them the guards who had watched him march out of the camp an hour and a half earlier. "That's the man!" they said in unison, pointing at Gottlieb.

~

The day it happened, snowflakes tumbled from the gray clouds that moved across the December sky, dusting the camp and its inhabitants in wintry white.

Morning roll call had finally ended. It was now Gottlieb's turn at the post the prisoners had come to call the "hanging tree." Two guards held him up – the beating he had received when he was brought back to Sachsenhausen had broken him physically, leaving him unable to stand. His face was a mass of blood, bruises, broken bones and shattered teeth, his breathing shallow and rapid. He

GERHARDT ROBERTS

tried to take a deep breath, but the unbearable pain coming from broken ribs thwarted the attempt.

He watched through eyes nearly swollen shut as Commandant Weber walked across the courtyard and stopped next to the place of execution. He pointed at Gottlieb and then scowled into the ranks of the prisoners. "Before you stands a very stupid man," he announced. "He fully knew the penalty for escaping and yet he ignored the warnings and fled anyway."

The commandant clasped his hands behind his back and began striding back and forth. "As you can see, Gottlieb Reinhold is back among us. How many more of you are willing to die to prove that I am not a liar? It's quite simple. If you escape, or even make the attempt, you will die."

He glared into the ranks for a long moment, as though he were trying to hypnotize his captives into obeying his will in the future. Then he motioned to the guards. "Proceed."

"I'd like to say something," Gottlieb managed through a broken jaw.

One of the guards clouted him in the face with the butt of his rifle. "Request denied," the guard barked. Gottlieb collapsed to the ground but was immediately yanked back to his feet.

He felt frozen to the bone and longed to be at home, passing these last few moments on this earth surrounded by his family, holding each one of them one more time. But that wasn't going to happen. He consoled himself with the fact that he would soon be in his true home, in the arms of God.

A lifetime of memories swept over him. Waltzing in the living room with his Hannah. Shivering in the cold, wet trenches of Verdun while reading a letter that had just arrived from her. The birth of his son, Franz. Teaching Erich how to ride a bicycle.

But he wasn't sorry to die, to leave the hell that his Fatherland had become. In a few moments he'd be able to embrace his Hannah – and his Lord.

One of the guards slipped the noose over his head. As was the case with all previous executions, Gottlieb's hands were not tied behind his back. Then the guard threw the loose end of the rope over the cross piece near the top of the post and three other guards grabbed the rope and hoisted Gottlieb into the air.

He looked down to see his fellow prisoners standing in rigid rows looking up at him. Some nodded at him nearly imperceptibly, eyes full of compassion, almost as if they were sharing his suffering, feeling his pain.

He gasped for air, tempted to reach out and grab the pole. But then an inner voice spoke. *Don't cling to this world, cling to God. You're dying and nothing can change that. Let go of this life with dignity and go to Him.* He lifted his hands toward heaven.

Gottlieb's emotions changed from fear to joy. He saw himself entering a long, dark tunnel, finally emerging at the other end bathed in glorious light, the Maker of light and all things good welcoming him home.

Then something snapped in his neck and his legs went numb. He saw sparks of light before everything went black.

~

Franz and Erich were doing repairs in the kitchen: a leaky faucet, a loose towel rack. Greta and Nessa were away visiting Frau Sturm.

There was a knock at the front door and Erich went to answer it.

A courier stood on the porch shifting a package from one hand to the other. "*Guten Tag,*" he said, "are you related to Gottlieb Reinhold?"

They had heard no news from Opa since his arrest and hope of ever seeing him again had all but vanished. Was the package something for Opa? Something from him? Or was this some strange Nazi trick?

"Yes," Erich said with some trepidation. "I'm his grandson."

"Sir, I need you to sign for this package."

"We're not expecting a delivery. Are you sure it's for us?"

"My paperwork says to deliver this package to the family of Gottlieb Reinhold."

Erich looked at the parcel. The address was correct. "Do you know what it is?" he asked.

"No sir. I just make deliveries. I don't ask questions." The man held out a piece of paper and a pen. "If you would please sign at the bottom of this form."

Erich signed, then took the box.

The courier clicked his heels, touched the tips of his fingers to the brim of his cap and left.

Erich carried the parcel into the kitchen and put it on the table. "What do you suppose it is, Papa?"

Franz put down the screwdriver he was using to adjust the kitchen door. He shook his head. "No idea." He walked over to the table and removed the envelope taped to the package, tearing it open and removing a letter.

He'd barely begun to read when the letter slipped from his hands. He fell onto a chair and began to weep.

Erich had never seen his father cry before, and the sight terrified him. He put an arm around his shoulder. "Papa, what is it?"

No response.

Erich retrieved the letter from the floor and read it: "Contents: One urn containing the remains of Gottlieb Reinhold." Knees weak, he too collapsed onto the nearest chair, his own eyes filling with tears.

After some minutes Franz forced himself to stop weeping and pulled the urn from the parcel, embracing the cold metal cylinder that contained what was left of his father's earthly existence. "Oh, Papa." There was a world of grief in those two words.

Sometime later, when Erich picked up the envelope to throw it away, he noticed that it contained another piece of paper. "Papa, there's something else here."

He handed the paper to his father who unfolded it and laid it on the table.

It was a bill from a local funeral home, which read:

Collection of remains of Gottlieb Reinhold from
Sachsenhausen Concentration Camp...12.40 RM
Cremation of remains ...35.00 RM
Brass Urn...23.00 RM
Delivery of remains via courier to Reinhold
Family...6.30 RM
Total amount due...76.70 RM

In red ink, stamped across the bottom of the bill, were the words, "Paid in Full." Under that a hand-written message:

Dear Reinhold Family,
I am so sorry for your loss.
May God be with you at this difficult time.
Anton Halbbauer,
Director, Halbbauer Funeral Home
P.S. Government regulations require that I issue a bill for services rendered.
I have taken the liberty of cancelling it.

Twenty years earlier Hannah Reinhold had been buried with Gottlieb's family in the Jewish cemetery near Opera Square and Franz gained permission from the Jewish Council to have Gottlieb join her there.

On a frigid December day, in a simple ceremony, the Reinhold family laid Gottlieb to rest beside his beloved wife.

CHAPTER NINE

Early December, 1938.

Greta and Nessa stood in the kitchen preparing the evening meal, Nessa slicing carrots, Greta stirring a pot of cabbage soup. Erich emerged from upstairs and inhaled deeply. "Something smells good." He planted a kiss on Nessa's cheek. "As soon as I finish replacing the last two windowpanes, the house will be almost as good as before."

In another, happier life, this could be a normal family, simply doing chores around the house, Nessa thought. Would she and Erich ever experience such a thing?

"Tell your father *Abendessen is* ready, Erich," Greta said, transferring the soup to a tureen.

Erich went to the staircase near the back door and yelled up to his father, which made his mother shake her head at his uncouth manners and Nessa smile at the small taste of everydayness, something they seemed to have so little of.

After a few moments Franz came down. "I've filled three more bags with things we'll have to leave behind," he announced. "We'll definitely be traveling light."

"We can start over when we get to Ohio," Greta assured him, setting the soup on the table.

After the family had settled around the table, Franz said grace, ending with, "We trust you, oh God, to keep us safe." The next words out of his mouth were, "I just hope the sponsorship papers from your parents get here soon, Greta. The American embassy won't issue our visas without them."

"They'll be here any day," she said, confidently. "I'm sure my parents will agree to support all four of us until we can get on our feet."

"Some of us won't be going," Erich declared.

Franz and Greta gaped at one another and then at Erich and Nessa.

"I can't go with you," Nessa said. "I can't leave my family. My father's still missing, and my aunt Helen is in poor health and needs someone to look after her."

"And I can't leave Nessa," Erich said in a voice that left no room for argument.

"Really, Erich?" Franz said, impatiently. "After everything that's happened?"

Nessa flushed with guilt. It was her fault Erich insisted on staying in this dangerous country. She should tell him to get out of Germany while he still could.

"Son, this makes no sense," Franz decried. "Weren't you listening to your mother? Her parents will most likely sponsor all of us. Nessa, I'm sure we can make provision for your father and your aunt, too. Although, my dear, I don't think your father will be coming back from Sachsenhausen," he added gently.

"He *will* come back," Nessa insisted. "I can't leave Germany and abandon my family." Oh, but how she longed to flee with the Reinholds, to someplace safe, where she could sleep peacefully at night. But she just couldn't go.

Greta threw her hands in front of her face and began to weep. "I can't bear the thought of leaving you two behind." She ran from the room and up the stairs, still crying.

Franz sighed and stood up. "We'll find a way to work this out." He left the kitchen and followed his wife upstairs.

"There's no way *to* work it out," Nessa said to Erich, tears welling in her eyes. "You should go with your family, leave while you can." It was selfish and wrong to expect him to stay behind with her. "I'll be all right."

He squeezed her hand. "There's no point discussing the matter anymore. I'm staying with you."

"Oh, Erich," she sobbed, "no matter what we do, it will be wrong. If we go, I'll be deserting my family; if we stay, your parents will be worried sick about leaving us behind." And what if her father never did come back? And what if Helen suddenly died? – the doctors said her heart was weak – then she'd have kept Erich in Germany for nothing. The thought made her cry all the harder.

He wrapped his arms around her. "You can't leave your family, and I won't abandon you. That settles it." He wiped away her tears, then kissed her.

In a more stable time, they'd be planning their wedding, holding each other, and talking nothing but love. If they chose to leave Germany now, they could still have all that. But she couldn't leave, and he wouldn't. There was no point in thinking about what might be. They would have to travel down this dark road looking only to God because the future was impossible to see.

A few days later the telephone on the kitchen counter rang, the shrill sound echoing off the tiled walls, making both Greta and Nessa jump. They looked at one another nervously.

"Who would be calling?" Nessa wondered.

Greta seemed frozen in place.

Nessa grabbed the receiver. "Reinhold residence. This is Nessa."

A frantic Frau Sturm was on the other end of the line. "Nessa, two stormtroopers just brought your father home."

"Papa's back!" Nessa cried as she hung up the phone and started for the door.

"Wait, we'll go with you," Greta said. "You may need help."

Why would she need help? Papa was back. Still, Nessa waited politely, trying to curb her impatience as Greta summoned the men. It only took a moment for her to do so, but to Nessa it felt like an eternity. Once Franz and Erich appeared, she dashed out the front door ahead of them.

They all hurried down the street, covering the short distance to Nessa's home in less than five minutes. The front door stood open. In the foyer Nessa spotted the large figure of Frau Sturm standing with her father, her arm around his shoulders, stroking his head and speaking quietly to him. David Baumgartner stared straight ahead, unaware of his neighbor's presence.

Nessa hurried up the front stairs and through the door, taking Frau Sturm's place. "Oh, Papa, you're back! Thank God you're back."

Her father gave no answer. His clothes were filthy, soiled with mud. His face was swollen, all expression absent. His head had been shaved and he smelled of urine and sweat.

Nessa dropped her arms and took his hands, panic rising in her like bile. "Papa, it's Nessa. Can you hear me?"

"He's in the same clothes he was wearing when they took him away," Frau Sturm said. "I don't think he's bathed since."

Nessa stared at her father in disbelief. How could anybody treat another human being that way? She stroked his face, remembering the man who had carried her on his shoulders through the *Tiergarten* when she was young, the man who had spent hours reading her fairy tales. "Papa, it's Nessa."

Frau Sturm gave Nessa a tattered document. "I found this in his coat. It attests that he wasn't mistreated."

Nessa studied the scrawled signature on the bottom of the form.

It didn't resemble her father's handwriting any more than this shell of a man resembled her Papa. "He was at Sachsenhausen, just as we thought."

"It's a miracle they even released him," Frau Sturm said as Erich led Nessa's father into the living room and pulled up a chair for him.

"Papa, please sit," Nessa urged and pressed him down. He sat for an instant, but then shot up with a jerk as if an inaudible voice had commanded him to come to attention, his glazed eyes fixed on some point in the distance.

"We'd better take him to our house," Franz said. "Frau Sturm, would you be able to drive us there?"

"Come, Papa," Nessa said. For an instant her father loosed his faraway gaze from that unseen object and looked at her. For a moment she hoped for some spark of recognition from him, but there was none.

At the Reinhold's home, the men bathed David and put him to bed. Franz called their family physician, who said he would come by the next morning. That night David Baumgartner died in his sleep. A week later they laid him to rest next to his wife near the shores of the *Schlachtensee*.

The winter sky was as gray as a lithograph as Nessa and Erich strolled arm-in-arm along Schierker Strasse towards Körner Park. A few brown and shriveled leaves still clung to the nearly naked linden trees that stood like sentinels in long rows on either side of the street.

It was a few days past Christmas and Nessa inhaled deeply and gazed into the park, longing for winter to retreat so that spring might awaken the slumbering hibiscus plants and lavender bushes, causing them to fill their cold, bare branches with fragrant, vernal buds and blossoms.

Then they saw him – a man leaning, almost lying, against a chestnut tree on the sidewalk outside the park, shivering in the cold. His hair and sidelocks were filthy, his beard disheveled. The man's feet were bare, bluish, and bleeding, his trousers in tatters. Nothing about him bore witness to the German sense of order. As people passed by, he repeated his mantra over and over. "*Hilfe, bitte. Habt Erbarmen.*"

A middle-aged man stopped to scold the vagrant. "You Jews have done nothing but rob us for centuries and now you want help and mercy?"

The beggar stretched out a dirty, trembling hand toward his accuser and opened a nearly toothless mouth. "*Hilfe, bitte.*"

"You'll not get a single *pfennig* from me, you lazy parasite," the man declared and continued down the street, shaking his head. "The Jews refuse to work and still they expect us to give them money."

The Germans had robbed thousands of Jews of their jobs and businesses. How could they work? Rage seethed inside Nessa. "We need to help that man," she said to Erich.

They started toward the beggar, but a gaggle of schoolchildren rushed past them, almost running them down. The children stopped abruptly in front of the Jew, gaping curiously. Then they huddled together, whispering, as if hatching a conspiracy. A few seconds later each child bent down and gathered a handful of fallen chestnuts and began pelting the man. "*Stinkjude! Stinkjude!*"

"Stop that!" Nessa commanded as she and Erich started toward them. The children stopped and stared at Nessa for an instant, their breaths pulsating in milky puffs, before dropping their projectiles and shrieking off down the street.

"No one deserves to live like this," Nessa said, bending at the man's side. The stench of filth and urine was overpowering. They tried to lift him to his feet, but he was much too heavy.

"*Hilfe.*"

"Don't worry, we're here to help," Nessa told him, putting a hand on his shoulder. But how? She looked around, not knowing quite what to do.

A woman with a young daughter in tow hurried past. The child broke away and ran over to stare at the Jew. "What's wrong with that man, Mutti?" the girl asked, pointing a timid finger.

The mother rushed over, grabbed the girl's hand and pulled her away. "He's a dirty Jew. Don't touch him."

The child pointed at Erich and Nessa. "Then why are those people touching him?"

The woman scowled at them and hurried the child away without answering the question.

"*Bitte, Hilfe.*"

Nessa straightened and looked up and down the street, hoping to discover a way to help. "Erich, there's a phone booth at the corner. I'll call Herr Nussbaum. He'll know what to do."

"I'll stay with him," Erich said. "Hurry."

Nessa ran to the phone booth, throwing open the door. She fumbled in her purse and found the business card Nussbaum had given her the last time she and Erich had seen him. She dialed his number.

"Nussbaum," a voice announced on the other end of the line.

"Herr Nussbaum, this is Nessa Baumgartner. Erich and I have found a homeless Jewish man who needs help."

"Where are you?"

"At the southwest corner of Körner Park. Can you come help us?" Surely Nussbaum would know a way to get help for the man.

"I'll be there in ten minutes," Nussbaum said and hung up.

She turned to see a police car come to a sudden stop beside the vagrant.

Nessa left the booth and rushed to join Erich, who knelt at the man's side, holding his hand.

Two officers got out of the car. "Are you the man who called to report a vagrant?" one of them asked Erich. The policeman's partner stood smoking a few meters away.

Erich dropped the man's hand and stood up, ignoring the question. "*Herr Wachtmeister*, this man needs help. Who knows when he last ate?"

"He's a vagrant. If you don't work, you don't eat – that's my philosophy. And since when do you care about a *Jude*?" the policeman added, apparently mistaking Erich's light hair and blue eyes for Aryan.

"*Herr Wachtmeister*, I think the man's sick," Nessa put in.

The policeman grunted impatiently. "All right, let's take a look." He bent over the man, then reeled back, seemingly overcome by the stench. "Drunk," he concluded. He kicked the man's foot. "Hey, *Jude*. This isn't your living room. Move along."

"Look at him, he's too weak to stand up," Erich said.

"Then I guess he can sleep it off in a jail cell."

Nessa knew incarceration couldn't end well for the vagrant. She risked a suggestion. "We'll take him home, *Herr Wachtmeister*. We have a car nearby." Hopefully they would soon. "I'm sorry we bothered you."

The policeman narrowed his eyes at her and snapped, "You won't take this man anywhere. We're arresting him for vagrancy and public intoxication. He's a disgrace to the Fatherland."

"He's only destitute because the government robbed him of his home and livelihood," Nessa snapped back.

The officer leveled an admonishing finger at Nessa. "We're not here to discuss government politics or policy, young lady. If I were you, I'd hold my tongue – unless you'd like to join this Jew in jail."

He was right. Nothing would be accomplished if she and Erich got arrested. How she wished Herr Nussbaum would hurry up and get there. Although, what could he do, now that the police had arrived?

After a brief consultation, the two officers seized the man's legs and dragged the bleeding bundle of rags over to their vehicle and threw him in like a sack of potatoes. A moment later, they pulled away from the curb.

Numb with distress, Nessa leaned against Erich and wept as she watched the police car round the corner.

When Nussbaum arrived, she was still crying, staring angrily in the direction the police car had disappeared. "The police took him away," she told the lawyer. "We couldn't save him."

Nussbaum put an arm around her and Erich. "I wish we could save everyone, but we can't."

"It's just not right," Nessa cried.

"For 'right,' we'll probably have to wait until Judgment Day," Nussbaum said. "Still we try."

Nessa stomped her foot. "I feel so helpless."

"There must be something we can do to help people like that," Erich put in.

Nussbaum looked speculatively from one to the other. "Do you two wish to help? Truly?"

"Yes. How?" Erich asked.

"Come back to my office with me. We can talk there."

Once in Nussbaum's office, supplied with cups of *Kaffee*, they did talk.

"First of all," Nussbaum began, "let me give you some advice. If I were you two, I would leave Germany right away. I have connections and I can get you out."

"I have an elderly aunt who is not in the best of health," Nessa said. "I can't leave. She needs my help."

Nussbaum turned to Erich. "And you won't leave Germany without Nessa, right?"

"Right."

Nussbaum steepled his palms and regarded them. "I'm going to make a prediction. There will come a day when it will be impossible for Jews to leave Germany unless they're bound for concentration camps – or worse. Even now it's hard. I, and … some others are working to get as many out now as we can. We supply funds where needed, make connections where possible, help with paperwork. This is dangerous work – and it's illegal. But it is very important work." He looked soberly from Nessa to Erich. "You said earlier you wanted to help people like the Jewish vagrant the police arrested?"

"That's right."

"I can use all the help I can get saving Jews at risk. But this kind of work isn't something to be entered into lightly, not even for a short time. It's risky and it's lonely. We live and work in the shadows, doing everything we can to stay off the Nazi radar, submerging below the surface of everyday life like U-Boats."

"We're not entering into this lightly," Nessa insisted.

"You two go have a long talk. Then if you still want to get involved, come back. But consider carefully. I'm a widower with no children, no family. And my youth is long gone. You are both young with a long future to spend. If you keep your heads down, and don't make waves in the New Germany, you'll have a much better chance of surviving than if you join me in my work."

"Sit idly by while people like that poor man suffer and die?" Nessa said in disgust. "We can't do that."

Nussbaum shrugged. "Our people have always suffered – this is no new thing," he said. "Now you two go home and consider my offer carefully," he added, leading them to the front door.

"I want to do whatever I can to help Herr Nussbaum in his work," Nessa said, as Erich closed the door to the attorney's office.

Erich nodded in agreement. "So do I."

"And we shouldn't help only because we have Jewish heritage. We should help because it's the decent thing to do, the Christian thing to do."

"You're right," he said. "But if things start to get too dangerous …" He pulled her close. "I don't want anything to happen to you."

She sighed. "So much has already happened. I don't see how things could get any worse."

"They can. Think about what the Nazis did to your Papa. If we get arrested, they won't treat you any differently simply because you're a woman. We'll help, but if I feel your life is in jeopardy, I'm getting you out of Germany and you'll have to settle for helping from a distance."

They made their way past slumbering churches as well as homes shuttered for the night. From a courtyard behind a stone wall, children squealed, and a dog barked. Behind those walls all seemed normal in Germany. Happy Aryan children, safe in their yard, playing with their dog. Nessa was sure that Jewish children in Hitler's Germany weren't feeling so protected and carefree.

Their decision made, Nessa and Erich agreed to say nothing to his parents for the time being. "No sense worrying them needlessly," he said.

～

A week later they rang in the New Year quietly at Erich's house.

"Here's to a better year," Franz toasted. "And a better life in America."

Nessa and Erich exchanged smiles. They had shared their decision with Nussbaum and would soon be experiencing a better life right there in Germany helping fellow Jews in distress.

And then, perhaps, America could be their reward – someday.

～

Mid-January, 1939.

Erich was about to join the family for lunch in the kitchen when he heard footsteps on the front porch followed by the doorbell. He felt a stab in the pit of his stomach. *Who could it be this time?* The door-bell sounded again.

He opened the door to find the postman, Herr Brandt, standing on the snowy front porch. "Some January, isn't it?" he said. "This cold freezes my bones." He held out an envelope. "A letter from America. From Cambridge, Ohio."

Herr Brandt normally dropped their mail in the letterbox next to the front door. Today he was personally delivering it – and taking time to stand around in the cold to visit.

"Thank you, Herr Brandt." Erich took the envelope and started to close the door.

The postman craned his neck toward the letter. "Good news, I hope. Cambridge, Ohio is a world away."

"I wouldn't know, Herr Brandt," Erich replied politely, "I've never been there. Thank you again." He closed the door on the nosey postman and hurried to the kitchen.

"It looks like a letter from Oma and Opa Schulz," he said, handing it to his father before taking a seat beside Nessa.

Franz ripped open the envelope, and then let out a whoop. "It's the affidavit, Greta. Your parents have agreed to support us once we get to America. All of us, even your aunt Helen," he added to Nessa.

"What a relief!" Greta said. She turned to Nessa. "Dear, won't you reconsider? We could all have a new start in America."

Nessa looked out the window as if searching for an answer on the horizon, then laid a hand on Greta's. "Helen would never leave. Germany is her home. Besides, she's in poor health and I have to stay with her. Please try to understand."

"Mutti, Nessa and I are staying in Germany," Erich insisted.

"You can't," his mother protested. "What will happen to you?"

"I won't leave Nessa," Erich said firmly. "Anyway, someone has offered us work. Important work."

"Who?" Greta snapped. "What kind of work?"

"Herr Nussbaum, the lawyer. He helps Jews who are in trouble."

Erich wasn't about to tell his parents that working with Nussbaum would put him and Nessa in grave danger.

But his father seemed to have figured that out. "This work's illegal, isn't it?"

Erich dodged the question. "Papa, we can't sit by and watch the Nazis rob Jews of their homes and businesses. Christians are supposed to love their neighbors. We have no other choice."

Greta dug both hands into the fabric of her apron, turning her knuckles colorless. "Erich, don't stay behind in Germany," she pleaded.

"Son, can this Herr Nussmann pay you a living wage?" Franz wanted to know.

"We'll manage, Papa. Once Nessa sells her parents' home, we'll have money. Herr Nussbaum is giving us an apartment above his office."

Greta clenched her jaw and shook her head. "I won't leave my children."

Erich slid over and put an arm around her. "But you must, Mutti." He picked up her all-important affidavit. "God's provided you a way out of Germany. It would be a sin to reject it."

"But what of you?" his mother sobbed. "What of both of you?"

"We'll come to America later, after all this madness is over," he said. "This can't go on forever."

Franz nodded in resignation. "I'll start the emigration paperwork tomorrow for your mother and me."

Early March, 1939.

Erich and Franz sat in the customs office, a dreary room that smelled of mildew. Paint peeled from the walls like bark from a diseased tree. Clients had come and gone all morning, and now Erich and Franz were the only people left in the waiting area.

Erich looked at his watch for perhaps the hundredth time they had arrived. It was almost noon. They'd been waiting nearly four hours. He turned to his father. "Are we ever going to get waited on?" he asked, glaring across the room at the customs official.

Franz followed Erich's gaze. "I've dealt with Herr Eisenach twice before," he said. "He'll call us when he's ready, not before." He leaned back in his seat and sighed. "You should've stayed home, Erich. There's no sense both of us wasting the day here."

"I wanted to come with you today, Papa. For moral support, if nothing else." He looked across the lobby again at Eisenach. "Although it probably won't take two of us to outsmart that buffoon." Eisenach's bloated face and crimson neck bulged out of his shirt collar. His eyes were as closely set as the two dots of an umlaut and his ears stood out from his head like a pair of horse blinders. He'd been sitting at his desk for twenty minutes ignoring them, lethargically stamping documents.

"We're not here to outsmart anyone. And when he calls us, please don't antagonize him." Franz held out a handful of papers. "I don't want to leave here without his signature on this emigration paperwork." He clawed at his hair as if trying to dislodge some fiendish beast that was digging its talons into his scalp. "I've been chasing paperwork for months. I don't want to do this for the rest of my life."

Papa's right. No sense rocking the boat. His father had spent many weeks slogging from one agency to the next, getting approval for this request, securing a notary stamp for this or that document. He'd stood for hours in line at the American Embassy, only to learn that their emigration request was still near the bottom of a huge list.

Erich stared at the official. Eisenach stuffed a sandwich into his face and washed down what he had bitten off with a mouthful of beer. He must have started his three-hour lunch break, Erich thought. The man chewed as lethargically as he worked.

At that moment Eisenach met Erich's gaze. He had just forced more of his sandwich into his mouth and paused in his chewing as if contemplating whether to finish his meal or deal with Erich and his father. Eisenach rolled his eyes and threw his sandwich onto his desk with a smack. He was going to finally grant them an audience!

He motioned to them as if summoning a pair of misbehaving children. "*Na, na, dann kommen Sie nur,*" he barked.

Erich grabbed his father's arm. "Papa, it's our turn. Come on."

They stood up and started across the lobby. To his left Erich saw a man and a woman come through the front door. He and Franz were almost at Eisenach's desk when the official raised his hand like a traffic cop. "Halt."

Franz and his son stopped in the middle of the lobby, confused.

Eisenach flicked his hand at them as if shooing away a pesky fly. "Back to your seats" he commanded. "Aryans are served first." He beckoned to the couple. "Herr Grass, Frau Grass, *willkommen.*"

The Aryan couple pushed past Erich, jostling him before seating themselves at Eisenach's desk. Erich and his father returned to their seats. Erich looked at his watch again. Nearly twelve-thirty.

A strange transformation came over Eisenach as soon as the Aryan couple sat down. His personality changed from a disinterested Joseph Goebbels to an effervescent Shirley Temple. He bowed and cooed and chuckled as if the three of them were fast friends.

Franz turned and looked at Erich, who was glaring holes in the bureaucrat's face, and laid his hand on his son's arm. "Easy, now. If he sees that look on your face, your mother and I may never get to America."

Forty-five minutes later, the Aryan couple and Eisenach stood up. He clicked his heels and shook each of their hands with both of his, then came around his desk to accompany them to the front door like a maître d' at a fine restaurant leading honored guests to their table. Then he rushed ahead of them, flung open the front door and bowed as they left. "Heil Hitler!"

Erich sighed. "Finally." He looked over at his father who had fallen asleep.

Eisenach turned on his heel and looked at Erich. "*Bin gleich wieder da*," he said, disappearing through the front door.

The slamming of the door woke Franz. He looked around. He and his son were alone in the room. "Where's Eisenach?"

"He left. He said he'd be right back." Erich leaned his head against the wall behind him. *I should've brought a book. I could have read through "War and Peace" by now.*

"Right back" turned into two hours, during which time several more people had entered the waiting room. When Eisenach finally waddled through the front door, he went to his desk and fell onto his chair, which responded with an energetic crack. He looked across the lobby from one face to the next. "Are there any Aryans here?" he asked. No reply. He beckoned to Erich and Franz.

"What is it?" he demanded, as they sat down. He smelled like a vat of stale beer.

"What is it?" Erich spat. "We've been waiting here for six hours while you eat and drink and stamp your pathetic little documents, and all you have to say is 'what is it?' I should report you to your superiors."

Franz laid a hand of his son's arm. "Erich, it's all right, Herr Eisenach is a busy man." He turned to the official, handing him some papers. "I'm hoping you'll provide the final signature I need for my emigration paperwork."

Eisenach scowled at Erich, then grabbed the papers.

"Hmm. Hmm. Franz Reinhold. Greta Reinhold. Hmm." He looked at Franz. "Which one of you is Franz?"

"I am."

Eisenach read some more, then looked at Erich. "You're obviously not Greta Reinhold."

"She's not here," Erich said.

Eisenach leveled a finger at him. "Then who the blazes are you?"

"Erich Reinhold." He pointed at Franz. "Franz is my father."

"I don't see your name on these papers, Erich Reinhold, son of Franz Reinhold. Are you emigrating as well?"

"No, I'm not."

"Then why in the blazes are you sitting here interfering with my job and lecturing me?" Eisenach growled. "Sit there like an obedient son and hold your tongue until I'm finished with your father!"

Erich fell silent and fumed.

Eisenach put a fat finger on Franz's paperwork. "Your Customs Declaration is in order. You've correctly listed all of the cash and other assets you intend to take out of the country."

"So, you'll approve my paperwork?"

"No." He patted the Customs Declaration. "The assets enumerated here belong to both you and your wife. I can't approve this paperwork unless both of you are present."

"No one told me that."

"Well, someone's telling you now."

"I'll bring her in tomorrow," Franz sighed. "Once you approve this customs paperwork, how long will it be before we can emigrate?"

"No idea. All applications are subject to a final review. That could take weeks. Months."

Erich was livid. He clenched the seat of his chair until his hands cramped. How he wanted to break his chair over Eisenach's head.

They left the official's desk and stepped outside, where a biting, cold wind greeted them.

"Papa, why do you put up with so much crap from these bureaucrats?"

"Because the abuse I get from Eisenach is nothing compared to what your mother and I will suffer if we stay in Germany. Which is exactly why we wanted to include your name and Nessa's on the emigration papers."

∿

Mid-March, 1939.

Franz took some books he was leaving behind from the bookcase in the living room and put them into a box. "I wish we'd gotten more money for our house," he complained. "After we pay all the emigration fees and our train fare to Amsterdam, we won't have much left over."

"But in the end, we'll have something more valuable than money," Greta reminded him as she folded some towels. "We'll have our lives and our liberty. Thank God the people who bought our home said we could stay here until we leave."

Turning to Erich and Nessa, she repeated the words she never tired of saying. "I only wish the two of you were coming with us."

"Don't worry, Mama, we'll be fine," Erich assured her.

Greta looked about to weep, but she nodded. "We'll find a way to bring you both over and I'll be counting the days until we're all safe together in America. You must promise to stay in touch. You still have my parents' address and phone number in Ohio, right?"

"Yes, Mama, don't worry." Erich said.

Greta nodded, grim-faced, picking up a dust rag.

"We won't be separated for long," Nessa soothed.

As always, talk of being separated and of knowing Erich and Nessa would be alone and in jeopardy left Greta beside herself. Erich wished he could cheer her. She scowled and began to dust more vigorously, knocking a figurine to the floor in the process. It landed with a quiet crunch.

"We couldn't take it with us anyway," she said, picking up the pieces in disgust.

∿

Ninety days later the miracle came to pass. The Reinholds' application had been approved. Suddenly they had two only weeks to leave the country. This posed no problem. Their affairs were in order and Greta's parents had arranged boat passage from Amsterdam to New York.

"So much has happened in a few short years," Greta lamented as the family sat in the living room, picking at *Apfelstrudel*. "I feel as if a giant broom has come along to sweep us out of our own country."

"That's how life often works, my love." Franz took her hand. "The people in power move us around like pieces on a chess board. And yet God has watched over us. Think of Mary and Joseph about to become parents and having to travel to Bethlehem because a greedy ruler wanted his taxes."

"And yet God's hand was in it," put in Nessa, catching on.

Greta scowled. "God's hand is not in what's happening in Germany today."

"And yet He's given us a way out," Franz countered.

"Not for these two," Greta said, looking at Erich and Nessa.

"They've made their choice. We have to allow them that freedom."

"I had thought by now this chaos in Germany would be all over, that we'd see you two happily married," Greta said to Erich.

Sometimes it seemed grossly unfair to Erich that he and Nessa still hung in limbo, unable to consummate their love, to have a home of their own and a family. And why should Hitler steal all that from them? Surely they could find a minister to marry them – even without the approval of the State.

"So, let's just get married," he said to Nessa. "Pastor Niemayer would perform the ceremony. Why should we let Hitler tell us when we can and can't start our life together?"

Instead of being thrilled, Nessa looked horrified.

"Erich, do you know what would happen to you two if you were found out?" asked his mother, equally horrified. "A *Mischling* and a

Jew marrying – you'd both end up in Sachsenhausen – or worse. Promise me you won't do such a stupid thing."

"We won't," Nessa promised, speaking for both of them and making Erich frown.

"So, we're to have no life, no happiness," he grumbled.

He felt his face flush.

"Not in this country," reminded his father. "Pieces on a chess board."

"Hitler can try, but this is one pawn that won't be so easily moved," Erich muttered.

～

Greta and Franz spent their last days in Germany saying goodbye to their homeland.

A few days before their departure, together with Erich and Nessa, they wandered through the paths and gardens of the *Tiergarten*, taking advantage of the robust spring weather.

They passed a group of oak trees and strolled over a bridge that spanned a large pond. Geese circled on its surface, chattering at one another, while two boys sat in a rowboat and fished.

How hard this had to be on Greta, Nessa thought. And yet Nessa as well was finding it difficult to face the imminent parting with the woman who'd become such a good friend.

"It's so peaceful here." Greta pointed to a mother and her toddler standing on a patch of lawn feeding a chipmunk. "No one would guess that hate is raging all around us."

Franz put a soothing arm around her shoulder. Turning to Erich he changed the subject. "Your mother and I used to walk you along this very trail in your pram." He pointed to the left. "Look how much that oak tree has grown, Greta. We used to sit under it on that bench."

"Everything here has changed so much."

Franz smiled at his wife and drew her closer. "We've changed a lot too, haven't we?"

"And so has Germany."

Franz hadn't succeeded in diverting Greta's attention from the realization that they'd soon be leaving forever. As they left the park, she wiped away a tear. "One man – one lunatic –has destroyed and separated so many families. What kind of people will be living here when he's finished?"

Nessa shook her head. *For one thing, there won't be as many. Thousands will have changed their places of residence from their homes to their graves.*

They moved on to the Jewish cemetery to say goodbye to Gottlieb and Hannah. A landscape of ruins greeted them. Vandals had toppled or defaced many of the gravestones.

Erich paused to look at the carnage. Several stones were painted with the words, *"Juden raus."* His face turned bitter. "I'm surprised the Nazis haven't dug up all of the Jewish graves and thrown the bodies over the border into Poland."

As they stood huddled around the graves of Gottlieb and Hannah, Franz sighed. "Three generations of Reinholds are buried here. I was hoping to rest beside my parents one day, but that's never going to happen now." He reached over and caressed the stones. "Goodbye, Mama, Papa. We do not abandon your resting places voluntarily. We've been driven from them."

As they turned to leave, a young man came through the gates pushing a dilapidated cart bearing what appeared to be a corpse shrouded in a bed sheet. Behind him hobbled an elderly man bent over from age. The family nodded to the two men, who nodded back.

After they watched the men wander down a path and out of sight, Nessa burst into tears. "This is what Germany has become!" she wailed. "The Jews have to bury their dead like stray dogs."

Erich pulled her closer and led her out of the cemetery.

～

June, 1939. Anhalter Train Station. Berlin.

Nessa and Erich and his parents stood on the platform exchanging goodbye hugs, when they heard a familiar voice behind them. "Hallo. Hallo."

They turned to see a tall, matronly woman rushing toward them. Her face glowed with perspiration and her blond hair had come loose from her hair bun.

"Frau Sturm!" Greta croaked in astonishment. "I was going to write you once we arrived in America. Who told you we were leaving today?"

"I did," Erich admitted.

"You shouldn't be seen with us," Greta fretted, looking nervously around the platform. "It's dangerous."

"Oh, nonsense," Frau Sturm responded, handing Greta a bouquet of flowers. "You know me by now. I'm too old to care what people think. I knew your parents long before you were born. I saw you take your first steps, for goodness sake. You're not leaving Germany without a hug from me."

"Thank you so much for coming," Greta said as the two women embraced, their cheeks wet with tears.

"How I'd love to come with you, but I can't leave my boys."

"I wish we didn't have to go," Greta sobbed.

"You're sailing to a new life, a new adventure," Frau Sturm insisted. "You're the fortunate ones. You're going to the land of liberty."

"Without my son," Greta sighed, washing Erich in guilt.

Until he looked at Nessa. Then he knew he'd made the right decision. How much more guilt would he feel if he left today with his parents and abandoned her to fend for herself?

When Franz and Greta located their railway car, Franz turned to hug Erich and Nessa once more. "You two watch out for one another, all right?"

Greta took her turn embracing them, giving each a kiss. "Promise me you'll be careful."

"We will," Erich assured her.

"I'll pray for both of you every day." She squeezed their hands. Then, with tears on her cheeks, she hugged Frau Sturm once more and turned to board the train, followed by Franz.

Once in their compartment, Franz opened the window so they could talk for a few more moments before the train left. Greta joined him at the window, dabbing her eyes with her handkerchief.

Franz poked his head out the window and opened his mouth to speak, but before he could form the words, a diminutive Gestapo officer burst into their compartment and barked, "Are there any Jews here?"

Franz turned around. "I'm Jewish. My wife's half-Jewish."

On the platform Erich tensed and held his breath.

"*Schwein*," Frau Sturm muttered, while Nessa began to pray.

The little man planted himself in the middle of the compartment, glared up at Franz and held out his hand. "Papers."

Franz handed the man their passports and travel documents. "I think you'll find everything in order."

"I'll be the one who decides what's in order," the little tyrant declared. He bent over the documents. "Going to America, eh?" With a sardonic smile he added, "Why would you want to do that? Don't you *Stinkjuden* like it here in Germany?"

Franz didn't answer.

An intense interrogation followed during which the Reinholds' papers and luggage were checked and rechecked.

Erich paced back and forth on the platform outside the compartment, fists clenched in rage. Nessa finally led him a few meters away from the train. "Erich, calm down. You'll just make matters worse."

From a distance Erich watched the man torment his parents,

praying the little bully would move on. He finally pushed Franz's paperwork hard into his chest, causing him to reel backwards. The little man smiled coldly, then disappeared down the corridor in search of more prey.

"Thank God," Nessa breathed.

Erich rushed back to the window and reached out a hand to his mother. "Are you two all right?" he asked.

"Fine. Fine," Franz said. "Don't worry about us."

"Good," Erich said, relieved. "Safe travels to both of you," he added, squeezing his mother's hand.

"God keep you safe, my son," she prayed, squeezing back.

Would he ever see his parents again? He found it difficult to let go of his mother's hand even after the whistle blew. The train wheezed, lurched forward a few feet and stopped. Then it set itself in motion again and began moving slowly down the track.

Nessa, Erich, and Frau Sturm kept pace with it until they reached the end of the platform. The train picked up speed, and a handful of seconds later it was two kilometers closer to America.

CHAPTER TEN

Nussbaum made a sweeping motion with his arms. "Welcome to the Nussbaum Building. This apartment not as luxurious as the Hotel Adlon, but the price is right."

It certainly was. Nussbaum was letting them stay in his building for free, allowing them to hoard the money from the sale of Nessa's home. With each passing day the Nazis evicted more and more Jews from their homes, and they were glad to have a place anywhere.

"You'll be comfortable here," Nussbaum promised, "and you each have your own sleeping area." He gestured to his right. "Nessa, your bed is behind that curtain. Erich, yours is over there by the door behind the other curtain."

They stood in a storage room on the second floor. Light streamed through the windows and Erich could see cars, bicycles, and pedestrians hurry past.

Next to the curtain concealing Nessa's bed stood a couple of dusty chairs and an equally dusty vanity. An enormous free-standing oak wardrobe dominated the wall next to the window. On another wall a group of filing cabinets huddled together. A grandfather clock in a corner ticked lazily near a coal-burning stove. A small table and two chairs occupied another corner.

Nussbaum was right. Sharing a storeroom wasn't grand. Even more, Erich hated the fact that he and Nessa would have to hole up there like abandoned dogs sheltering from a storm, living together, but not as husband and wife. How far this was from the vision he'd once entertained of carrying her over the threshold of a cute little house with lace curtains in the windows and a nice kitchen where she could bake *Kuchen*. But it was safe, and that was what mattered.

Nussbaum pointed toward the far corner of the room. "That's the door to the back stairway. It leads down to the rear entrance and to my office on the first floor, as well as up to my apartment on the third floor. Last September I had to Aryanize my practice. Since then I've been training the new owner, Herr Werfel. I had a lot of clients, so it will take me quite a while to bring Herr Werfel up to speed." He moved toward the window and tapped with his foot on a floor vent. "You'll be able to hear us talking downstairs through this heating vent."

Nessa shot a nervous glance at the vent. "Can anyone in the office hear us talking up here."

"Yes, but don't worry. Werfel knows that I have tenants. He won't give you any trouble."

"But he doesn't know who we really are, right?"

"And he never will. You are simply two boarders. And once we make your counterfeit ID's, it won't matter who you have been in the past. For all intents and purposes, you two will be Aryans and will be able to move about the city easily, hiding in plain sight, so to speak. You'll be as safe as any legal Aryan."

"You mean as safe as any Aryan can be in Germany," Nessa countered.

Nussbaum smiled. "Indeed. These days every German's existence is in jeopardy."

Erich nodded and put his arm around Nessa. "We know it's going to be an eerie existence for a while."

"Today you two are submerging below the surface of everyday

life," Nussbaum informed them. He put his hand on Erich's shoulder. "Many of the Jews living under the Nazi radar look as Aryan as you and can live and work on the surface much of the time. By the same token, many Aryans have dark hair and eyes and are mistaken for Jews. These gray areas work to our advantage because the authorities can't always figure out who is who."

Nussbaum turned to Nessa. "Nessa, you are in that gray area. You have dark hair and eyes. Are you Jewish or Aryan? Some might guess Jewish, but who knows for sure? But once you get your 'Aryan' ID, you will, for all intents and purposes, be a proud member of the master race."

"Are you going to stay on the surface?" Nessa asked Nussbaum.

He winked. "Yes, for the time being. Right now, with the knowledge of the government, my official function is to help Herr Werfel learn the business. Unofficially, I run 'Operation Nussbaum,' the illegal organization that produces forged documents and smuggles people at risk out of Germany."

"But it's still legal to leave Germany," Erich said. "My parents did."

"Yes, but many Jews no longer have the money to leave. The Germans have taken their homes and businesses and left them so impoverished they couldn't finance a trip to Munich, much less to America. They end up destitute, living on the streets. Sooner or later they get scooped up by the police and sent to labor camps. That's where my colleagues Rabbi Grünberg and Frau Kleist come in. The Rabbi refers Jews to us who want to leave Germany, but who either have no money to finance the trip or are having trouble getting the necessary documents. Frau Kleist is the wealthy Aryan who bankrolls 'Operation Nussbaum.'"

Nussbaum folded his arms across his chest and looked at them earnestly. "Speaking of money, you two will be compensated for the work you do."

"That won't be necessary, Herr Nussbaum," Nessa said. "I have a bit of money from the sale of my parents' home. We have no intention of taking money for doing what we know to be right."

"I admire that," Nussbaum said. "You'll find the work interesting, rewarding, and full of challenges. For instance, we won't be at this location forever. Herr Werfel bought my practice, but he also wants to buy this building. When that happens, we'll have to relocate."

Stairs creaked behind them. Erich, already on alert, pulled Nessa into a dark corner of the room. What looked like a boy in adult clothes shuffled through the door. Erich noted the fair skin and blue eyes, and when the boy pulled off his shabby hat to reveal straw-colored hair, Erich held his breath.

"Ah," Nussbaum said, "Konrad's home." He called to Nessa and Erich. "Come out of there, you two. I want you to meet someone."

They stepped out of the dim light, and as Konrad approached, Erich realized he wasn't a boy at all, not with that stubble on his chin. He was simply short and slender.

"Konrad Spielhagen, glad to meet you," the young man said, holding out his hand.

Erich reluctantly took Konrad's hand and shook it. Why would Nussbaum have an Aryan working with him? It didn't make sense.

"Konrad has the other apartment upstairs," Nussbaum said. "He helps make bogus credentials and passports. In a day or two he'll have your counterfeit identification papers ready."

Nussbaum put his arm around the young man. "As you can see, Konrad's an Aryan."

"And you're helping Jews?" Erich asked incredulously.

"Not everyone in Germany hates Jews," Konrad replied.

"Konrad's parents were friends of mine," Nussbaum explained. "Before they died, I promised to take care of him. Now, don't let his size fool you. He can pass for a child, but he's actually nineteen. In a way his height, or lack thereof, is the perfect cover, just as your Aryan features are, Erich."

Erich nodded. *We all must be chameleons, now.*

"Konrad will teach you how to make counterfeit passports, identity cards, and ration cards," Nussbaum continued. "Nessa, you'll be helping me downstairs in the office, not only with my practice, but also with the administrative aspects of the smuggling business, such as booking train travel and picking up supplies."

Nussbaum put his hand on Erich's shoulder. "And Erich, Konrad will also be training you as a conductor."

Erich furrowed his brow. In his mind he saw himself dressed in a dark uniform punching holes in train tickets.

"That's what we call the people who accompany our refugees on their travels," Nussbaum said. "You'll be conducting illegals from Berlin to southern Germany."

"What happens from there?"

"We have other conductors who spirit our illegals over the Swiss border and then on to Lisbon. From there they sail to Palestine and to America." Nussbaum looked at Nessa and Erich soberly. "Our work is extremely dangerous. If you're caught, you will probably be executed."

Nessa shot Erich a frightened look and he took her hand. This was the life they had chosen. He remembered his uncle's words so many years ago: "A ship in the harbor is safe, but that's not what ships are built for." They were leaving the harbor now. Hopefully they'd carry many shipwrecked Jews to safety.

A bell sounded below them on the first floor. "That's the call bell," Nussbaum noted. "Herr Werfel apparently needs my help. I'll drop by tomorrow and we'll continue our conversation. Meanwhile, get settled and get acquainted with Konrad." Nussbaum turned and disappeared down the stairs.

"What did you two do before you decided to be lawbreakers?" Konrad quipped.

"For a while we worked as apprentices at Morgenstern's Department Store," Nessa said.

"Let me guess," Konrad said. "In the eyes of the Nazis you two are more Jew than Aryan."

Nessa sighed. "That's right."

"After we lost our jobs at Morgenstern's, I had hopes of taking over our family bookstore," Erich said. "But then we had to sell it to Aryans."

"Well, we employ anyone who wants to save lives," Konrad said, "no matter what your bloodlines." He looked at his watch. "It's noon. I've got to run some errands, but I'll be back in an hour to tell you more about your job duties."

❧

Nessa sat on her bed and stared into the room, her expression sober. Erich joined her and put his arm around her shoulder.

"What's wrong?"

"Erich ..." Her voice faltered. She was trembling.

"What is it? What's bothering you?"

"I know we've discussed this, and I thought we'd made the right decision. But when Herr Nussbaum said we could be executed for helping Jews ..."

"You're right. Smuggling people is not a wise decision."

"You mean we shouldn't get involved?"

"I mean that putting your life in jeopardy is always insanity.

It's not the natural thing to do. But we're not doing the wise thing, or the sane thing – we're doing the right thing."

Nessa bit her lip and nodded. "I know ..."

He took her hands into his. "I'm afraid, too. But we'll be saving doomed people from perishing. No one should suffer the fate your mother and your father suffered."

She nodded. "I just wish I were stronger," she said with a sigh, "and not so timid."

"You chose to remain in a violent, dangerous country. I'd hardly call that timid. In fact, I'd call it brave." He looked out the window. "Opa Gottlieb used to say that you should always stand up for what you believe. That doesn't mean that you're never afraid."

Nessa snuggled against him. "I wish I had gotten the chance to know him better."

"He knew enough about you to know you're wonderful and I share his opinion." Erich wrapped his arms around her and kissed her. One kiss led to another and Erich leaned her back on the bed, letting his fingers get lost in her hair. When they were together, he could easily forget the dangerous new world they lived in and all the attendant troubles. She was soft and lovely and smelled like roses. How he loved her and how he wanted her to be fully his.

∾

Erich's embrace had a way of dispelling Nessa's fears. His lips moved away from her mouth to behind her ear. She closed her eyes, giving in to the sensation. His kisses moved down her neck and his hands began to roam. As always, the temptation to give herself to him was strong.

So was her sense of right and wrong – as well as her practical side. She squirmed out of his arms and sat up.

"What's wrong?"

"One thing you don't need now is a pregnant fiancée."

He ran a hand up her arm. "So, let's get married."

"We both know what would happen if a Jew and a *Mischling* showed up at city hall and applied for a marriage license. The Germans would not only deny our marriage application, but arrest us. The Nuremberg Laws were still in effect last time I checked."

"Like I said before, we'll find a minister. We'll be married in the eyes of God. Never mind the government."

"Oh, Erich, you're dreaming. Even if we could marry, the thought of bringing a child into the world right now horrifies me. Everywhere I look, I see evil and terror." She felt the sting of tears in her eyes. It seemed as if all she did these dark days was cry.

He took her in his arms once more and pressed her head

against his shoulder. "I'm sorry. Forgive me. I got carried away and I acted selfishly. You're right, of course."

She wished she weren't. If only they could marry. How nice it would be to share this room as husband and wife. Just the two of them, high above the turmoil below, pretending that life was normal. But it wasn't.

Maybe it would never be normal again.

Konrad returned an hour later and pulled a third chair up to the small table in their room, motioning for Erich and Nessa to join him.

"We will be working with a gentleman named Manfred Dietmayer," he said. "You'll meet him in a few days."

"Manfred Dietmayer?" Erich said. "The owner of Manfred's Miscellanea?"

"The same. You know him?"

"His shop's down the street from our family's bookstore."

"Manfred has a hidden room in his shop where we produce false documents."

"We can't wait to get started," Erich said.

"Konrad," Nessa said, "why are you involved in Nussbaum's work?"

Konrad got up and fetched a picture frame hanging on the wall by the window, giving it to Nessa. She had expected the frame to hold a photograph, but it held a sheet of paper with five type-written lines.

"Go ahead, read it," Konrad said.

She obeyed:

"Rescue those who are being dragged off to death. Save those who are staggering toward the slaughtering block.

Don't claim that you knew nothing about it. Don't you realize that the Searcher of hearts knows, and will repay each person according to his deeds?

Proverbs 24: 11 and 12."

Konrad took the picture frame from her. "Herr Nussbaum set up his operation to rescue his Jewish brothers and sisters from certain death," he said. "I can't stand by and watch people brutalized and killed without lifting a finger to help. It's the right thing to do."

Erich and Nessa looked at one another and smiled.

"We were just talking about that very thing while you were gone," Nessa said.

Konrad smiled at them. "Thanks for joining the cause," he said. He looked at his watch. "I need to get going. Come on, I'll show you the back way out of here."

Konrad returned the picture frame to the wall and then took them down the back staircase to the rear door. Once outside they went along a cobblestoned walkway lined with huge cedar trees. The walkway intersected with an alley.

"The trees provide a perfect cover," Konrad said. "They block the view of our walkway from our neighbors so we can come in and out of the alley all year round without being seen."

Konrad led them to the back gate. "In a few days, once I've produced your new ID's, we'll send you to Café Nola and Café Krone, two favorite hangouts for illegals. They provide opportunities for social contact and information sharing. Information is vital for survival and illegals share most of it by word of mouth."

"The Gestapo hasn't raided the cafés?"

"Not yet. The trick to surviving is simple. Don't frequent the same establishment too long or too often."

We're like thieves, Nessa thought. In a way, that's what they were now, thieves stealing victims from the Nazi machine.

Konrad held out his hand. "Well, it was nice meeting both of you," he said, clasping Erich's hand and then Nessa's. "I'm off to buy supplies," he added. "The counterfeit passport business is booming." He tipped his hat and disappeared down the alley.

Nussbaum knocked on their door the next morning. "Ready for your next lesson?"

"We are," Erich assured him. If he was to be deprived of the life he wanted with Nessa, then he would at least take pleasure in sabotaging the people who had robbed them of their future.

"Operation Nussbaum has many facets," their friend explained. "Since we smuggle our refugees over the German-Swiss border, we collect information on the habits and movements of the German guards on that border. We then share that information with other underground organizations. And as an illegal operation, we're not above bribing officials to get any information we need. The sum total of these activities contributes to our main objective: rescuing people at risk."

"What about sabotage?"

"We avoid that. Violence would only put us on the Nazi radar, although we would use physical force in self-defense, if need be. I don't want to sound like a broken record, but our work is dangerous. If you're caught, you will die, probably after extreme torture."

Nessa took hold of Erich's hands.

"It'll be all right," he told her. "We'll get through this."

"I know. I'm just concerned that we'll get caught."

"Concern is a good thing," Nussbaum said. "It makes you careful, and caution increases your chances of survival. So does confidence. I will not allow either of you to go on missions alone until both you and I are confident that you are ready, which means your training program will likely last several months."

Erich was frustrated by the news, Nessa relieved.

Nussbaum laid a hand on their shoulders. "But let's not worry about that right now. Come, I have a special place to show you – an oasis in the desert, so to speak.

He led them up a creaky, dimly lit stairwell and opened the door at the top of the stairs and they stepped out onto the roof of the building.

Nussbaum stretched out his arms. "I call this 'The Garden of

Eden.' In the summertime, my wife and I used to spend almost every evening up here, God rest her soul."

The roof area was flat and did indeed resemble a garden. Along the railing overlooking the street, a handful of miniature cedars in wooden pots stood at attention and rustled in the wind. Nussbaum gestured to the right. "These are my pride and joy." A group of miniature pear trees laden with fruit stood proudly against a wall. "In a few weeks we'll have bushels of pears."

To add to the ambiance, a cage with pigeons stood next to the pear trees, the birds cooing softly.

"Here, let me show you my pigeons," Nussbaum said, leading them over to the cage.

"The big white one in the corner is actually a dove. His name is Hermann Göring. I named him after the commander-in-chief of the German Air Force." Nussbaum took Hermann out of the cage and held him out to Nessa. "Here, take him, he won't peck you. He loves women."

Nessa took the immense white bird. Hermann tipped his head at an angle, studying her.

"These birds carry messages to and from the other underground groups. Everyday hundreds of pigeons swarm Berlin's squares and parks, so no one thinks twice about my pigeons flying over the city, going on their missions. It's brilliant, if I do say so myself."

Hermann had begun cooing in Nessa's arms, and the two were becoming fast friends.

Nussbaum relieved Nessa of Hermann and led them over to the railing and looked out over Berlin. "What we do can be very demanding and this rooftop is a great place to come in the evening to recover from the stress of the day."

Despite the danger involved in smuggling human cargo, Erich was excited about this new adventure. They'd be saving lives instead of simply watching bad things happen to people. He and Nessa would be tools in the hands of the resistance, chipping away at the dark wall that surrounded Germany. He couldn't wait to take that first swing.

~

Hirsch Strasse had changed a lot in the months since Erich had last been there. Shops that were once Jewish were now firmly in the clutches of Aryans, including the bookstore that once belonged to his family.

"I hate what they've done to our store," he complained, as he and Konrad passed it one afternoon.

Nazi flags fluttered over the façade and a sign warning *"Juden Verboten"* hung in the front door. Erich stepped up to the display window. Inside the store, customers mingled under a banner laden with swastikas, which boasted, "The Führer is leading the Volk from darkness to light."

The display window no longer exhibited the works of un-German authors, writers unacceptable to the Nazis. Novels by outlawed authors such as Thomas Mann, Erich Maria Remarque, and Franz Kafka had yielded to dozens of leather-bound editions of Hitler's *Mein Kampf*, piled in pyramid fashion. A spotlight shone on an open volume of the Führer's tome, the edges of its gilded pages glistening in the light.

Above the sales counter a portrait of the Führer, illuminated by another spotlight, brooded over the store's interior, while dust particles danced in the shaft of light. So many childhood memories lived inside the shop among those specks of dust. Erich recalled walking through the aisles as a boy, arms outstretched, running his fingers over the book bindings, imagining he was absorbing all the knowledge and adventure contained in the books he touched.

He sighed and turned away and he and Konrad continued down the street. In the middle of the block, over the doorway of a dilapidated building, a sign said, "Manfred's Miscellanea."

Many people considered Manfred Dietmayer a walking, or

rather, a hobbling miracle. A discourteous remark about Hitler had once landed him at Gestapo Headquarters, but astonishingly, he had returned to tell about it. However, his extended stay at Burgstrasse 28 left him with a crippled arm, a hideously scarred face and a handful of missing teeth. Rounding out Manfred's disturbing appearance was a prosthesis leg – a souvenir from the Great War.

Konrad turned the knob to Manfred's shop door and pushed. The door refused to yield. "This happens every time I come here. Manfred keeps promising to fix this door." He pushed harder. No success.

"Konrad, let me try." Erich put his shoulder to the door and rammed it. It responded with a loud crack before bursting open. They stepped inside and closed the door behind them.

"I need to fix that door," a raspy voice said from somewhere in the shadows.

A small light bulb hanging from the ceiling flickered in the entryway. *Most dungeons are better lit than this place*, Erich thought. He almost expected to see bats hanging from the ceiling.

Konrad and Erich waited at the door for a few moments to let their eyes adjust to the dim light. Gradually, Erich saw the outlines of tables and shelves heaped with merchandise and the smoky contours of a middle-aged man puffing on a cigarette.

"Is that you, Konrad?" the man called.

"Yes, Herr Dietmayer. I hope you are well."

"Thank you, I'm fine, fine. Come on back."

The two young men moved toward the glow of the cigarette, walking through a dark aisle for a few meters before finding Manfred sitting at a workbench illuminated by a shop light.

Manfred got up and started around the bench. He had a bushy mustache and wore a pair of dirty, striped overalls and dragged his bad leg behind him as he walked. His crimson face resembled the surface of a sponge. He took a long drag from his cigarette, expelling the smoke before reaching out to shake Erich's hand.

"Erich, it's nice to see you again. I hear your parents have escaped to America. How are they settling in?"

"Very well, thank you."

"Konrad tells me that you'll be working with us doing forgeries."

"I'm looking forward to it."

"Fine, fine," Manfred said. He stepped over to the wall and flipped a switch, energizing half a dozen lights throughout the shop. "That's better," he said. "Sorry about the lack of light. I've been trying to save on electricity." He turned toward the back of the shop. "You probably want to see our work area." He threw his cigarette on the wooden floor and crushed it with his foot – then lit another. "Come with me." He let out a bark of laughter. "That's what the Gestapo agent said just before he arrested me."

They moved around a table strewn with machine parts, heaps of unsorted nuts, bolts, springs, and nails. At "Manfred's," chaos seemed to have supplanted ant remnant the German sense of order.

"Manfred has anything you could want," Konrad whispered to Erich, as they made their way through the aisles. "A tuning knob for the People's Radio or lug nuts for a 1938 Volkswagen. No extra charge for the rust and the dust."

Manfred stopped and pushed on a wall. It clicked and sprang open.

Erich grinned in delight. The secret door – every boy's dream.

Manfred swung open the door, reached inside, and flipped on the lights. Out of the darkness a workbench appeared laden with film, paper, cameras and bottles of chemicals and glue. He motioned to his two guests. "Come in. Come in." They entered the room, then Manfred grabbed a handle on the inside of the door and pulled it until the door clicked shut. He spread his arms wide. "This is where we do most of our forgeries." He put a hand on Erich's shoulder. "Make Konrad teach you everything he knows. He's a genius."

Konrad smiled sheepishly. "Manfred's prone to exaggeration."

Manfred switched his hand to Konrad's shoulder. "I never exaggerate when it comes to you, my young friend." He turned back to Erich and tapped on the door. "You can see everything that happens in the front of the shop through this peephole. Take a look."

Erich looked and saw the front counter, the entryway, and the front door.

"See this latch?" Manfred pointed to a bolt attached to the inside of the door. "Flip it to the right and you're locked in."

Erich tried the latch.

"Well, in this room we do our small part to thwart the Führer's plans," Manfred said. "Most Germans consider him a God," Manfred added, "but there's a world of difference between the true God and Hitler. God forgives us no matter how much we sin against him. Hitler doesn't. I have the scars to prove it."

"Well, on that cheerful note, Erich and I should get started," Konrad said, turning on a lamp above the workbench.

Manfred smiled, patted Eric on the shoulder and left the workroom.

"Today we'll be forging papers — your new identity papers," Konrad said. "You are now Erich Frank, an accountant based in Munich and Nessa is Nessa Schroeder, a student from Potsdam who's working as Herr Nussbaum's secretary to earn money for school."

Armed with their new identities, Erich and Nessa, under the tutelage of Nussbaum and Konrad, began to learn the art of producing forgeries and smuggling Germans in jeopardy out of the country. Most of the activities were mundane and devoid of adventure: learning the routine at Nussbaum's office, picking up the paper and ink needed for producing forgeries, and purchasing train fare for escaping Jews.

Nussbaum also insisted that they spend as much time as possible in public, keeping their hands on the pulse of the city – an activity that was becoming more and more distressing due to Hitler's unpredictable temperament.

CHAPTER ELEVEN

September 1, 1939. Midmorning.

The subway car came to a bumpy stop at *Unter den Linden*. Erich and Nessa followed the throng leaving the train and threaded their way through the crowd toward the stairwell leading to street level.

"I hope your aunt is doing better today," Erich said. "Last time, she didn't look that well."

"Helen's been in poor health ever since I can remember," Nessa said. "I'm surprised she made it to ninety."

A policeman stood against a wall, arms folded across his chest, scrutinizing the commuters. As they passed him, Nessa tightened her grip on Erich's arm.

"Don't be afraid. Just act like you belong here," he whispered. "We see lots of policemen. Our identification papers are practically perfect. Konrad made sure of that." He knew he was trying to assure himself of the absence of danger as much as her.

As they ascended the stairs to street level, Tessa searched the faces of the people pouring down the staircase. Why was everyone so glum? Then she heard it: the raucous voice of the Führer blaring out of a loudspeaker at the top of the stairs.

"Last night," Hitler seethed, "Polish soldiers attacked German soil. We have been returning fire since early this morning."

Erich called to a man brushing past them. "Excuse me, sir, can you tell me what's going on?"

"The Führer's speaking before Parliament," he said before continuing down the stairwell to the subway station. "We're at war with Poland."

Nessa stopped on the stairs and melted against Erich while pedestrians swirled all around them. "What are we going to do now?" she asked. "Poland's only a few kilometers away. The Poles will probably march on Berlin."

"Don't think that," Erich said, although it was impossible not to.

"Henceforth bomb will be met with bomb," Hitler shrieked. "He who fights with poison shall be met with poison gas."

A woman squeezed past them. "*Das ist das Ende Deutschlands*," she murmured.

The end of Germany? Could this really be the beginning of the end? But why on earth would Poland attack Germany? That would be suicide. The German Army could crush any army in Europe.

When they reached street level, they discovered that loud-speakers had been set up at each street corner to broadcast Hitler's speech. There was simply no escaping the Führer. "I will lead this battle, whoever the adversary may be, until the security of the Reich has been assured." Hitler paused and the members of parliament took advantage of the lull. "*Sieg Heil! Sieg Heil!*"

No one on the street offered a "*Sieg Heil*" in return.

On the sidewalk a group of people stood talking, faces somber and hopeless. A few pedestrians ducked into shops in an apparent effort to escape the blare of Hitler's voice. Others hurried along the sidewalks as if trying to outrun the omnipresent Führer.

When Hitler concluded his speech, a voice from the speakers chanted, "Long live the Führer! *Sieg Heil! Sieg Heil!*" Then Parliament began singing, "Deutschland Über Alles."

The few people left on the streets scattered in every direction, clearly less interested in singing than in seeking refuge, somewhere – anywhere.

Erich and Nessa moved on, walking in silence. A few minutes later they arrived at Helen's apartment building.

Helen's neighbor, Frau Biedermann, sat in the lobby reading a newspaper. She rose and gave Nessa a hug, then pointed down the hallway. "She's in the lounge having her morning coffee."

When they entered the lounge, a score of concerned faces, mostly elderly, turned to look at them before returning to their discussions.

"The German people don't want another war," a man asserted, raising a wrinkled fist. "The Volk will not put up with this."

"They are too afraid not to," a woman countered. "Defying the Führer can be hazardous to your health."

Nessa spotted Helen sitting alone by the window, hunched over a cup of coffee and she and Nessa wove their way through the maze of sofas and chairs to her table.

"Auntie, how are you doing today?"

Helen turned and smiled, struggling to her feet to embrace them. "Nessa. Erich. It's so nice to see you. Thank you for coming." She sat back down, her smile changing to a frown. "I suppose you've heard the news?"

"It was impossible to escape it," Nessa said, as she and Erich joined Helen at the table. "The Führer's speech was blasting from every loudspeaker in town."

"We listened to it here, too. I'm not sure the German people are as excited about this war as the Führer would hope." She shook her head. "Neither of you was alive during the Great War. We thought it would be over in weeks. The war we expected did not remotely resemble the one we got." She shook her head. "I don't have a good feeling about this new war."

Nessa took Helen's hand. "If you want to leave Germany, we can arrange it," she said in a soft voice.

Helen's brow furrowed. "Why on earth would I want to leave my homeland? I survived one war. I can survive another."

She must be related to Erich's grandfather Gottlieb, Nessa thought.

"Just remember that if things get really bad, there's a way out," Erich said.

Helen dismissed his remark with the wave of her hand. "I've lived through bad times before and survived. During the Great War we were so hungry we stripped wallpaper from the walls and boiled it. In those days they used flour as wallpaper adhesive, so we had a food source hanging right in front of our noses on our living room walls." She clasped her hands together, then laughed.

"My Anton used to rave about my 'wallpaper bread.'"

"Tell us about Anton," Nessa said, knowing that Helen's memories of her late husband would occupy her with pleasant thoughts for the rest of their visit.

Helen smiled, her eyes radiant, and for the next hour she led Nessa and Erich on a guided tour of her life with Anton.

When they rose to leave, Helen's face was still aglow with her memories. They hugged her and left her to resume her journey down memory lane with Anton.

On the way back to the subway Nessa thought about the wallpaper bread Helen had baked to feed her starving family during the war. Could things really get that bad in Germany again?

CHAPTER TWELVE

Spring, 1940.

Erich opened the rusted gate that separated the rear courtyard from the alley and looked up at the decrepit villa. Most of the windowpanes were cracked or broken, their frames blistered and gray with mold. The roof was green with moss and the dirt of many decades clung to the building's façade. The structure, long ago stripped of its splendor, almost looked abandoned – which was the point – no sense drawing attention to the fact that it was Operation Nussbaum's safe house. It looked more like the gateway to hell than a portal to freedom.

Erich made his way to the back door along a graveled path lined by withered rose bushes. He removed a key from his pocket and turned it in the lock. He pushed on the rotting wood door, which creaked open like the entrance to a haunted mansion, making a shiver rush down his spine.

Inside, the smell of mildew and the swirl of dust greeted him. As he walked down the hallway, he wondered what stories the walls could tell. Well, before the war was over these walls would have new stories to tell, stories of freedom and escape from a country where the stench of hopelessness and death was seeping into every facet of everyday life.

Erich's stomach shifted uneasily. Today, after accompanying Konrad on a dozen or so assignments, he would undertake his first solo mission. He hoped the Feinstein family was ready, because today he would take them half the length of Germany to the Swiss border.

He hoped he was ready as well.

He entered the living room to find the Feinsteins packed and waiting. "How did you sleep last night?" he asked, taking a seat. "Are you rested?"

"As rested as one can be knowing that today we will either end up in prison or in Switzerland," Herr Feinstein said.

Erich clenched his jaw, hoping the family wouldn't notice his own apprehension. He hadn't slept well either, waking up exhausted at three in the morning with his bedsheets in a knot. After that, sleep had evaded him for the rest of the night.

"We have planned your trip very carefully," he assured them. "I am confident that nothing will go wrong. Now, let's review the details of our journey one last time before we go to the train station."

Herr Feinstein nodded, as did his wife.

Eight-year-old Nathan squirmed in his chair. "Why do I have to wear three shirts and two pairs of pants?" he asked. "I'm hot." The boy's coloring was lighter than that of his parents and his features more Germanic. He would easily pass for a member of the Volk.

"Nathan," his mother said, "we've discussed this already. We can't carry a lot of luggage on this trip. That would look suspicious. So, we're wearing extra clothes instead of taking suitcases."

"But I'm sweating. Can't I just carry one bag with my clothes in it?"

"I'm afraid not, Nathan," Erich told the boy. "Like your mother said, that would look suspicious, and it would be dangerous. You don't want to get arrested by the Gestapo and go to jail, do you?"

Nathan scratched his head. "No, I guess not," he said, but he still didn't look convinced.

Erich decided to appeal to the boy's sense of adventure. "Nathan, I'm taking your family on a secret mission to Switzerland. Do you know where that is?"

Nathan shook his head.

"It's a country a few hours south of here."

"Do they speak German there?"

"Yes, in some parts."

The boy nodded. "Good."

"Now, because this is a secret mission, you are sworn to secrecy."

"What's that mean?"

"It means you can't tell anyone we meet where you're going or where you've been. You can't even tell them that you're on a secret mission. If anyone asks you where we're going, tell them you're going to see your aunt Hilda. Can you remember all that?"

The boy nodded again, this time enthusiastically. "Of course I can." Then he looked at his mother. "Do we have an aunt Hilda?"

Erich spoke before the boy's mother could respond. "No, Nathan. She's part of our secret mission."

The boy shrugged his shoulders, still looking confused. "Okay."

"I'll be with your family on this mission, but I won't sit with you on the train," Erich explained. "I'm a secret agent and so are you, but we must pretend we don't know each other. Is that clear?"

Nathan nodded, giving half a smile.

"Now Nathan, this evening on your mission, you'll be crawling on the ground out of Germany and into Switzerland. You mustn't make a sound during that part of the mission, all right?"

Nathan's eyes lit up, obviously excited about the call to adventure. "Yes." It looked like he was all in.

"Now, listen very carefully as I explain the rest of the mission to you and your parents."

"Okay."

Erich looked from one parent to the other as he spoke. "Now we'll review the details of our trip in case we get separated. Frau Feinstein, you and your family are visiting your fictitious aunt Hilda Fochler in the German town of Tengen, near the Swiss border."

"What does fictitious mean?" Nathan stumbled over the unfamiliar term.

"It means 'secret,' Nathan. This is a secret mission, remember?"

Nathan clapped his hands together. "Yes."

Erich turned his attention back to the boy's parents, handing them a photograph of a matronly woman wearing an elegant hair bun. "Frau Feinstein, this is your aunt Hilda. Her son recently died during Germany's invasion of France, and you're traveling to Tengen to be with her at this difficult time. She'll meet us at the train station along with her fictitious husband." He handed them a picture of a man with a white beard and hair. "His name is Josef Eichendorff. He'll take you over the border into Switzerland. There he'll introduce you to the people who will take you to Lisbon to catch your ship to Palestine."

Nathan giggled. "That man looks like Father Christmas."

"Doesn't he?" Nathan's father agreed.

"Memorize their faces and names in case we get separated," Erich instructed the parents. "For obvious reasons I can't let you keep the pictures."

Erich gave them a minute to commit the faces to memory.

"These are your train tickets." Erich handed Herr Feinstein an envelope. "In a few minutes we'll walk to the Anhalter Train Station and take the 3:30 express to Frankfurt. We'll transfer there for Karlsruhe and then take a local train to Tengen. We'll be there by this evening."

Herr Feinstein nodded. "We understand."

"And you have your identification papers?" Erich asked.

Frau Feinstein pulled the documents from her handbag. "Yes,

everything is here. We're now the Braun family. The passports look so real."

"We do good work," Erich bragged.

"And you're doing *a* good work," Herr Feinstein told him, smiling gratefully.

"If not for you we'd be trapped here," his wife added. "And with almost no money ..." She stopped and bit her lip, trying not to cry.

"We are so thankful," said Feinstein, reaching over to squeeze Erich's hand.

Erich returned the squeeze. "It's our privilege to help," he said. He looked at his watch. "It's time. You leave first and I'll follow. I'll walk a few meters behind you. And on the train, I'll sit several rows behind you. Whatever happens, you must remember to stay calm. Understood?"

They nodded.

"If for any reason we get separated, don't panic. You have the information and the documents you need to get to Tengen. Herr Eichendorff and Aunt Hilda will meet you there whether I arrive with you or not. We sent them copies of the pictures we took for your passports, so they know what you look like."

"You seem to have planned everything very carefully," Frau Feinstein said.

"I don't anticipate any problems." Erich turned to Nathan, who was fiddling with his shoelaces. "All right, young man, are you ready for our secret mission?"

Nathan jumped to his feet and saluted. "Ready."

The trip to Frankfurt was uneventful and the transfer to Karlsruhe smooth.

Shivering in the frigid railway car, Erich centered his thoughts around warmer things: Nessa. The happiness he felt when he was with her, the touch of her hand, how her brown eyes would light up at the sight of him. His mind traveled back to the first time they'd met.

He was minding the family bookshop alone one Saturday, balancing on a ladder in the front of the store. In one hand, pressed against his chest, he held a bundle of six or seven new arrivals by Hermann Hesse; with the other he picked the volumes out of the stack to place them onto the bookshelf.

He had just slid a copy of Hermann Hesse's novel, *Steppenwolf,* into place when he saw someone outside on the sidewalk looking in the display window. Turning for a better look, he caught sight of the most beautiful girl he'd ever seen. At that moment gravity and the angle of his body took over and he was suddenly in mid-air plunging downward. He crashed onto the floor, the books in his hands scattering everywhere.

Unhurt, he scrambled to his feet and scooped them up. Then, in an attempt to save face, he tried to act as though nothing had happened. Too late. The girl on the sidewalk had witnessed the entire scene: the awkward flight to earth, the sprawling crash, and the mad scramble afterwards. She covered her mouth with her hand, trying to conceal her laughter.

Red-faced, Erich smiled at her through the window. After she had gained control of herself, she looked at him with a smile that seemed to shine right through him. He put his pile of books on a nearby counter and hurried toward the front door, anxious to find out her name.

She met him as he swung the door open. "Are you all right? I'm so sorry for laughing. I just couldn't help myself."

"Don't worry, I'm fine. That was my imitation of *The Flying Dutchman.*"

The girl let out a laugh and Erich blushed again. He held out his hand to her. "My name is Erich Reinhold. How can I help you?"

She shook his hand. "Anastasia Baumgartner. You can call me Nessa. Have you got anything by Thomas Mann?"

The touch of her hand! Erich held it and stared into her eyes, which were the shade of chestnuts.

Nessa withdrew her hand. She cocked an eyebrow and smiled at him. "Thomas Mann?"

She had the most beautiful smile. And such lovely eyes and ... "Who?"

"Do you have anything by Thomas Mann?"

"Oh...oh, yes." He turned and pointed toward the far corner of the shop. "Right over here."

Nessa followed as he led her past a rack bulging with maps and then down a narrow aisle flanked by bookshelves.

"Let's see," he said, running his finger over the book spines. "Otto Ludwig, Heinrich Mann ... and here's Thomas Mann. Have you read any of his books? He can be a bit depressing, you know."

"I've read *Buddenbrooks*. It was a little gloomy, but I like his writing style."

She was smart as well as beautiful. And she liked his favorite author; that had to be a sign they were meant to be together. "If you got through *Buddenbrooks* you won't have any trouble with *The Magic Mountain*." He pulled down a volume bound in brown leather. "It's set in the Swiss Alps. Stunning descriptions of nature. Great character development."

Nessa took the book, her hand brushing his for a moment, sending an electric jolt through his body. As they stood in the narrow aisle surrounded by legendary Germanic authors and the smell of books, the fragrance of roses coming from her hair and skin overwhelmed him. He felt a nearly irrepressible urge to take the book from her, place it back on the shelf, and kiss her.

He watched her eyes in fascination as she skimmed through the first page of the book. He had to find a reason to keep her there. *Say something*, he told himself. "This volume's on sale," he said. "Over seven hundred pages. With that many pages, it's a good thing we don't sell books by the kilo." Was that witty or stupid?

Witty. She smiled up at him. "I'll take it."

"Would you like me to gift wrap it?" He was stalling. He knew she was buying it for herself.

"No, it's for me."

There was that smile again. Erich cleared his throat. "Great. I'll ring it up." He motioned for her to walk ahead of him and watched the sway of her hips as she moved through the aisles. How did she do that?

He rang up her purchase and wrapped it slowly and carefully in brown paper, savoring every moment with her. "Do you live around here?" She couldn't. He'd have noticed such a pretty girl.

"Just over on Lessing Strasse, a subway stop away."

"Really? I live just a few blocks from there." He'd have to find a reason to walk down Lessing Strasse. He handed her the book. "Is there anything else I can do for you? All of Schiller's works are on sale."

"No, thank you. This should keep me busy for some time."

"I hope you'll come again." How many times had he said those words since he'd been working at the bookshop? But this time he really meant them. *I hope you'll come back every day for the rest of my life.*

She smiled once more and turned to go.

He rushed ahead of her to open the door. Ten seconds later she was gone.

But she did come again. And again. Soon she was coming back nearly every day. And one day, in a narrow aisle, surrounded by the collected works of Goethe and Grillparzer, he took her hands and drew her to him for their first kiss. That first kiss had been perfect. After that life had been perfect. For such a short time.

~

The train clunked and swayed past villages nestled into rolling hills and farmland. The sun, a pearly disk looming behind stubborn shrouds of fog, had been attempting for hours to assert itself over the thick mist, but with little success.

A sign for Karlsruhe moved past the window as the train slowed, its brakes screeching as though in pain. Sycamores and lindens and oaks slid by, their leaves dripping with moisture, as if weeping.

Erich bit his lip. Although he had already helped usher a dozen families to freedom, that dull, sick feeling in his gut, that fear of being caught, of failing – above all, the terror of ending up in prison and losing Nessa – rarely left him. He assured himself that he hadn't lost her yet – he wouldn't – he couldn't – he ...

At that moment, the front door of the railway carriage banged open. Gestapo!

The agent stood in the doorway, surveying the crowd, as if challenging someone – anyone – to meet his gaze. *You've been through this before, just relax,* Erich told himself.

At the sight of the Gestapo nearly every passenger in the car bowed his head, staring at the floor as though something fascinating were happening there. The agent began working his way down the aisle, checking travel documents. Erich bit his lip, even though he knew that the Feinsteins' papers were some of the best that Manfred had ever produced.

The man stopped next to the Feinsteins, demanding their papers.

Stay calm, Feinsteins. Stay calm. From his seat near the back of the car, Erich watched them answer questions as sweat formed between his shoulder blades and trickled down his back.

Nathan stared straight ahead, ignoring the agent, apparently intent on safeguarding the secrecy of his mission.

Then a scream near him, loud enough to wake the dead, took Erich's breath away. He lurched around to see a baby, red-faced and flailing, wailing in its mother's arms.

The woman smiled at Erich. "Sorry. Colic." She stroked the child and nestled it deeper into its blanket.

Erich returned the mother's smile and turned back around. The child's outburst had caught the attention of the Gestapo agent, who stared in Erich's direction.

After what seemed an eternity, the agent returned his attention to the Feinsteins.

A few moments later the man handed back their papers. He patted Nathan's head and gave the boy a good-natured wink before moving on. *Thank God.*

Before long, the agent was hovering over Erich.

"Gestapo. Papers, please."

Now we'll see if Konrad's forgeries can pass another test. Erich's heart pounded against his chest as he reached into his pocket and pulled out his identification. For a moment the documents hung in the air, suspended in Erich's hand, while the agent studied his face.

Then the man took the papers.

"Erich Frank?"

"Yes."

"Accountant. Twenty-one years old?"

"That's correct."

"Why isn't a young man like you serving the Führer in the Wehrmacht?"

"I have a heart condition." As hard as his heart was hammering, he could be telling the truth.

"A heart condition?"

"Yes, as a boy I had rheumatic fever. It was my childhood dream to serve my Führer and fight for my Fatherland. Unfortunately, I'm unable to do that." Erich hoped he wasn't laying it on too thick.

"Can you prove that you have this ailment?"

Erich pointed to the papers the agent was holding. "There's a letter from my doctor with my papers."

The man unfolded the doctor's letter and studied it. His face soured. He shot a dubious look at Erich and then back at the letter, then mumbled a skeptical grunt. "Even if I had rheumatic fever and were missing both legs," he said, "I would still find a way to serve my Führer instead of wandering about Germany."

"Yes, sir."

"You would have no objection to me contacting your doctor to verify your heart condition?"

Erich felt sweat beading on his forehead. "Please do," he bluffed. "His phone number and address are on the letter."

The man grunted again, then handed back the phony doctor's letter. He directed his attention to Erich's other documents, turning them over and over, then holding them up to the light. "And where are you headed today, Herr Frank?"

Erich could see the man's pulse pounding in his neck. *This man loves the thrill of the hunt. He enjoys seeing his prey cower and squirm.*

"Tengen," Erich responded. "My mother's health is failing. I visit her several times a month."

The Gestapo agent tapped Erich's ID on his wrist as he searched Erich's face once again.

Erich's heart was pounding even faster, but he met the man's gaze and forced a smile. *Stay calm, this isn't the first time someone has inspected your papers.* Still, it was hard to remain calm. He thought of Nessa waiting back at Nussbaum's. What would happen to her if he were arrested?

The man grunted yet again, returned Erich's papers, and nodded. "Herr Frank." He put the tips of his fingers to the brim of his hat and continued down the aisle. After a few more spot checks he slipped into the next car.

Erich was bathed in perspiration; his heart was still pounding when they pulled into Tengen.

The sun was about to dip below the horizon, signaling the end of another day, and painting the skyline of Hitler's capital orange and purple. Nessa sat on the rooftop of the Nussbaum Building and sipped ersatz coffee, awaiting Erich's return from his mission. A small lamp on a table at her elbow washed the rooftop in a dim glow. In the distance someone clumsily practiced Beethoven's *"Für Elise"* on the piano.

When Erich was away, Nessa's evenings were a time of pleasant weariness. Pleasant because she enjoyed the atmosphere in Nussbaum's little Garden of Eden. Weariness because her working days were demanding and awaiting Erich's homecoming stressful.

When he wasn't away, the two of them spent their evenings on the rooftop, snuggling and talking, recovering from the strain of exhausting days, and planning a future that would possibly always elude them. It seemed as if Hitler was making sure of that. Only a few countries in Europe hadn't yet been swallowed up by the German war machine in its lust for more living space. To make matters worse, the Führer had promised that his war would spell the end of the Jewish race in Europe, and he was well on the way to fulfilling his vow.

As darkness began to engulf her, she switched on the radio. The dreamy sounds of a Mozart nocturne drifted across the rooftop. Nussbaum's pigeons, soothed by the combination of dusk and Mozart, nestled together, cooing in their cage. Nessa hummed along with the music, slightly off key, as always.

"I think the pigeons like Mozart," said a voice behind her.

Nessa's eyes flew open. "You're back!" She jumped up and ran to Erich.

"I was only away three days."

"I know, but when you're gone, I'm terrified you'll never return."

"I'll always come back to you, I promise. Don't worry." He took her hand and drew her to the little table with chairs in the middle of the rooftop. He sat down and pulled her onto his lap. Then came an embrace and a very long kiss, which momentarily dispelled Nessa's fears. He kissed her again and drank in the scent of roses from her skin and hair. Not for the first time he questioned why he'd allowed her to stay in Germany so long. He should have sent her off to America months ago. It was selfish of him to want to keep her in Germany simply to enjoy moments together like this.

He brushed his finger across her cheek. "What were you up to while I was away?"

"Nothing that exciting. Helping Herr Nussbaum in the office. Running errands. Missing you."

"And you baked Stollen!" Erich took a slice of the sweet cake from the plate on the table and put most of it into his mouth. "This is so good," he mumbled around a full mouth, rolling his eyes.

Nessa took a napkin from the table and wiped the powdered sugar from his face and mouth and kissed him. "I baked a loaf for you and one for my Aunt Helen."

"How's Helen doing?" he asked, grabbing another slice.

"She had another small stroke, but her physician told me she is recovering quite well."

"She'll probably outlive us all."

Nessa took Erich's hands, looked into his eyes, and savored his presence. The next words out of her mouth had long since become predictable. "Tell me about your trip. Were there any problems?"

Erich downplayed his encounter with the Gestapo agent on the train. "There was an anxious moment or two. Nothing I couldn't handle."

Nessa's hands tensed in his. "Which means you were almost arrested." Danger – how he seemed to thrive on it.

"Let's just say that I met an agent who asked a few more questions than usual. Nothing to worry about."

Herr Korff in the building across the street stepped out onto his balcony and sat down at a small white table, placing in its center a bottle of wine and a glass. He popped off the cork and the sound echoed in the evening air. He poured himself a glass and gestured toward Erich and Nessa. Then he swiped a match across the tabletop and lit a cigarette, watching the exhaled smoke disappear into the shadows.

The nocturne on the radio faded away; in its wake a tango floated across the rooftop.

"*Darf ich bitten?*" Erich asked.

An amused smile stole across Nessa's lips. "I didn't know you could dance."

"My mother taught me the waltz and the tango. The tango's not difficult. Two slow steps, then three quick ones." He slipped her off his lap, stood up and took her into his arms. "Just follow me." He demonstrated. "One, two, tang-o step. Five beats, just like that."

Nessa soon memorized the steps. She nestled her head against Erich's shoulder and sighed. "On nights like this I can almost imagine us far from here, in a land where hate and killing don't exist."

"Tonight they don't," he whispered, allowing the melody to banish their anxiety. When the music stopped, he tipped her back and kissed her. When they parted, Herr Korff applauded their performance. Erich bowed in his direction and Nessa curtsied.

Just as the sun disappeared, a white streak swooped in from the darkness to land on Nessa's shoulder. Hermann Göring was back from another successful mission.

"All my men have returned," she said, stroking Hermann's head. The dove cooed and rubbed its head on the side of Nessa's hand, making her laugh.

Erich hadn't heard her laugh in a long time.

CHAPTER THIRTEEN

Spring, 1941.

The stale air of winter had yielded to the fragrance of spring. The linden trees scattered across Alexander Square, warmed by the fresh sunlight, had begun to unfurl their leaves, and flowers bloomed in the window boxes of the homes and businesses that surrounded the square.

Erich, shading his eyes against the sun, squinted up at the clock on the police station at the edge of the plaza. Almost three.

"I think we should head home," he said to Nessa. "It's getting late."

"I just need to pick up a blouse at Holbach's," she replied, coaxing him in the direction of the store.

He made a face but let her drag him across the street, resigned to his fate. Once they entered the store, he knew it would be at least an hour before they saw the light of day again. Nessa would disappear into a dressing room with an armload of garments. He would settle into a chair, waiting for her to model every item under consideration. But to him, the clothes were of secondary interest. He loved watching her emerge from the dressing room to glide noiselessly past him, like a swan moving on a placid lake in the *Tiergarten*. Then she'd whirl around, her hands on her hips, and smile at him expectantly, waiting for a compliment.

As he reached for the door handle at Holbach's, he heard what sounded like thunder in the distance. Couldn't be. The sky was clear. There it was again. Suddenly he recognized it – the sound of a bass drum. He looked up König Strasse to see a group of stormtroopers and their band marching in his direction. From out of their ranks, a forest of arms shot outward in the Hitler salute. Pedestrians paused on the sidewalks, returning the greeting.

Erich pulled the door open. "Let's get inside. I'm not saluting those cretins."

As they watched from the safety of Holbach's, the infectious drumbeat shook the display window in front of them. The Volk continued to salute obediently. Except for one old man, who stood in the crowd clinging to an armload of packages. A trooper detached himself from the ranks and bullied the offender against the window in front of Nessa and Erich. After a heated exchange of words, the trooper's fist shot out. The back of the old man's head jerked backwards and smacked against the window and Nessa screamed and jumped back, as he and his purchases tumbled to the sidewalk.

After a minute, the man recovered, gathered his packages, and scurried away.

Then the stormtroopers came to a stop on the sidewalk and the reason for the parade became clear. At the head of the procession stood a distraught young woman. Head crudely shaved, she held a large sign that said, "I slept with a Jew. I have defiled the blood of my people."

Bystanders leered at the woman in disgust, taking in the spectacle. Disgust gave way to indignation. Indignation to murmuring. Murmuring soon seethed into rage. An old woman stepped out of the crowd and slapped the offender to her knees, and Nessa jerked back against Erich's chest, grabbing her cheek as if the woman had actually struck her.

The crowd roared its approval and the vengeance of the Volk seemed infectious. A businessman spat in the woman's face and several boys began pelting her with apples, knocking her to the ground.

After a few minutes, the band began playing again. The stormtroopers closed ranks around the woman and hauled her to her feet, herding her down the street. The show was moving to a new location.

Erich watched the troopers march off down the street, his face ridged with tension. How things in Germany had changed in just a few short years. A decade ago, having relations with a Jew had not been a crime. Now it was an act punishable by death.

"You were right," Nessa said, interrupting his reflections. "We really should head home."

"Home" used to mean a safe place, Erich thought, a place he could go to escape the madness of the world, a place where he could pull up a chair in the kitchen after returning home from school and sip the warm glass of milk his mother always had ready for him. A place where he could discuss his day and express his frustrations. A place of belonging.

He felt no sense of belonging to the mob of racists torturing the woman they had caught in sin and it gave him a measure of satisfaction and relief knowing he was no longer considered one of them.

September, 1941.

Despite the war, 1941 had seemed like any other year in Berlin. By March, the snow and ice of winter were gone, glutting the Spree

River with snow melt as it rushed through the city anxious to meet the Havel River, which joined the romantic Elbe River north of Berlin.

And in spite of the political climate, the seasons had come and gone, Berlin trees sprouted buds, then blossoms, and finally the vibrant leaves of summer.

On the second day of summer, Germany invaded the Soviet Union and by September first, exactly two years after invading Poland and unleashing the Second World War, the German Army had marched within artillery range of Leningrad.

Closer to home, the Germans had overrun much of the European continent and it appeared as if their war machine was unstoppable.

September also brought with it an intensification of Germany's efforts to humiliate and isolate European Jews. All Jews above the age of six in German-occupied Europe were now required to wear the "yellow star" on their coats whenever they went out in public.

It was a chilly and cloudy morning in Berlin, the thermometer hovering around fifty-seven degrees. In less than three weeks summer would yield to autumn, which for Nessa was the grand finale of each year, when the leaves, though dying, donned vibrant hues of red and orange and gold in one last burst of energy before floating to the ground.

Fall had always been her favorite time of year, and as she and Erich and Nussbaum made their way across Alexander Square, she recalled autumn afternoons as a little girl, picking apples at home in the backyard with her father. She picked the ones she could reach, and Papa would stretch up to get the others. He'd have to use a stick to knock down the apples that even he couldn't reach, and she would try to catch them before they hit the ground, although more often than not they would thump to earth out of reach or sail between her outstretched hands onto her head.

After she'd collected about a dozen apples, she'd run inside to help her mother peel and wash them for *Apfelstrudel,* a dessert all good Germans consumed on a regular basis. In her mind's eye she saw herself with her apples, hurrying up the back stairs and into the kitchen where her mother stood at the kitchen sink in that apron she always wore. Mama would turn and kneel and enclose Nessa in a hug, praising her for being the best little helper her Papa ever had.

Nessa smiled sadly at the memories of doing the things that normal German families still did. But now her parents were dead, and her childhood home belonged to Aryans and, according to the law, she was no longer a German.

In spite of the frigid weather, the Volk swarmed through the Alexander Square apparently determined to enjoy one of the last days of summer before the bitter cold of autumn and winter arrived. Mothers pushed baby strollers with happy infants wrapped in wool blankets. Old men meandered along in heavy coats and thick scarves, their hands clasped behind their backs. Lovers cuddled on benches, absorbed in their own private world.

Erich, Nessa, and Nussbaum left the square and after a few minutes turned onto Ansbacher Strasse. "Rabbi Grünberg's safe house is this way," Nussbaum said, leading them down an alley lined by linden trees. "He uses it for special meetings, like the one today."

After fifty meters they came to a two-story brick building.

Nussbaum opened a rusted, wrought-iron gate that squealed in protest, leading them through a courtyard.

When they entered, they found the meeting room nearly full. It was well heated and most of those in attendance had hung their coats on hooks along a wall, each coat bearing the required Jewish star.

A few minutes later a man sitting at a table at the front of the room stood up. He was tall and slender with dark eyes and hair and a pale complexion.

"Good afternoon," he said, "if we haven't already met, my name is Rabbi Grünberg. I want to thank you for coming today. As you know, I have called this meeting to discuss what I call the 'yellow star law,' and how it affects us as Jews."

The Rabbi paused and took a few moments to look from face to face. "Before we deal with the ramifications of the new law, I'd like to read a passage of Scripture from Psalm 129. I pray that these words bring encouragement."

'Since I was young, they have attacked me – Let Isra'el repeat it – since I was young, they have attacked me, but they have not overcome me.

The plowmen plowed on my back, wounding me with long furrows.
But Adonai is righteous.
He cuts me free from the yoke of wicked men. Amen.'"

The crowd murmured, "Amen."

Grünberg closed his Bible and once again looked at his audience for a few moments before continuing. "The Jewish people have tried to live in peace with the rest of mankind, but this hasn't always been easy. Today our status in Germany is quite precarious. The government enacts restrictive new race laws on a regular basis, but please remember that God has not abandoned us."

A man in the front row stood up. "Rabbi, our children can't attend public school," he said, shaking his fist. "We can't attend public events, either. And now we must wear that yellow star wherever we go. It's like wearing a target for the Nazis to shoot at."

Murmurs of agreement came from various parts of the room.

"I completely understand," the Rabbi replied. "Now, let's see a show of hands. Who is in favor of refusing to wear the star? Remember, non-compliance means arrest and imprisonment."

No hands were raised. "Are there any more comments on this subject?"

Nearly member of the audience stared glumly at the floor.

"We can do nothing to change this new law," Grünberg continued. "So let us wear the star as a badge of honor. Let us tell the world that we are Jews and proud of it. The star has the word 'Jew' emblazoned across it. It reminds us that we are God's chosen people. Let us stand up and say, 'yes, we are,' and embrace our identity with pride."

There were nods of agreement throughout the room.

"The Nazis have a simple goal," the Rabbi said. "They want to force us to leave Germany. They have purged us from every profession and forced us to sell our businesses and homes to Aryans for next to nothing. Our situation is quite desperate. I encourage anyone who hasn't already done so to start the emigration process immediately. Yes, you will have to abandon your homeland, and you will have to leave behind most of your assets. But you will escape with your lives."

"In the meantime," he said, "if anyone here needs food or money for food, please see me after the meeting."

A few minutes later Rabbi Grünberg adjourned the meeting and his flock donned their coats and filed slowly out of the building.

"I'll be hanged if I'll sew one of those stars on my coat," Nussbaum said as they followed the crowd out. Then he laughed, his generous midriff convulsing in mirth. "Come to think of it, they probably *will* hang me if they catch me in public without one."

Early October, 1941.

The cigarette smoke was so thick inside Café Krone that it was like being *inside* a cigarette. Erich held Nessa's hand and stared into the haze, watching a few men at a nearby table play dominos.

Konrad used his corner of the table to play solitaire.

The room, where one normally heard at least the murmur of a few voices, was as silent as a tomb except for the clacking of the dominos. Which was not surprising. In recent weeks, enemy bombers, some Russian, some British, had entered German airspace to bomb Berlin and the general mood among the Volk had changed from hopeful to somber.

Nussbaum came through the front door and sat down with a groan. "Stressful times, my young friends, don't you agree?"

Konrad gathered up his cards and slipped them into his pocket. "Indeed,' he laughed and smacked his hand on the table, sending Erich's coffee cup and saucer dancing away from him. "A few bombs falling on Berlin should throw a wrench into that famous German sense of order."

Nussbaum chuckled as well. "Well, they entered the war with the rather childish notion that they were going to bomb everyone else, and nobody was going to bomb them."

"I hope the Allies level Berlin," Konrad said bitterly, sliding Erich's coffee cup back to him. "After robbing the Jews of their homes and businesses, the Germans will finally get a taste of what it's like to lose something they value," he laughed.

Nessa smiled, but fear quickly stole the smile from her face. "Do you think we should get out of Berlin, Herr Nussbaum," she asked. "Lots of people are leaving."

"Not yet," he said. "The bombers haven't done much damage yet. But we should move out of the center of the city. When the bombers come in earnest, the city center will be the first part of Berlin they'll target."

"Why don't we ask your old neighbor, Frau Sturm, if we can live with her?" Erich said to Nessa. "She's offered to take us in before."

"Good idea," Nessa replied. "She does have some rooms in the basement she doesn't use. I'm sure she'd be glad to house all four of us."

"I'm ready to turn my law practice and my building over to Herr

Werner," Nussbaum said. "Do you think we could relocate to Frau Sturm's by next week?"

"I don't think that will be a problem," Nessa said.

"On an equally somber note," Nussbaum said, pulling a worn, crumpled photograph from his pocket, "I have some news from our underground contacts."

He handed Erich a photograph and Nessa leaned over his shoulder to look at it. "I know this man," she said. "Martin Schneider. His parents and mine were close friends. He came to our home once to introduce his wife and little daughter."

"He's Jewish," Nussbaum said. "He works for the Gestapo as a 'catcher,' ferreting out Jews in hiding."

Erich's clenched the picture tighter. "So, he betrays his own people to save his own skin."

Nussbaum nodded. "Don't be too quick to judge, my young hothead. It's true, some catchers are in it for the money. But many others have families who have lost everything. They give the money they earn to penniless relatives who would otherwise be shipped off to work camps."

"Which is it with him, I wonder?" Konrad asked as Erich handed him the picture.

"I don't know," Nussbaum admitted, "but he's very good at what he does. He trolls for illegals in restaurants, cafés, and public toilets."

Nussbaum took another picture from his pocket and handed it to Konrad. "This is Schneider's partner."

Erich gasped and snatched the photo from Konrad. "Gerhardt Schmutze!"

"You know this man?"

"We grew up together," Erich said, handing the picture back to Konrad. "He's a snake."

"Well, now Schmutze's Gestapo," Nussbaum continued. "He and Schneider have no shame. They've been known to show up at

Jewish funerals posing as mourners, looking for illegals. Sometimes they even make arrests before the service is over."

Konrad grimaced. "That's criminal."

Nessa was trembling and Erich reached over and took her hands. "Don't worry, it'll be all right," he said. He wanted to tell her that he could always protect her from the Gestapo and from the bombs, but he knew he couldn't.

CHAPTER FOURTEEN

On October 18, 1941, the prospects for survival for Jews in Hitler's capital degenerated from doubtful to nearly hopeless when the Germans loaded the first Berlin Jews onto eastbound trains for "resettlement." Five days later the Nazis issued a ban on emigration. It was no longer possible for Jews to leave Germany legally.

In the wake of these actions, the number of Jews going into hiding increased dramatically.

A few weeks after Erich, Nessa, Nussbaum, and Konrad had relocated to Frau Sturm's, Erich strolled with Nessa along *Unter den Linden*, his arm around her waist. They fell into step and turned onto a pathway flanked by oak trees. Light from the setting sun played in the colorful canopy of foliage overhead. The few remaining leaves of autumn that had refused to release their grip on the trees, were finally surrendering to gravity and fluttering, red and yellow and orange, toward earth to join their fallen comrades on the ground.

A group of workers raked the leaves into piles behind the park benches that lined the path and a cluster of children took turns climbing onto the benches and diving into the leaf piles, scattering the leaves everywhere and eliciting good-natured reprimands from the workers.

A squirrel darted across the path and hopped onto a park bench with the warning sign, "Aryans Only." The animal rested there for an instant before dashing up a tree.

Nessa laughed. "That must have been a Jewish squirrel. He didn't stay on that bench for long."

Erich pointed to a park bench painted yellow and called up to the squirrel. "You're only allowed to sit on the benches for Jews, sir. I don't want to have to remind you again."

They laughed and continued down the path. "Although I'll sit wherever I please," Erich said, defiantly.

"I hope Aunt Helen is doing better," Nessa said, changing the subject. "The doctor said the next stroke might kill her."

Erich pulled her closer. "I'm sure she's fine. She'll probably live to be a hundred."

They walked a few more blocks, turned a corner and mounted the steps to Helen's apartment building.

Frau Biedermann, Helen's neighbor, sat in the lobby as usual, reading a newspaper. When she saw Nessa and Erich, her smile seemed guarded. She rose and took Nessa into her arms. "The doctor's with Helen. He needs to talk to you."

Nessa pulled away. "The doctor? What's wrong?"

Tears welled in Frau Biedermann's eyes. "I'm so sorry, Nessa."

They hurried up the stairs to Helen's apartment. When they entered the room, Nessa stopped and gasped. Helen lay in bed, her face ashen. The doctor sat next to her, holding her hand. He turned and rose to meet Nessa and Erich at the door. "I'm so sorry. Helen passed away a few minutes ago. Another stroke. Let's sit over here," he added, leading them to chairs surrounding a small dining room table.

Nessa threw her hands over her face and wept. "Oh, no, no."

Erich wrapped his arms around her. "She's in a better place now."

"Now I have no family left," Nessa sobbed.

"You have me," he said, hugging her.

The doctor put his arm on Nessa's shoulder. "It may be small comfort, but I want you to know that she didn't suffer."

Later, they again walked under the oak trees and retraced their steps, heading toward the subway station. Only the glow from the lanterns that lined the path lighting their way. So much had changed since she and Erich had been on this path two hours earlier. And yet, so much remained the same. The palette of autumn color continued to swirl all around them in the semi-darkness. A few piles of raked leaves remained, although the workers and the children had disappeared.

It was unusually warm for autumn, but for Nessa the chill of winter had already arrived.

A week later they laid Helen to rest outside of Berlin near the banks of the Schlachtensee next to David and Ruth Baumgartner and Stefan Bacharach, Nessa's parents and uncle.

∿

December, 1941.

In early summer, Mother Russia had reluctantly opened her arms to welcome the invading German armies. But by the beginning of October the first snows had fallen; they melted and left behind a sea of mud. Frost and more snow followed in November and December. Fanatical Russian resistance and the brutal Russian climate had joined forces to impede the Germans at every turn. It was going to be a long, hard Russian winter.

~

Not even the Nazis and bad news from the Russian front could prevent the arrival of the holidays. At the beginning of Advent, Christmas markets sprang up all over Berlin. The government had renamed them "Yule Markets," attempting to take Christ out of Christmas, but for millions of Germans the Christmas traditions remained the basis of the holiday.

Erich and Nessa got out of the subway at *Zoologischer Garten* and climbed to street level. A sea of humanity churned all around them, filling the sidewalks and spilling over into the streets. In the distance loomed the Kaiser Wilhelm Memorial Church, the main spire sprouting out of the earth like the point of a spear, stabbing into the heavens, penetrating to the stars. Floodlights illuminated its façade, adding a splash of light to an otherwise cold, dark night.

They turned toward the church, the crowd sweeping them along. A massive Christmas tree, adorned with oversized ornaments and heavily laden with the previous night's snowfall, dominated the square in front of the church. A Christmas market encircled the entire building, and Erich and Nessa wandered together past booths selling ornaments, nutcrackers, and wooden angels. The tempting aroma of honey-roasted almonds lured them out of the crowd to a stall near the north side of the church, and Erich bought them a bag to share.

They trailed a group of worshippers up the cathedral's front steps and went inside. A Bach fugue coming from the organ loft saturated the interior of the church, scampering up the walls and resonating over the thousands of tiny tiles comprising the mosaic ceiling.

Nessa leaned against Erich and closed her eyes as intricate harmonies cannoned from wall to wall, the soprano and tenor voices going it alone, then joined by the alto. But something was missing from the fugue. Then Erich realized what it was: the bass part. After a few seconds, droning and somber, it joined the other three voices, then all four parts intertwined, chasing one another through time and space.

Erich pointed to the staircase leading to the main steeple. He had attended hundreds of services here but had never climbed the main steeple. They started up and the music followed them, ascending to heaven, the sound fading as they went higher and higher.

After a few meters they came to a small, glassless window that overlooked the city. An icy wind blew in and chilled them. "It's almost like we've left the earth and are hovering far above the chaos below," Nessa said, marveling at the crisscross of streets beneath them.

Erich nodded and pulled her to him. Despite the frigid air in their sanctuary high above Berlin, he could feel her warmth. He too felt as if they were suspended in a peaceful world, far from Earth, closer to God.

They continued up, the faint sounds of the fugue pursuing them, and came to a landing suspended over the interior of the church. Floodlights outside shone through the stained glass in the large, circular rose window above the front doors, bathing the altar and the sanctuary in muted tones of red, blue, and yellow. Below them, the devout huddled together in the pews.

From their vantage point they could see the organ. Silver pipes sprang out of the belly of the instrument like huge lances. In the light that illuminated his score, the organist played, his entire body a hive of activity. His head bobbed in time with the music as his hands glided over the keys and his feet over the pedals. The waves of sound ascended the columns that supported the cathedral, the notes still pursuing one another in tones as delicate as lace.

The fugue ended on a sustained note shared by all four parts. The worshippers, bundled in winter coats, sat motionless in the pews. Were they praying or just stunned by the genius of the fugue? Perhaps a little of both.

"Let's go higher," Erich urged.

Climbing in near darkness, they soon came to a rectangular crenel through which they could see the world they had left far below. The Kurfürstendamm shone beneath them, cold and distant, illuminated by the headlamps of the hundreds of vehicles clogging its surface. Snow had begun to fall, blowing in at them through the open space.

They climbed still higher and after a few minutes reached a large chamber where a handful of massive church bells dwelt in hallowed darkness. The wind was stronger and colder now. Pigeons cooing in the darkness accompanied the sound of the wind.

"I wish we could stay up here forever and forget our troubles," Nessa said, snuggling into Erich's side.

"So do I." He touched her lips with his forefinger, and then kissed her.

She sighed after the kiss and laid her head on his shoulder. "Of course, that's not very practical."

"Wishes and dreams don't have to be practical."

"That's true. If we stayed here, we'd only have to worry about little things like staying warm and getting food," she said with a teasing smile.

"Never mind food. We'll live on love."

The words were barely out of his mouth when they heard a creaking and a grinding, a groaning and a rattling next to them and above them and under them. The enormous bells had come to life and began ringing; the entire belfry shook and shuttered. The unseen pigeons shot out of the darkness and streaked past them into the night.

The harmonic thunder quaked in their ears and pulsated through their bodies in unbearable seismic waves. They covered their ears and sprinted down the stairway to escape the storm of sound, arriving back in the sanctuary breathless and laughing.

"I guess we won't be able to live up there after all," Nessa said, panting.

They stepped outside to see the blur of snow tumbling softly, silently from the sky. While they had been in the church the world had been transformed. Plump pillows of white were piling up on automobiles, trees and the tops of vendor stalls.

They turned left to circle the church. Halfway around they encountered a Christmas tree decorated with tinsel, straw stars and illuminated swastikas. "Swastikas on a Christmas Tree?" Erich spat, his holiday mood gone. Of all the atrocities and indignities!

He started toward the tree, but Nessa lunged after him, grabbing his arm.

"Erich, no!" she hissed. "I know what you're thinking. But kicking over that tree will put us both at risk. Remember, you're all I have." She nodded in the direction of a pair of policemen, leaning against the church, watching the crowd. "And for heaven's sake, smile. You look ready to kill someone."

"I am," he muttered.

She tugged at his arm, moving them back into the safety of the crowd. "I've always loved this time of year," she said, trying to steer his thoughts into safer territory. "What was Christmas like at your house growing up?"

Erich got the hint. No point risking arrest by doing something stupid. "December was a mixture of both good and bad memories," he said, smiling. "I remember Mutti baking *Lebkuchen* for Karl and me to steal – and scolding us when we did. 'Remember, Saint Nikolaus sees everything,' she'd say. 'He's always watching. Do you want presents or punishment for Christmas?'"

"Did that frighten you into behaving?"

"Yes, of course. We were young. We believed everything our mother said. And it turned out she was right. At the beginning of December, Nikolaus, and his assistant, Ruprecht, would show up at our front door. Nikolaus wore a red robe and cap and had a long, white beard. Papa would let them in, and Nikolaus would open a big black book and recite all the sins we had committed that year."

"Nikolaus came to our house too."

"I'm sure he didn't find much fault with you," Erich teased.

"You're right, he didn't," Nessa said with a grin.

"Well, our Nikolaus had plenty to say about my brother and me. My parents must have kept track of our every transgression and passed them on to Nikolaus." He shook his head and smiled at the memory. "Of course, when he listed our offenses, Karl and I were stunned. He really *had* seen everything we had done."

"Like what?"

"When your mother puts you to bed," Erich said, imitating Nikolaus's voice, "you two never stay put. You always find a reason to get up and wander about the house. I expect this to stop. Disobedient children get no presents."

Nessa laughed.

"Then we would swear by all that was holy that we would change our ways."

"How long did that last?" Nessa smirked.

"Until after Christmas. I really wasn't afraid of Nikolaus. But Ruprecht terrified me. He dressed in black and had dark, wild-looking hair. His job was to punish the bad children. He'd scowl at us, slowing waving the switch in his hand. Long before Christmas, Karl would tell me that Ruprecht would soon arrive to beat me to death because of my sins. One year I crawled under the couch when Ruprecht came and stayed there until he left. After that he stopped coming. I think my parents realized that the trauma of facing him every year was doing me more harm than good."

During their stroll, the snow turned to freezing rain. Nessa, shivering, drew closer to Erich. "We should head home."

Later, as the subway car rumbled through the night, Erich laid his head on Nessa's shoulder and yawned. "This is the third Christmas without my family. I wonder what Christmas is like in America? I wonder what my family ..." his voice trailed off.

That night, in his dreams, a dark-haired man with a contorted face appeared. A modern-day Ruprecht pounded vehemently on a lectern, promising to punish the Jews for their sins.

"Ruprecht, no..."

He awoke to find Nessa stroking his cheek. "Go back to sleep," she whispered. "You're safe. Ruprecht isn't here."

Erich drifted off again, and the dark-haired man disappeared, replaced by a vision of him and Nessa on the bow of an ocean liner pulling out of Lisbon harbor in the direction of the setting sun.

CHAPTER FIFTEEN

March, 1942.

"Are you almost finished with those passports?" Manfred said, the ever-present cigarette bobbing in the corner of his mouth.

In the many months Erich had worked with Manfred, he had never seen the man without a cigarette wedged in his mouth. It hung there when he ate and when he drank – probably even when he showered.

"I'm working on the last two," Erich answered. He took the photographs of Daniel and Hilda Zweig from the chemical bath and hung them up. "They'll be dry in a couple of minutes, then Nessa can mount them on the passports." With any luck the Zweig family would be in Switzerland by the following evening.

"Have I ever told you about my run in with the Gestapo?" Manfred asked, examining a forged ration card for defects.

"More than once," Konrad said, with a yawn.

Manfred ignored him. "I got a postcard in the mail. The wording was almost prosaic. I was 'invited' to Gestapo Headquarters." He took a swig of beer, then dunked a large chunk of knackwurst into a jar of mustard, before stuffing the sausage into his mouth.

"Don't get mustard on that ration card," Konrad warned him.

Manfred ignored him again. "I got the postcard several days before I was supposed to appear," he said. "When I arrived at Gestapo Headquarters, two men took me to a room in the basement and pushed me onto a chair. They proceeded to tell me things about myself that I didn't know. That I was hiding Jews. That I was plotting to assassinate the Führer." Manfred laughed. "All things I would have been proud to have done."

His three friends laughed as well.

"I knew both of the men," Manfred continued. "Bruno Immermann and Uwe Keller. They were a strange pair. Bruno was short and pudgy, Uwe tall and slender. I served with their fathers in the Great War. 'That's when soldiers were soldiers,' I told them, 'and not bullies in uniform.' Uwe didn't appreciate my attitude and punched me in the face, knocking out a molar. I spit in into his face. That just made him angrier. He yanked off my artificial leg and hit me in the face with it until several more teeth were adrift in my mouth."

Manfred took another bite of knackwurst, chewing it with his few remaining teeth, and swilling it down with more beer. "But I was determined to outlast my tormentors. At some point during the torture I must have passed out, because later I woke up on the floor of a cold cell. No bed, no blanket, my leg in a corner. That's when I got these," he said, pointing to his scarred face. "I used my fingernails to scratch up my neck and face. When my captors returned, I told them I had scarlet fever. Their eyes got as big as the Führer's ego. Have you ever seen two terrified Aryans try to squeeze through a doorframe at the same time?"

Nessa grinned. Erich and Konrad laughed.

"Later a couple of soldiers took me to the hospital. Of course, the doctors soon discovered the truth. They patched me up and sent me home the next day."

"And you haven't heard from the Gestapo since then?" Nessa asked.

"Not a peep." His knackwurst finished, he fished another cigarette out of his overalls pocket, lit it with the butt of the old cigarette, and then crushed the butt on the floor with his prosthetic leg. "Of course, that may change because I'm not going to keep my mouth shut about the government."

Just then they heard someone pounding on the shop door.

"It must be the Gestapo," Manfred joked. "I'll get it," he said, struggling to his feet. "Lock the door behind me. Then turn off the lights and don't make a sound."

Manfred left the room and Erich latched the door while Nessa doused the lights.

Erich looked through the peephole in the door, watching Manfred hobble to the front of the shop where he yanked the door open. Herr Richter, the postman, stood in the doorway.

"It's the postman," Erich whispered to Konrad and Nessa.

"Dietmayer," Richter scolded, "how do you expect to make any money if no one can open your shop door?" Erich and the others could hear his voice through the ventilation holes near the ceiling.

"You're right," Manfred said, scratching the back of his head. "I've been meaning to get that door fixed."

"And where's your 'No Jews' sign?"

Manfred threw up his hands and looked toward heaven. "Just because he wears a uniform, he thinks he works for the Gestapo."

"Funny you should mention that." Richter smiled coldly and pushed a brown postcard into Manfred's chest. "Here's a love note from your friends at Burgstrasse 28."

A wave of nausea rushed over Erich. Manfred's big mouth had borne fruit once again.

Richter pressed his forefinger onto the card. "You're a rebel, Dietmayer. You should watch what you say about the Führer. Word gets out."

"It's probably nothing," Manfred replied, stuffing the card into the pocket of his overalls.

"Oh, it's definitely *not* nothing," Richter said. "Come to your senses, man. Look at you. Before your first trip to Burgstrasse you could lift your right arm. And back then you had all your teeth."

"That's exactly why I'm not going back there. And you can tell your friends at the Gestapo I said so."

"Tell them yourself," Richter said. "I'm not your errand boy." He shook his head and left.

Manfred pushed the door closed, limped back to the workroom and knocked on the door. Konrad flipped on the lights and Erich unbolted the door. Manfred hobbled in and dropped onto a chair.

"May I see the card?" Erich asked.

Manfred fished it out of his pocket and handed it to Erich. "It looks exactly like the last one."

"It is indeed from the Gestapo. The subject line says, 'Discussion.'"

Manfred chuckled. "It sounds like an invitation to a book club, doesn't it?"

Nessa leaned over the postcard. "They want you to report the day after tomorrow. What are you going to do, Manfred?"

"Ignore their invitation, of course," he said, lighting a fresh cigarette.

"I wonder why they didn't just come here to fetch you" Erich mused.

"They have bigger fish to fry," Manfred said.

"Like ferreting out underground organizations," Konrad reminded them. He and Erich exchanged anxious glances.

"Of course, when I don't show up at their party, they'll come and get me." Manfred said.

"Manfred, you have to run – hide!" Nessa said.

He shook his head. "And how fast and how far can a one-legged man run? No, I'll stay right here until they come for me."

Erich ran his hands nervously through his hair. "Manfred, we admire your bravery, but being so outspoken puts our entire mission at risk."

"I won't hide in the dark like a cockroach," Manfred snapped.

"And I refuse to look over my shoulder every time I express my opinions to make sure the Gestapo isn't listening. And if they do come for me, I won't be going quietly." He looked from Erich to Konrad to Nessa. "The Führer and I agree on almost nothing, but we do have one thing in common. We both take personal responsibility for everything we say and do."

Later that day, as he and Konrad and Nessa took the subway home to Frau Sturm's, Erich knew that the Gestapo would come for Manfred and that they would find the workshop. They would have to relocate it.

"I agree that we must move our base of operations, Erich," Nussbaum said later that evening at Frau Sturm's. "Manfred's big mouth will land us all in Sachsenhausen."

"But where can we go?" Konrad wondered.

"We could move everything to the safe house," Nessa said.

"Great idea," Nussbaum agreed. "Let's do that."

"Should I call Manfred and give him the news?" Konrad asked.

"Too risky. If the Gestapo is bugging his phone, the trail could lead back to us." Nussbaum turned to Erich. "You still have a key to Manfred's shop, right?"

"Right."

"We need to get our equipment out of there as soon as possible."

"The Gestapo could be staking the place out," Nessa pointed out.

"That's true," Nussbaum said. "Take my truck over there tomorrow evening and park it a few blocks away. Then walk to the shop. If nothing looks out of the ordinary, bring the truck around to the shop and load up our equipment. Otherwise, come back home. No sense taking chances."

The next evening Erich and Konrad left the truck a few hundred meters from Manfred's shop and joined the late evening shoppers hurrying home through the chill of dusk. In front of

Manfred's shop stood a black Mercedes limousine, the driver leaning against the back of the vehicle, smoking.

Erich and Konrad moved back into the shadows.

Just then two men in long leather coats, one short and stout, the other tall and awkward, emerged from the shop dragging Manfred behind them. His lips were bleeding and the front of his overalls spattered with blood.

Several pedestrians stopped, gaped, then hurried away, heads bent toward the ground.

"Those must be the two Gestapo agents who beat Manfred," Konrad said.

"Bruno's the short, pudgy one," deduced Erich, "and the tall one has to be Uwe. I guess they decided not to wait for Manfred to report to Gestapo Headquarters tomorrow."

Manfred began to struggle, and Bruno punched him in the ribs, making him howl in pain. Uwe opened the back door of the car and the two men hurled Manfred in. Then Bruno climbed into the back seat with Manfred, and his partner slammed the car door after them. "Let's go," he barked at the driver.

The driver climbed behind the wheel and started the engine while Uwe started around to the passenger's side.

"We have to help him," Erich said, moving toward the car.

Konrad grabbed his arm, pulling him back. "There's nothing we can do, Erich. Don't risk it."

Erich watched the car rock while Manfred and Bruno fought in the back. The driver got out to help and threw open the back door. A fist came through the doorframe and clouted him in the face. He lurched backward, listed to one side, and crashed onto the street.

Uwe threw his hands up in desperation and hurried back around the car, stepping over the unconscious driver. He drew his gun and pointed it toward Manfred, but holstered it again when he evidently could not get a clear shot at the prisoner. He threw himself into the back seat with the brawling men. The car swayed and pitched, the interior a jumble of flailing hands and fists and feet.

"I think Manfred's going to kill them," Erich said.

"Wouldn't that be nice," Konrad murmured.

In the back seat an overall-covered arm collided with Bruno's face, catapulting him out of the vehicle onto the body of the driver. Bruno rolled over onto the cobblestones like a pudgy ball with arms and legs, then stopped moving.

In the meantime, Uwe managed to ram his forehead hard into Manfred's face, stunning him. He climbed out of the car over the bodies of his unconscious comrades. He stood for a moment next to the car, his uniform more crimson than black, his hair matted with blood and his long nose bleeding and pointing comically in the direction of his left ear. He more resembled the loser in a bar fight than a member of the invincible Gestapo.

Then he pulled his gun and leveled it at Manfred's head. Murmurs behind him made him suddenly aware of onlookers. He lowered his weapon, then looked daggers into the crowd that had formed to watch the melee. "I'm not going to shoot this traitor in the presence of women and children," he said. "This pond scum, this mocker of the Führer, will receive a fair trial, after which he will hang."

Most of the onlookers stood pressed against the buildings on either side of the street, fear in their eyes, as well as a measure of satisfaction. One of their own had taken on the Secret Police and had nearly won.

"Move along, people," Uwe barked at the crowd. "Nothing to see here."

On the contrary – there had been a lot to see.

Uwe bent down, revived his comrades, and helped them into the limousine. A few moments later it glided away. The show was over.

"Do you think Manfred will talk?" Konrad asked, as the car disappeared around a corner.

"He'll let them kill him before he does."

Konrad looked toward Manfred's shop. "I wonder if it's safe to fetch our equipment?"

"No. If they return to search the place while we're in there, we're dead. We'll have to buy new equipment and supplies and start over."

They never saw Manfred again.

April, 1942.

Erich and Konrad sat in the rear of Café Krone with Nussbaum over steaming cups of ersatz coffee. The sun had fallen below the horizon and the chill in the air had driven many of Berlin's illegal residents out of their unheated hiding places and into the warm café. Waiters and waitresses scurried among the tables delivering desserts and beverages. A group of men at the next table played a noisy game of skat. Other patrons sat smoking, engrossed in their newspapers.

Erich shot a glance toward the front of the café, something he was in the habit of doing every few minutes. When danger came, it usually walked through the front door.

Through the smoky haze he saw a young, blond man enter and scan the room. He looked a little too attentive to be searching for a free table.

Willing his hand not to shake, Erich took a casual sip of coffee and nudged Nussbaum's foot with his. "Martin Schneider's heading this way."

"Has he seen us?" Konrad whispered, keeping his eyes on Erich.

"I don't think so. Konrad, you and Herr Nussbaum duck out the back door. I'm right behind you."

They rose and were gone in an instant.

Schneider was not alone. Erich saw the hazy form of a second man behind him – it was Gerhardt Schmutze.

He tried to tell himself that he had nothing to fear from Schmutze or the Gestapo. They couldn't connect him with any wrongdoing. Except his refusal to wear the Jewish star. He stood up slowly and backed toward the rear door, keeping his eyes on the two men. As they came further inside the café, Schmutze spotted him. Their gazes locked. Panicked, Erich bolted for the door.

Schmutze was on him in an instant, knocking him off balance. Erich tumbled backward against the corner of a table. He was barely aware of the pain in his back as he and Schmutze wrestled, scattering tables and chairs in every direction. Within seconds, the café was void of customers.

As the two men struggled, Erich felt Schmutze's breath hot on his neck. Schneider moved closer and managed to land a few kicks to Erich's ribs. Then Schmutze pulled a gun from his coat and clubbed Erich in the side of the face, stunning him.

"Why did you run, Reinhold?" Schmutze panted, rising to his feet and leveling his gun at Erich's head. "Running makes you look guilty. Have you been up to no good, my old friend?"

Erich looked up from the floor, but refused to answer.

"Why aren't you wearing your Jew star?" Schmutze asked. "Never mind, I suspect you're guilty of crimes much more serious than that. And rest assured, we're going to find out what they are. Now stand up, you're under arrest. Come quietly and don't make a scene. If you try to escape, I'll shoot you in the head."

Schneider, now standing shoulder to shoulder with Schmutze, also pointed a gun at Erich.

If he went docilely with these men, his life was over. He thought of Nessa, waiting back at Frau Sturm's, looking forward to his return. Oh, no, he would not go quietly.

He struggled to his feet, feigning disorientation, then quickly grabbed a chair and swung it at the two men, hitting both.

Schmutze's gun discharged with a deafening explosion, as he

and Schneider fell to the floor. Erich stumbled through the café's back door and ran for his life.

He raced through courtyard and began scaling the stone wall.

Behind him, he heard his assailants crash through the door. One of them fired his weapon. The bullet impacted next to Erich, sending mortar and dust spraying in all directions.

Before they could get off another round, Erich was over the wall and gone.

Half an hour later he turned the corner into the long alley behind Frau Sturm's home. Halfway down the alley he saw two figures in the dim light slip through her back gate. *Probably Nussbaum and Konrad.* He hurried down the alley, opened the gate and crossed the courtyard. He stole up to the back door and slipped inside.

Suddenly feeling weak, he stood on the landing to the basement, clutching the railing. What was that pressure in his chest? It hurt to breathe. He felt like he was underwater in a sinking U-Boat, unable to breathe. He clutched the railing tighter, forcing himself to take a few breaths and after a minute the stress and the pain subsided.

He heard Konrad and Nussbaum murmuring in the basement. Relief washed over him. They had made it back safely.

May, 1942.

"Harold Stifter needs to disappear," Nussbaum said. He, Nessa, and Erich were in the safe house putting finishing touches on some bogus passports.

Erich looked up from his workbench. "You mean that postman you've been bribing?" He had met Stifter several years earlier and didn't like the man. He was an Aryan who was more than willing to help them smuggle Jews out of Germany, providing the amount of the bribe was high enough.

"One of our contacts said the Gestapo stopped by his apartment yesterday," Nussbaum said.

"Which means they're onto him," Nessa worried.

"Right," Nussbaum agreed. "Fortunately, he wasn't home at the time. Konrad's bringing him over here right now. We have to get him out of the country right away. If he's arrested, he may give us up."

Erich laid the documents he was working on face down on the workbench. "When do Stifter and I leave?"

"As soon as we can get his passport prepared. Nessa, can you arrange for the train tickets?"

"Yes. Why don't I come along? I could pose as Stifter's wife."

Lately she'd been lobbying to get more involved in transporting refugees to the Swiss border, but Erich had no intention of seeing that happen. Being part of their illegal operation meant that she was already at great risk. If he'd had his way, she'd have sailed for America, and safety, long ago. He shook his head. "That's not going to happen and that's final."

"I like Nessa's idea," Nussbaum asserted. "Most of the people you've taken to the border have been married couples, but Stifter's single. A woman traveling with a man looks less suspicious than a man traveling alone."

"And taking a chance on both Nessa and me getting arrested is foolish," Erich argued.

"Erich, I'll be fine," Nessa insisted.

"Of course you will, because you're staying here in Berlin."

"I'm not helpless," she countered, offended. "Besides, I need the experience."

"There's too much for you to do here, Nessa."

"Like going on supply runs?" Nessa said, glaring at him. "Erich, I want to do more than just office work."

"I think we can spare her for a few days, Erich," Nussbaum

offered.

"I really prefer to work alone," Erich said. "I don't need an accomplice." He turned his back on Nessa and scowled at Nussbaum to convey his need for some male solidarity.

Erich's last statement had been the wrong thing to say. He knew it after dead silence invaded the room followed by the slamming of the door.

Nussbaum looked sheepishly at him and shrugged. "You have to love her. You don't have to understand her."

Erich found Nessa sitting on the living room couch, arms crossed, staring daggers at him. She'd never looked at him like that before, and it was almost frightening.

He took a seat next to her. "Nessa ..."

"So, you prefer to work alone?" she fumed. "What other things do you prefer to do alone? Hug? Kiss? Try doing those things by yourself."

Erich didn't like the card she was playing. There was no way to trump it.

"Women aren't helpless," she continued. "Your mother said in her last letter that American women are working in the factories making weapons. I don't appreciate being treated like I'd fall apart at the first sign of danger. That timid little sixteen-year-old you first met no longer lives in this body."

He hated this kind of a discussion. Nessa was quicker with words than he was. He wished he could slip out of the room for a few minutes to think, to produce a long list of good reasons why she couldn't come with him. But there was no time for that.

"You'll be sitting nearby," she reminded him. "If something happens, you'll be able to intervene."

He pounced on her illogical argument. "If you and Stifter get arrested by the Gestapo, I won't be able to save you. They carry guns! I don't."

"Erich, of course I'm terrified that we will be caught one day. But we both went into this knowing the risks."

Oh, how he wished he had made her go to America with his parents.

"Thousands of Jews have already been put on eastbound trains and transported to God knows where," she said. "It breaks my heart that we're only able to save a handful of them. I want to do more."

He shook his head, unable to come up with a counterargument.

"We're a team," she soothed. "You don't always get to work 'alone,' as you put it."

Erich realized he wasn't going to win the argument. "All right. But at the first hint of danger the three of us are making ourselves scarce." How they'd possibly accomplish that was beyond him. But she was right. They had to save as many people as they could as quickly as possible. And Nussbaum had also been right – getting Stifter safely out of Germany would go more smoothly if he had a "wife."

She threw her arms around his neck. "Thank you!"

"If you're going to thank me, you could at least do it with a kiss," he teased, and she obliged.

"Are we interrupting something? Do you two need some romantic time alone?"

They broke apart to see Konrad and Harold Stifter standing in the doorway.

"I need to get the train tickets," Nessa mumbled sheepishly. She jumped up and quickly left the room.

"And I have paperwork to finish," Konrad announced, following her out.

Stifter sat down on the couch next to Erich. He was tall, with green eyes and a full head of red hair. He was an opportunist, and Erich would have gladly let the Gestapo have him. There were far more deserving people who needed to be taken to safety.

"You don't like me much, do you?" Stifter said.

"Actually, I don't."

"Because I take money to save lives and you do it for free?"

"People risking their lives for a cause, aren't doing it for free,"

Erich said. "The life I put on the line is worth a great deal more to me than money."

"Well, you have to admit Nussbaum's operation is brilliant. He finds Jews about to be relocated and bribes me to write 'moved to unknown destination in the east' on their mail. The family then vanishes from the Gestapo radar. Then your group snatches them up and spirits them out of Germany. You and I are actually brothers-in-arms, fighting the same war."

"I wouldn't go that far."

"I would." Stifter winked. "What's the life of one of your precious Jews worth? I would say that depends on where he lives. In Palestine, that Jew is worth a lot. In Germany, that same Jew has no worth unless he can do something to benefit the Fatherland."

"Like produce weapons in an armament factory, for instance? Where he's worked to death if necessary."

"Exactly."

"An attitude like that shows how noble your intentions are," Erich sneered.

Stifter was unfazed by his scorn. "We're both rescuing condemned men and women from certain death. Does it really matter how we get the job done?"

Erich didn't have an answer for that. Could he be harboring a bit of pride? Did he think he was better than Stifter because he didn't take bribes in exchange for his services?

Yes, he did feel he was better, actually. Still, although Stifter filled his pockets with Reichsmarks, he gave the people he helped much more than they could have bought with that money – a future.

～

"I'll be sitting a few rows behind you on the train," Erich reminded Nessa on the way to the station. "If there's even a hint of danger, I'm getting you out of there."

"I understand." She pulled her hat further down over her face and tightened the scarf around her neck. In the three days since she'd volunteered to play Stifter's wife, her bravado had melted into doubt. Once they got Stifter to the Swiss border, they'd still have to make it back to Berlin. What if someone noticed she'd been traveling with two different men?

At the train station they descended the stairs to track five. The train was waiting, the locomotive hissing impatiently in anticipation of the journey. "I told Stifter to sit in the second car from the back of the train," Erich said. They climbed aboard and found their companion in an aisle seat. "Slip in next to him and sit by the window," Erich told Nessa. "I'll be three rows behind you."

Nessa joined Stifter. He was wearing a dark suit, looking like a businessman on his way to a meeting.

"I'm sorry I'm late, darling," Nessa murmured, and gave him a kiss on the cheek.

"No matter. You're here now." He looked around, gnawing at his lip.

His nervousness soon infected Nessa, whose heartbeat began to accelerate.

After a few minutes she looked at her watch. They should have left three minutes ago. What was wrong?

Then she spotted him. A Gestapo agent in the carriage ahead of them opened the connecting door and stepped into their car. "*Meine Damen und Herren*," he announced. "Before the train leaves, I must check your papers. Please have them ready."

Nessa felt perspiration beading on her forehead. She took her passport from her purse and pulled her hat even lower. She wished she'd listened to Erich and stayed behind.

It wasn't long before the agent was standing next to her and Stifter. He took Stifter's passport, compared the photograph to his face, and then held the document up to the light to examine it closely. "Where are you heading today, *mein Herr*?"

Stifter handed him his train ticket. "Frankfurt."

"Is that your final destination?"

Silence.

"Sir, is Frankfurt your final destination today?"

Stifter stared straight ahead, unable to speak, his hands trembling wildly.

"Sir, please stand up."

Stifter wouldn't budge. The Gestapo agent seized him under his right arm and pulled him partway to his feet.

As if waking from a trance, Stifter jumped to a standing position, knocked the agent to the floor, and flew to the exit door. The man struggled to his feet, pulled a pistol from under his coat and ran after him. "Halt!" he yelled.

Stifter had almost reached one of the staircases leading to street level, when a bullet brought him to his knees. He tried to get back up, but a second bullet found its mark and sent him sprawling to the ground, lifeless.

The passengers in the coach screamed and poured out of the train. Nessa felt a hand seize her upper arm and pull her to her feet and toward the exit. "Lose that hat and scarf," Erich hissed. She dropped them on the tracks as they left the train.

They melted into the crowd and were halfway to the safe house within minutes.

Nessa's felt nauseated, her teeth chattering. "We failed," she whispered, as they hurried along.

"We tried. That's all we can do," Erich said grimly. "At least the Gestapo killed him. If he had survived being shot, they would have tortured him until he talked. He would have betrayed us all."

July, 1942. Operation Nussbaum Safe House

Ever since Nessa had insisted on being more involved in the smuggling operation, Erich had resigned himself to the fact that she wasn't going to sit idly by while he risked his life for the cause.

It had taken her a couple of weeks to recover from the trauma of watching the Gestapo gun down Harold Stifter, but she soon came to realize that her trauma was insignificant compared to that of the hundreds of Berlin Jews being loaded aboard eastbound trains every day and transported – most people surmised – to work camps in Poland and Czechoslovakia.

Nessa and Erich had come up with a scheme to save at least a few of those Jews from deportation and they were anxious to implement it.

Konrad not so much. "This is insane," he protested. "Why don't we just buy some rope and hang ourselves right now? That's exactly what the Nazis will do if they catch us. The whole plan is foolhardy."

Nussbaum laid a hand on his arm. "Let's give Erich and Nessa a chance to give us all of the details of their plan."

Konrad leaned back in his chair, crossed his arms in front of his chest and scowled.

"Everyone in Berlin is talking about the Jew trains that have been leaving for the east from Grunewald Station since last fall," Erich said. "Rabbi Grünberg's two sons and their wives have volunteered to take the places of four other people who have been slated for what the government is calling resettlement in Eastern Europe."

"We can't let that happen," Nessa added. "Our plan is to 'abduct' the Rabbi's sons and their wives at the station before they are loaded onto the train."

Konrad threw up his hands in exasperation. "You're plan is very noble, but those transports are heavily guarded. Are you suggesting we bribe some of the guards to look the other way while we whisk away some of their captives? No guard would do that. They're responsible for each and every Jew. Lose one and you get shot." He turned to Nussbaum. "Herr Nussbaum, talk some sense into these two. Let's stick to rescuing the people Rabbi Grünberg refers to us and leave it at that. If we're all dead or in prison, we won't be able to help anyone."

"The Jews being deported to eastern Europe aren't ending up in vacation spas," Nessa stated. "The Rabbi has helped us save so many people. How can we not try to rescue his only sons?" She had to admit that she shared Konrad's fears. She didn't relish the thought of being arrested and hanged if caught.

"If the Rabbi's sons disappear, the Nazis will surely think he was involved and go looking for him," Konrad said.

"The Rabbi's not afraid of the Germans," Nessa said. "He'd gladly sacrifice himself to save any member of his flock, not to mention a family member. If we succeed, word will get out and that will give people hope. We'll be the mice that send the elephant into a panic."

"Agitated elephants crush mice," Konrad said cynically.

"We need to do this," Nessa insisted, pounding her fist on the table. "How many of the Jews who have left for the east have come back to tell about it?"

"Some of their relatives have received postcards claiming they arrived in Lodz or Warsaw and are doing fine," Konrad said.

"And you believe that?" Erich asked.

Konrad pursed his lips, stared at the floor, and shook his head.

Nessa took Konrad's hand. "Do you remember the verses from Proverbs you quoted when we first joined the operation four years ago? One of them was: 'Rescue those who are being dragged off to death; save those who are staggering toward the slaughtering block.'"

"I still believe that," Konrad said, "but snatching up people right under the noses of the Nazis terrifies me."

"We're all terrified," Erich said, "but our commitment to our cause means doing whatever we can, whenever we can, to save lives."

Konrad dug his fingers nervously into his scalp. "You're right, you're right. Okay, I'm on board. In for a penny, in for a pound. So how are we going to pull this thing off? We can't just mingle with the crowd at the station and waltz away with four people."

"Nessa and I developed our plan with Georg Bräutigam of the Meier Group," Erich said. "We'll need to create a diversion. That's where Georg and his group come in. Once the trucks with the deportees arrive at the station, his team will set off a couple of explosions nearby. The guards will surely take cover, thinking they're under attack. In the confusion, we'll grab our people and hustle them into Herr Nussbaum's car."

"It all sounds so simple," Konrad said, "but there's one big problem. What if our target families are in the center of the crowd? That would make it very difficult for us to find them."

"Rabbi Grünberg will tell them about the rescue mission and instruct them to work their way to the edge of the crowd once they get off the truck, and then move toward the small park that's in the station plaza."

"I'm really nervous about the use of explosives," Konrad said. "We're not terrorists, remember? I'm all in favor of working with other underground groups, but Georg Bräutigam is a hothead and has been known to take unnecessary risks. What if the explosions kill innocent people?"

"Georg was an ordinance officer in the last war," Erich said. "He knows what he's doing. He'll make sure no one gets hurt."

Konrad leaned back in his chair and looked at Nussbaum. "What do you think of their plan, Herr Nussbaum?"

"Frankly, I applaud their boldness. This mission is dangerous, but everything we do has its risks." He looked from Erich to Nessa. "I'm in too. But I can't let you young people do this without a wiser head as counsel. I'll serve as driver – and adviser," he added with a smile. "When do we want to do this?"

"A week from today," Nessa said.

Konrad shook his head. "We must be mad. Once the Germans discover that some of their 'Jewish property' is missing, they won't give up until they locate it again. And if they somehow connect our organization to the plot they won't rest until they've tracked down and executed every one of us."

It was a sober thought, and it left Nessa feeling faint. But the plan had to go forward just as surely as the departure of each train full of Jews from Grunewald Station. *Lord, give us courage. And more important, give us success.*

~

The day of the mission came and just before dusk the four of them climbed into Nussbaum's large sedan and set out for the train station. Nussbaum guided the car through the Grunewald section of Berlin, past the mansions along Winkler Strasse, then looped around past Grunewald train station before stopping in front of the small park twenty meters past the station entrance.

Erich looked back at the station. Its entrance hall, which was modeled on a castle gate house, with a clock tower between two small turrets, glowed red in the light of the setting sun.

The four co-conspirators had reconnoitered the station a few days earlier in preparation for the mission, taking photographs of the building and taking note of the layout of the plaza.

Erich and Nessa had walked through the station as well and had made their way to track seventeen where the trains stopped to load the Jews into the east-bound cattle cars. Track seventeen had looked innocent enough, and yet Erich had almost felt the specter of doom and hopelessness clinging to the rails. After they had left the platform and descended the stairs to the tunnel that led to the main hall, a breeze had swept through the passageway, creating a low keening sound much like human howls of distress. It had made the hair on the back of his neck stand up.

Nussbaum turned off the car engine and set the hand brake. "Rabbi Grünberg gave me these photographs of his sons and their wives," he said, taking them from his coat pocket and passing them around.

After they had studied the pictures, Nussbaum said, "Erich, why don't you go over the details of this operation one last time."

Erich's heart rate began to accelerate. He nodded and forced himself to relax, pointing toward the park. "Nessa and Konrad and I will hide in the park. When the trucks arrive, the guards will clear the plaza and then begin unloading the Jews. As soon as they are finished, our friends in the Meier Group will set off two explosions, one in the forest five hundred meters from here, and the other thirty seconds later in the woods behind the station. Those blasts should create enough commotion to allow Nessa and I to slip out of the park, grab the Grünbergs and lead them to the car. Nessa will disguise herself as one of the Jews and I as one of the German guards."

Nessa pinned a yellow Star of David on her coat – her camouflage – and ran her fingers across the word "*Jude.*"

Erich slipped into a German Army overcoat and pulled a military hat onto his head. He turned to Konrad. "Do you have the rope?"

Konrad reached into his coat pocket and produced a length of rope. "Right here."

"Good." Erich nodded toward the park. "Konrad, as we discussed, you'll run interference. Tie one end of your rope to the base of a tree along our escape route and trip any guards that happen to chase Nessa and me after we collect the Grünbergs."

"Got it," Konrad said.

"Remember, if anything goes wrong, we'll all return to the car immediately." Erich looked from Nessa to Konrad. "Anyone who cannot make it back to the car safely, will go to Frau Kleist's guest cottage, which is located behind her home at Koenigsallee, Number 102. Much of this part of Berlin is covered with woods, so you should be able to follow the forest trails to within a few meters of her house without being seen."

Frau Kleist was the wealthy Aryan who provided most of the funding for Operation Nussbaum. During the last few days, the four of them had driven between the station and her home several times to familiarize themselves with the route.

Erich squeezed Nessa's hand and patted Konrad on the shoulder and said, "Let's go."

It seemed they had barely entered the park when they heard trucks approaching. Then a line of headlights emerged from Trabener Strasse and turned right onto Winkler Strasse toward the station, pulling into the plaza.

In the dim light Erich and Nessa and Konrad crept through the trees toward the plaza. Konrad went to take up his position and Erich and Nessa crouched behind the tree line at the edge of the park. Half a dozen flatbed trucks stood in a line, each packed with Jewish families. Women and children wept, and men wailed, many sending up desperate prayers to their God.

The guards quickly cleared the plaza of onlookers and began herding the Jews off the trucks, their yellow stars glowing in the faint light.

Then the first explosion went off with startling loudness, making both Erich and Nessa jump. The captives screamed and huddled together while the guards took cover, pointing their rifles in the direction of the blast.

The second explosion sounded as if a mortar round had landed behind the station, rattling the windows in the building. Some of the guards took cover behind their trucks while the remainder split into two groups and moved around each side of the station in the direction of the blast. Their prisoners thronged together near the park; children wept and buried their faces in their mothers' skirts; husbands pulled their wives and children closer.

Erich spotted Rabbi Grünberg's sons and their wives standing at the edge of the crowd "There they are," he told Nessa.

They moved quickly out of the trees and mingled with the crowd for a few moments before Erich spoke. "I'm Erich and this is Nessa," he said to them. "Please come with us."

They had just reached the edge of the park when a voice behind them yelled, "*Stehenbleiben, ihr Juden, oder ich schiesse!*"

"Duck down and go with Nessa." Erich commanded. He dropped back to shield the others in case the guard made good on his promise to shoot.

Which he did. The bullets whizzed over their heads, smacking loudly into tree trunks.

They zigzagged through the trees and raced passed Konrad who stood holding the end of his rope.

Erich heard the shouts of the guards as they crashed through the bushes after them. Just before Nessa and the Grünbergs reached the car, Erich looked back to see Konrad pull the rope, tripping the soldiers and sending them sprawling to the ground. Then Konrad disappeared into the trees.

Erich saw Nessa and the Grünbergs jump into the sedan, leaving the door open for him. He was five meters from the car when more shots rang out, the soldiers apparently on their feet again and firing in his direction. Several bullets hit the vehicle's trunk, and another blew out the rear window making those inside scream in terror.

More shots rang out and Erich felt an intense, burning pain in his left hand that sent him to his knees and sprawling toward the ground. He threw out his hands to break his fall and crashed onto his face three meters from the car.

"Go! Go!" he screamed at Nussbaum. He heard Nessa shriek "No!" but the engine revved and the sedan screeched away, the force of inertia slamming the car door shut. He saw Nessa gaping at him through the frame of the rear window, before hearing Nussbaum shout at her to get down.

The soldiers continued to fire at the fleeing sedan and at Erich as he scrambled to his feet and darted across the street, staying low to the ground and diving into the stand of trees that bordered Auerbach Strasse.

As he raced through the woods, he looked down at his left

hand. The index finger was hanging by a few shreds of flesh and blood pulsated from the wound, leaving a trail of blood on the ground.

He quickly squatted and removed his belt, sliding up his sleeve and cinching the belt around his arm just above the wrist. The bleeding subsided and he pulled his handkerchief from his pocket and clasped it around the wound, nearly retching from the pain.

He had to get to Frau Kleist's before he bled to death!

He ran across Auerbach Strasse into another patch of woods along Fontane Strasse, knowing that it would intersect with Koenigsallee in a few hundred meters. He took a moment to bend over and catch his breath. Konrad had been right. This was insane.

He heard shouts from across the street, then the tramp of many boots, followed by the barking of dogs. The soldiers had probably found his blood trail. He looked down at his wound. It was still oozing, a few drops of blood penetrating the handkerchief and seeping onto the ground. He stuffed his wounded hand into his coat pocket and began running again. Now that he was bleeding inside his pocket and not on the ground, perhaps the dogs would lose his trail.

Darkness was beginning to descend on Berlin, increasing Erich's chances of reaching Frau Kleist's undetected. The wooded area along Fontane Strasse continued in fits and starts for a hundred meters. He could still hear the shouts of the guards and the bellowing of the dogs, but the sounds were fainter now.

He went to the edge of the tree line and peeked around an oak. Street lamps lined the road, each one casting an eerie cone of light onto the street. He ducked back into the woods as a lone truck thundered past in the direction of the train station. *Reinforcements to help find me?*

He continued along, dodging tree branches and tripping over tree roots. He felt forlorn and deserted. His heart seemed ready to pound out of his chest, threatening to crack a rib. He poked his head out of the woods again and looked in the direction of the station. The truck that had passed him had stopped in the middle of the road, soldiers jumping from it and fanning out through the streets and into the woods. And more dogs! How many dogs did it take to catch one fugitive? Two fugitives, actually. Konrad was probably also on the run.

He finally came to Koenigsallee. Far away he could hear shouting and barking, a reminder that despite the distance he had put between himself and his pursuers, he was far from safe. He broke out of the woods, dashed across the street and ran down Koenigsallee.

He was halfway down the block when he saw a soldier facing the opposite direction with a rifle slung over his shoulder, standing under a lamppost. The man had stopped an older couple and stood studying their identification. Erich drew back and hugged a stone wall, which separated the residences from the sidewalk. The wall was still warm from the sun, but is warmth couldn't prevent his teeth from chattering in terror. Behind him dogs howled, and soldiers screamed. They were getting closer, making him desperate for sanctuary. This lone soldier stood between him and Frau Kleist's.

He crossed to the other side of the street, staying close to the stone wall, hoping to slip by the soldier undetected. Heart pounding, he hurried past. Just then the soldier returned the couple's ID's and in parting touched the brim of his cap with his forefinger. Then he turned around.

He immediately spotted Erich and leveled his weapon in his direction. *"Hey, was machen Sie da?"* The man was short and smallish, but that gun gave him a distinct advantage.

"Nothing. I'm not doing anything," Erich said, as the older couple hurried away.

The soldier crossed the street and pressed Erich against the wall with the muzzle of his rifle. "That doesn't look like a standard army uniform. Who are you? And why is your hand in your pocket?"

"I'm on leave from the Russian front." Erich pointed down the street with his good hand. I'm just heading home."

The man looked unconvinced. "You live here?"

"Yes, three streets down," he lied. "On Lassen Strasse. Number 153."

"Show me your ID."

Erich reached into his pocket and pulled out his identification.

He held it out toward the soldier and then fumbled it, dropping it at the man's feet. The soldier reacted the way Erich had hoped. With a curse he bent to retrieve the document and Erich hit him as hard as he could in the face. The man's hands flew into the air, the rifle crashed to the ground and he staggered backwards. Erich picked up the rifle and slammed the butt into his enemy's face, sending blood spurting from the man's mouth and nose. The soldier fell, arms outstretched, his helmet clanking onto the street as the back of his head slammed against the sidewalk. He lay motionless on the ground, his head listing to one side, blood, and dislodged teeth on the pavement next to him.

The dogs and soldiers were now very close. Erich threw the man's rifle over the stone wall and then dragged him using only his right hand into a driveway lined with bushes. He rolled the man between two bushes and stuffed him as far back as he could and then rushed out of the driveway and ran toward Frau Kleist's.

The soldiers and dogs were rounding the corner onto Koenigsallee just as he threw open the gate to Frau Kleist's back yard and bolted in.

A light shone through the window of the guest cottage. *Konrad must be here already.*

Erich stole up to the window and looked in. Frau Kleist and Konrad sat at a table eating cheese and bread and chatting – just two law-abiding members of the Volk enjoying an evening snack. Erich's heart was still racing and he felt faint. He moved to the door and knocked. Just as Frau Kleist opened the door he collapsed at her feet and everything went black.

CHAPTER SIXTEEN

"That finger will have to come off," a voice said. "The bone's shattered and the finger's only hanging by a thread."

Erich opened his eyes to find himself in bed. An elderly man sat next to him on a chair. Behind him Frau Kleist and Konrad hovered over the man's shoulder, their faces grim with worry.

Erich pressed his hands against the bed in an effort to sit up, then immediately fell back, both hands on fire with pain.

"Lie still," the man said. "I'm Doctor Schlegel. I'm here to patch you up."

"Nessa," Erich said, looking around wildly. "Where's Nessa?"

Frau Kleist pulled up a chair and took a seat next to the doctor, taking Erich's hand. "She's fine and the Grünbergs should be in Switzerland by now, thanks to you."

"And you'll be out of commission for a while, young man," the doctor said. "The forefinger on your left hand is too damaged to save. I'll have to amputate it."

Erich closed his eyes and grimaced. A finger was a small price to pay. He could have lost his life in that park. "All right," he said. "When do you want to do it?"

"In a few minutes," the doctor said. He took Erich's bruised right hand. "What happened to this hand? It looks like you just went ten rounds with Max Schmeling."

"I hit a soldier in the face."

"Fortunately, it's not broken," Doctor Schlegel said, squeezing it gently, "just badly sprained. In future, you'll want to avoid hitting anyone in the face. A man's jaw is as hard as a block of wood, you know."

Erich tried to sit up again, but once again fell back in pain. "Frau Kleist," he said, "I hid that soldier in some bushes down the street."

"They found him," she said. "They came to the door asking if I had seen you."

"What did you tell them?" Erich asked.

Frau Kleist laughed and put her hand on the doctor's shoulder. "He was almost killed and yet he still has a sense of humor." She patted Erich's shoulder. "I told them I hadn't seen you. Both my husband and my son are in the SS. That puts me completely above suspicion."

Konrad stepped up to the bed and put his hand on Erich's shoulder, his eyes beaming with reluctant respect. "It was a crazy scheme, but we pulled it off, didn't we? By the way, Nussbaum has put a moratorium on any more missions at Grunewald Station. You only have a limited number of fingers."

Erich managed a smile, although almost every bone in his body ached.

"Nessa's on the way over," Konrad continued. "She wanted to become a nurse. Now she can practice on you."

~

Late August, 1942.

"Thank you for the *Apfelstrudel*," Nessa said to the salesclerk as she and Konrad left the bakery. "I know we'll enjoy the cake, as well."

For all intents and purposes, it looked as if they had just made an ordinary purchase, but the *"Apfelstrudel"* and "cake" were actually ink and paper for producing forgeries. She handed the box to Konrad. "Can you take these supplies back to the safe house? Erich's waiting for me at Café Nola and I'm running late."

"I'll walk you there."

"No need," Nessa said. "It's just around the corner."

"I should really walk you the rest of the way. Better safe than sorry."

"Really, Konrad, it's all right. I can handle walking another hundred meters by myself, even in the dark."

"I'm sure you can, but I'd feel much better knowing I had delivered you safely to the front door."

"You're a dear, but I'm a big girl. I can do this. Besides, weren't you supposed to meet Nussbaum at the safehouse half an hour ago?"

"Yes, but I'm always late. Nussbaum won't ..."

"You'd better get going," she insisted, giving him a playful shove.

He gave up and turned to go, muttering something about not understanding women, while Nessa hurried down Ludwig Strasse, smiling over her small victory.

From a distance she could see the marquee of Café Nola casting a swathe of light across the street. She was within a few meters of the front door when she saw Erich come out, followed closely by another man.

She gasped and backed into the shadows. The man with Erich was Martin Schneider, her former classmate, the man who worked with the Gestapo rounding up illegals. And Schneider had a gun pointed at Erich's back!

Two women walking a dog screeched when they saw the weapon, then hurried away.

Nessa stood on the sidewalk, numb, her mind racing. Obviously

Erich had been arrested, but, dear God, what could she possibly do about it?

She decided she really had no choice. She had to follow them. There was no time to call Nussbaum. No time to double back to see if Konrad was still nearby. How she wished she hadn't been in such a hurry to send him away.

Nessa followed the two men at a distance until they disappeared into a dilapidated hotel. Then she ran across the street to close the distance. The asphalt on the sidewalk absorbed the light from a neon sign humming above the doorway, which read, *Hotel Linde.*

Nessa hurried up the front stairs, swung the door open, and stepped into the lobby. It was drafty and empty except for the desk clerk and a disheveled middle-aged man sitting on a couch. Down the dim hallway she saw Schneider shove Erich into a room, and slam the door. Drops of blood led through the lobby in the direction of Schneider's room. *Good Lord! Erich's been injured or shot!*

To her left she heard laughter and saw a group of men sitting in a smoky pub at the end of a narrow corridor. She doubled any of them could help her. She'd have to rescue Erich by herself.

But how?

Hoping the desk clerk wouldn't notice, she started toward Schneider's room.

She'd only gone a couple of meters when the man on the lobby couch staggered to his feet and grabbed her arm. His breath smelled of beer and cigarettes. His face was swollen and red and covered with stubble. "Hey, little girl, what's the hurry?" he said. "My name's Peter. Want some company?"

She shook off his grip and pushed him away. "Don't touch me."

"Just trying to be friendly," Peter whined and wandered off in the direction of the pub.

Nessa continued toward Schneider's room with no idea what she was going to do once she got there.

"Where do you think you're going?" a voice demanded. "Let's

see your room key. Unless I'm sorely mistaken, you don't have a room here."

She looked over to see the desk clerk, hands on hips, scrutinizing her.

She pointed down the hallway. "Two friends of mine just came in and went into one of the rooms down there."

The clerk grabbed his generous belly and laughed. "Did you notice that one of your friends had a gun?" he scoffed.

Nessa nodded.

"Did you also notice that your other friend was bleeding from the mouth?" He pointed at the floor. "That's his blood all over my carpet."

Nessa winced, struggling to breathe. She felt faint.

"One of your two so-called friends is Martin Schneider. He works for the Gestapo. As we speak, he's probably on the phone with his boss, Gerhardt Schmutze. When Schmutze gets here, the two of them will quite possibly beat your injured friend half to death before they drag him off to Gestapo Headquarters for some more fun," he smirked. "The cat always plays with the mouse before killing it, you know." He propped his hands on the counter and his demeanor softened. "Listen, Fräulein, this dump is no place for a nice girl like you. Why don't you go home?"

Absolutely not! Brave words, but if she went to Schneider's room, he would probably shoot her. She bit her lip in agony. A gun. She needed to get a gun! Was she out of her mind? Where would she get a gun? She'd never even touched a gun, much less fired one.

She backed up a few steps as if she were leaving and looked down the corridor toward the pub. Peter was sitting on a bar stool ogling her, a come-hither smile animating his lips. "Any port in a storm," she murmured, and gestured to him.

The man obviously couldn't believe his good fortune. He flew out of the pub, grabbed Nessa's hand, and pulled her over to the couch in the lobby. "I knew you'd change your mind."

"I need a gun."

He blinked in disbelief. "You need what?"

"Did you see those two men who came through the lobby in a few minutes ago?"

"Of course I saw them." He pointed down the hallway. "They went into one of the rooms down there. One of them actually had a gun. When I see a man with a gun, I steer clear of him."

"One of those men is Erich, my fiancé."

"I hope he's the one with the gun."

"No, he's the other one."

"So, you need a weapon so you can march down the hallway, kick in the door, shoot the man with the gun, and save Erich's life?" Peter fell back on the couch, laughing.

"Listen to me," Nessa said, grabbing his elbow. "I'm dead serious."

Peter sat up. "If you do what I just described, you'll be dead, not serious."

It was time to change tactics. Nessa took Peter's hand and stroked it, trying hard to play the damsel in distress, which indeed she was. "Peter, dear, won't you help me? The man with the gun is Martin Schneider and he works for the Gestapo. He's going to kill Erich."

Peter's eyes widened. He snatched his hand out of her grasp.

"Gestapo? You want me to find you a gun, so you can shoot the Gestapo agent who's got Erich? How long do you suppose it would take them to connect me to the gun and you to me? Do I look like I have a death wish?"

Nessa took both of Peter's hands into hers. They were as rough as sandpaper, the fingers stained with nicotine. "Peter, please," she begged, searching his face.

He shook his head. "Absolutely not."

"If you find me a gun, I'll pay you fifty marks and I'll make sure no one traces it back to you." She had no idea how she could possibly prevent that from happening.

Thirty seconds passed while her companion thought. A minute.

Then he heaved a sigh. "All right," he said, running his fingers nervously through his hair. "I must be crazy for telling you this. I don't have a gun, but I know where you can get one."

"I'm listening."

"You may have noticed that this isn't the best of hotels. Some pretty sleazy types stay here." He smiled and squeezed Nessa's hands. "Present company excepted, of course."

Nessa pulled her hands free of Peter's squeeze. "Peter, stay focused. Where can I get the gun?"

"The desk clerk keeps one behind the counter for protection. Listen, I'll tell him that the toilet in the lobby washroom is malfunctioning. When he leaves to look at it, you duck behind the counter. The gun's on a shelf under the cash drawer." He held out his hand. "That'll be fifty marks."

Nessa dug in her purse and handed over the money, then nudged Peter's foot with hers. "Well, get going. I don't have much time."

"Just remember you're on your own in this. You didn't hear about the gun from me."

"Agreed."

Peter pointed down the hallway. "Look, don't go to Schneider's room. If you go out the front door and turn left, you'll see an alley. The windows in every room in the hotel face that alley. From there, you can see what's going on in each room." He studied her face for an instant. "Are you sure you want to go through with this?"

"I don't have much of a choice."

"All right then," Peter got to his feet and crossed the lobby and went into the washroom. He stayed there about ten seconds, then poked his head out through the door. "Günther," he called to the desk clerk, "the toilet in here is overflowing. Hurry."

Günther swore, then rushed around the counter, red-faced.

He followed Peter into the washroom and closed the door.

Nessa ran behind the counter, found a small revolver on a shelf, stuffed it into her coat pocket and then rushed out the front door and down the stairs.

She waited for a few moments at the entrance to the alley, which was lit only by the light steaming from the hotel windows. *Dear Lord, I'm about to kill a man.* She held her breath and started down the alley. She passed a room where a man lay on his bed listening to the radio. In another room a woman sat smoking, reading a magazine.

Halfway down the building she found Schneider's room. The window shade had been pulled down less than halfway and Nessa had nearly a full view of the room. Erich sat on a chair in a corner looking up at his assailant. Blood dripped from his mouth, soaking the front of his coat.

Schneider, a big man, with short-cropped, sandy hair, stood with his back to the window, waving his gun. He was saying something, but his voice was muffled by the closed window. He stopped talking long enough to light a cigarette, inhaling deeply and exhaling fiercely. Then he backhanded Erich, spattering blood from his mouth onto the wall behind him. Schneider backed away toward the window and leveled the gun at Erich's head.

Nessa removed the gun from her coat, her hands trembling as she tried to steady the weapon. She pointed it at Schneider's back and pulled the trigger, but nothing happened. She stared at the gun in horror and panic. *What's wrong with this thing?* Then she remembered that a gun had a safety latch. She fumbled with the safety, finally switching it off. Schneider stood only a meter from her on the other side of the window. She clenched the gun with both hands and again took aim at his back. Just then Schneider turned around. His gaze met hers, and his eyes flew open. He was just mouthing the word "Nessa" when she fired. The window burst and Schneider threw both hands into the air, sending his gun sailing into a corner. He pitched backward and grabbed a rapidly expanding red stain on the left side of his chest. Then he fell to his knees before smacking face-first onto the floor.

In the commotion Erich had tumbled from his chair and lay sprawled on the floor. He stared at Schneider for an instant, then jumped to his feet and scrambled out of the room.

Nessa stared at the gun for a moment, hands still trembling, then stuffed it into her pocket. *In case we need it some other time.*

She ran out to the street and caught a glimpse of Erich throwing his bloody coat into some bushes and disappearing around a corner. She took off after him, but by the time she reached the corner, there was no sign of him.

As the subway car sped through the tunnel, Nessa looked at her reflection in the window. A young woman stared back, eyes thrown open, mouth agape, and sweat drenching her face. To keep from trembling, she clenched her hands together until they hurt.

Her thoughts raced. *I just killed a man. I could have handled that differently. I didn't have to kill him.* But how could she have avoided it? She had to save Erich – it was him or Schneider. Yes, she could have gone to Schneider's room and knocked on the door. She could have shoved her gun in his face and gotten the drop on him. She laughed. Who was she trying to fool?

Could Schneider's family ever forgive her? she asked herself. Could God forgive her?

Schneider had a wife and a young daughter. Nessa could almost see the little girl at home clutching a ragged old doll and asking her Mutti when Papa would be home. *Your Papa won't be coming home, little girl. Ever.*

Nessa shuddered. The Gestapo would be at the hotel by now to investigate Schneider's death. The desk clerk had seen her. He could identify her. Peter had seen her. He would crack under pressure and describe her right down to the clothes she was wearing. The Gestapo was patient. They wouldn't give up until they tracked down her and then Erich and then Nussbaum and Konrad. They were all going to die because of her.

She slid her hand into her pocket and felt the gun. It was hard and cold. What if the Gestapo stopped her on the way home? Would she have the nerve to use the gun to avoid capture?

At home, Nessa closed the door behind her.

"Where in the world have you been?" Erich's face was contorted in pain. He held a bloodied towel to his nose and mouth.

Nessa ran to him and held him. "I thought I had lost you for good tonight."

He pulled back, frowning. "What is that supposed to mean?"

Nessa was still shaking. "I saw you with Schneider outside Café Nola. I followed you to that hotel."

Erich removed the towel from his face, his mouth gaping open. "You followed us? Please tell me you're joking."

"Schneider was going to kill you. I had to save you, Erich."

"He wasn't going to kill me," Erich said. "I had a plan." Although for the life of him he had no idea what that plan could have been. "Besides, Schneider had a gun. There was no way you could have saved me."

"I shot Schneider through the window."

He stared at Nessa, trying to comprehend what she was saying. "That was you? Where on earth did you get a gun?"

"Peter told me that the desk clerk at that hotel kept a gun behind the counter."

"Peter who?"

"Never mind. Peter is just some drunk that hangs around the hotel lobby."

"Good Lord, Nessa, were you out of your mind?"

"I was desperate. Was I just supposed to let Schneider kill you?"

Suddenly Erich was very tired – and grateful. He led her to the couch, and they sat down. He drew her into his arms. "No, darling, you weren't supposed to just let him kill me." He kissed her. "Thank you. Thank you." He never thought he'd be thanking her for shooting someone.

She pulled away from him and reached into her pocket,

handing him the weapon. Then she leaned into him and wept on his shoulder. "Erich, I killed a man tonight."

"You didn't kill anyone. I called the hotel when I got home. The desk clerk said that Schneider was hit just above the heart. He'll live."

She hunched her shoulders and sighed, clearly relieved. "Thank God. I'd never want to kill another human being. But I'd do it again to save you."

He smiled at her. "You're going to get a reputation as the most dangerous woman in Berlin," he said.

Erich fingered the gun. They'd keep it. It might come in handy one day.

The subway car came to a lurching stop at Potsdamer Platz, and Erich and Nessa joined the other travelers exiting the train. On the platform, the mass of commuters boarding the train jostled past them, nearly pushing them back into the coach. Then the doors closed and the train rumbled away.

The stifling heat on the platform was only a precursor to what awaited them at street level. The glare of the August sun and the oppressive humidity nearly took their breath away.

They walked along Bellevue Strasse, under a canopy of sycamore trees, peering into shop windows full of things they could never afford to buy. She wouldn't have much room in her luggage for much more than the essentials anyway, Erich thought.

In a few minutes he would break the news to her. He wondered how she would react to his decision. He would get Nessa to Lisbon, Europe's safe harbor, and then put her on the ship to America, out of harm's way. It was time; her aunt Helen was dead, and she had no family left in Germany. And there had been too many close calls with death. There was the near disaster at Grunewald Station in July when they snatched Rabbi Grünberg's family out of the clutches of the Nazis. Then the shooting of Martin Schneider. Erich was thankful that she had saved his life, but he refused to expose her to any more danger. She was leaving Germany – whether she wanted to or not.

But for now, he'd buy her a treat.

They could have found the bakery blindfolded – the aromas drifting along the street were overpowering. Scores of breads, rolls, and pastries tempted them from the display case, which was alive with activity, as wasps and fruit flies swarmed over the pastries, reveling in the sweetness.

Erich paid for two pieces of *Bienenstich* – small square cakes topped with caramelized almonds and filled with vanilla custard.

Then they left the shop to resume their stroll, eating as they went. They continued to the end of the street and crossed a small square that led into the *Tiergarten*. Here they wandered together along tree-lined paths and strolled over arched bridges that spanned ponds and waterways, before finally taking a seat on a familiar park bench near a small pond that was overshadowed by scores of oak trees.

They watched as a man on horseback rode over a nearby bridge while a couple in a rowboat passed under it before disappearing around a bend.

"This is the same bench your parents used to sit on," Nessa recalled. "Do you remember when we came here just before they left for America? I can't believe it's been three years."

Tell her now. He took her hand in both of his. "And in a few weeks, you'll be in America with them."

Nessa gasped. "We're leaving?"

"I'm getting you out."

"But what about you?" she said, alarmed.

"I'll come later. Your parents and your aunt Helen have passed away, so you have no more family here. Besides, you shot Martin Schneider. The Gestapo's looking for you. You can't stay in Germany."

"The Gestapo's looking for you, too, in case you've forgotten." She shook her head. "No, I won't go without you."

"I can't leave. There's still too much to do. I need to get you out of harm's way. For my peace of mind, you must go."

"And what of my peace of mind?" she retorted. "What if you get caught making counterfeit IDs? Or smuggling people out of Germany? What do you think will happen to you then, Erich Reinhold?"

"Stop worrying. Nothing's going to happen. We'll be together in America very soon." He nudged her. "Besides, haven't you shot enough Nazi agents for one lifetime?"

She frowned and shook her head, ignoring the quip, then squeezed his hands. "Erich, I admire your heroism in wanting to stay, but I can't marry a dead hero. Come with me or let me stay here with you."

"We have to find that safe harbor you wished for so many years ago and the first step is getting you out of Europe."

"No! I won't leave," she shouted. An elderly couple on a nearby park bench stopped their conversation and scowled in their direction.

"Yes, you will," Erich whispered.

She lowered her voice to a hiss. "Now you're the Führer, ordering my life for me, telling me what to do?"

"No, I'm the man who loves you and cannot live without you. I must get you to a safe place. Nessa, if something happened to you here, I'd never forgive myself."

She stared straight ahead, jaw clenched.

It was time to play the parents card. "Listen, Nessa. Last July, after we were almost killed rescuing Rabbi Grünberg's sons, I wrote my parents and asked them to sponsor you. Of course they agreed. I got the sponsorship letter a couple of weeks ago and gave it to Frau Kleist and she was able to get you an American visa. My parents are very worried about us. Once you arrive safely in America, it will give them hope that I'll be there soon as well."

She squeezed his hands hard. "Just come with me *now.*"

He gave her an impudent grin. "I can't. I don't have a visa." Then his countenance sobered. "Nessa, please go. Go and be a comfort and a hope to my parents."

She looked on the verge of tears. He also wanted to cry, but forced himself to smile at her, squeezing her hands. "Let me stay and finish what I've committed to do." He took her face in his hands. "Listen, you'll barely arrive in Ohio before I show up on your doorstep. Then we'll be together for the rest of our lives."

Nessa wasn't the only one he was trying to convince.

When they got home, they found Frau Sturm sitting in the living room engrossed in her newspaper. She looked up and smiled at them. They sat down on a loveseat, away from the windows, in a dimly lit corner of the room and Erich shared their news with her.

She was ecstatic. "Just think, a month from now you'll be in America," she said to Nessa. "How I envy you. You're going to freedom while we remain here under Hitler's boot." She looked out the window. "I'd love to go to America, but that's impossible, of course. My husband died in the Great War and I can't leave my two sons behind. But they're out there on the Russian front, so in a way, I've already lost them ... Here, see what I mean," she said, reaching for a letter on the living room table. "Listen to the letter I got from Horst a few days ago."

Dear Mother,

I pray that you are doing well. This letter brings you my love as well as birthday greetings. Dear mother, remain strong at my side. As a soldier I need your support now more than ever. We have come to Russia to bring the Bolsheviks to their knees. What a privilege it is to fight at the Führer's side! The German warrior always carries with him the spirit of his loving mother who inspires him to be victorious and to go down fighting, if necessary. Her eyes shine on him even in death.

I will be home soon, I promise.

Faithfully, your thankful son,

Horst

Frau Sturm sighed and laid the letter aside. "The Nazis have ruined my boy. His letters read like propaganda slogans. They took away his Christian faith and replaced it with allegiance to a mad man. Two of my sons have already died in battle. They will never return. And now Horst and Hans are in Russia. What in the world are we doing there? I would have remained childless if I had known my boys would one day be shot to pieces on some battlefield."

"You still have Horst and Hans," Nessa said. "Soon the war will be over, and they'll return home to embrace you," she added, although she didn't believe a word she was saying.

Frau Sturm glowered out the window. From the expression on her face, it was evident that she too didn't believe either of her remaining sons would ever return home alive.

CHAPTER SEVENTEEN

September 9, 1942. Anhalter Station, Berlin.

Erich and Nessa walked through the first-class sleeping carriages on the way to their seats in second class, stopping to peer into one of the luxurious sleeping compartments. Inside stood a crimson sofa upholstered in crushed velvet next to a small mahogany table. A diminutive gas heater filled the compartment with cozy warmth. In both berths the pillows had been fluffed and the covers turned down, inviting the traveler to spend the night in blissful luxury.

The second-class carriages were a world apart – unheated cars with hard, cold, wooden seats. They found two seats together and Nessa snuggled into Erich and watched the hustle and bustle on the platform. Sweaty porters lugged carts piled high with luggage, families cried and hugged goodbye, and newspaper boys waved their papers and sang out the latest headlines.

"Are you ready for our big adventure?" Erich asked.

"Not really," Nessa admitted, biting her lip.

He took her hand. "Listen, we'll get you to on that ship to America and I'll be practically right behind you. Hitler's bogged down in Russia. This war can't last much longer. We'll be together again before you know it."

Nessa wasn't listening. Her thoughts centered only around that moment in Lisbon when she would have to leave Erich behind. Now she had an inkling of how his parents must have felt the day they left him in Germany.

Erich stroked her hand encouragingly. "Don't worry, darling," he said, pulling her into an embrace. "I know this is hard. I don't want you to go – but you must."

"If only there was a way ..." She put her hand over her mouth and stared at the floor, tears welling in her eyes.

He took both of her hands. "There isn't. You have to leave."

She nodded, then pulled a hand free to wipe away a tear. "I know." She knew, but didn't understand. How was she supposed to start a new life without him? He was sending her to America to keep her alive, but if he never made it to that safe harbor, her life would be over anyway.

"Why don't we review our trip one more time before we leave," Erich suggested.

Nessa sighed and nodded wearily.

"Today we'll be going to Nuremberg before transferring to Ulm," he said. "We'll spend the night there and tomorrow morning we'll take the train to Tengen to attend your aunt Ingrid's bogus memorial service. In Tengen we'll meet Josef Eichendorff, who will take us across the Swiss border that evening. From Switzerland we'll travel through southern France, Spain and on to Lisbon."

Nessa pulled out their tickets and studied them. "We'll be in Nuremberg a little after noon today."

Erich looked at his watch. "Six hours from now. Why don't you try to get some sleep?"

"I'm too wound up to sleep." On the one hand she wished they were already in Lisbon, far away from Berlin and the terror of wondering when the next fleet of Allied bombers would arrive to drop their payloads on the city. On the other hand, she wanted this trip to last forever, because Lisbon meant leaving Erich behind. And then he would return to Germany, and danger. Every time she thought of that she wondered why she had let him talk her into leaving. Of course, there was also the specter of failure. What would happen if the Gestapo picked them up on the way? And so, the thoughts continued to chase one other around inside her head.

Their carriage started to fill up. An old man leaning on a cane hobbled past them and sat in the back of the car, followed by a young couple talking about honeymoon plans in Italy. Two nuns clutching their rosaries settled in across the aisle from the honeymooners.

Then the conductor on the platform blew his whistle. The locomotive's whistle answered, and the train lurched into motion, the engine spewing out great balls of white smoke, filling the hall with mist, which clung to the windows, momentarily transforming them into milk glass.

South of Potsdam they crossed the Elbe River, then scooted past the Harz Mountains where the Brothers Grimm had once spent their days collecting tales of ragged peasants marrying princes and wicked witches swooping down on their brooms from crag-perched castles to cast spells on virtuous young maidens.

Soon, Thuringia, known as the "Green Heart of Germany," opened her arms to the travelers with waterfalls tumbling off cliffs into nothingness. Deep, wooded valleys lay packed with mist. Steep-roofed houses with tiny windows rolled by, and crooked cobblestone roads slithered away like serpents into the forests.

Then they crossed into Franconia, slipping past Bayreuth and steaming into Nuremberg, Hitler's favorite city. The imperial castle sat on a hill, looming over the city. In its shadow stood the city walls and the gothic spires of the Church of Our Lady.

A few passengers got off the train and were soon replaced by others.

Nessa took their tickets out of her purse, then turned Erich's wrist to look at his watch. "Noon. We leave for Ulm in half an hour and arrive at five." She dug in her bag and pulled out two liverwurst sandwiches wrapped in wax paper, handing one to Erich. "We should get to Tengen tonight around nine-thirty."

She took out her ID and examined it. She and Erich were now "married," traveling as Erich and Nessa Frank. If only they were truly married and somewhere safe, already sharing life as husband and wife. Would that ever happen?

At half past twelve the conductor gave the "all aboard" warning. Just as he shoved his whistle into his mouth to signal their departure, a rotund middle-aged man, laden with two suitcases, sprinted past him to the car door. The conductor yanked the whistle out of his mouth, pointed to the pocket watch in his hand, and barked something at the latecomer.

Thirty seconds later they were underway.

The late arrival, wheezing and sweating, lumbered down the aisle and stowed his baggage above Nessa and Erich before settling in across from them. "That was close," he panted, removing his monocle and mopping his face and balding head with a handkerchief. He stretched out a sweaty hand to them. "Robert Merkel. *Es freut mich.*"

They each shook his hand. "Glad to meet you, too," Nessa said. "I'm Nessa Frank and this is my husband, Erich."

"And where are the Franks heading today?" Merkel wanted to know. "All the way to Ulm?"

"Yes," Erich said.

"As am I," the man said. He mopped his face with his handkerchief again. "If I had missed this train, I would have lost my biggest account. I wish I could work from home, but traveling salesmen travel, you know."

Robert Merkel turned out to be a hopeless chatterbox, prattling and pontificating ad nauseam about every subject under the sun, from food to family and the joys of having a large one. "Even in difficult times you manage," he said. "So don't let that stop you young people from producing many children for the Führer. Do you have children yet?"

To have children, they would have to be intimate. Nessa blushed as she remembered how close they'd once come. Now she was half-wishing they'd succumbed to the temptation. Perhaps then she'd have been on her way to America carrying a child inside her, bringing Erich's parents a grandson as a consolation for showing up without their son.

"We don't have any children," Erich said.

"Ah, well, you're young. There's time – as soon as we win this war and sort out the Jewish problem, that is."

Three hours into the trip, as they passed through Heidenheim, Merkel was still blathering. "I have the utmost confidence in our Führer," he said, removing his monocle and waving it in front of his face for emphasis. "He's the embodiment of the State and of authority. Yes, sometimes the State is stern, even insensitive like a strict schoolmaster, but it blesses us with security and protection." He popped his monocle back into his eye socket, and leaned in toward them, smirking. "Unless, of course, you're Jewish," he added, laughing at his joke.

Nessa was tempted to look for something with which to club Merkel, but resisted the urge.

At that moment, a Gestapo agent entered the front of their carriage, banging the door shut behind him. Merkel gulped and stared wide-eyed at the man, his monocle popping out of his eye socket and dangling on a ribbon against his chest. Apparently this representative of the State was not the embodiment of security and protection to him.

"Please have your identification papers ready," the agent said.

Merkel's handkerchief reappeared and he dragged it across his face and forehead. "It's getting more and more dangerous to travel, even if you're an upstanding member of the Volk," he said in a low voice. "The Gestapo is so unpredictable. They'll arrest you for sneezing at the wrong time."

Merkel wasn't the only one who was afraid. Nessa closed her eyes and prayed for protection. Like Daniel, she and Erich were caught in the lion's den and they would have to trust God to keep them safe from the jaws of cruelty and brutality in the New Germany.

But trust was sometimes hard for her to find. It hid behind the memory of what had happened to her parents and to Erich's grandfather. She threaded her arms through Erich's, holding on tightly to keep fear at bay.

He cupped a hand over hers and gently squeezed it. "Relax," he whispered, "no need to worry. I've done this lots of times."

"I've done it too, and it didn't turn out well," Nessa whispered back. Fear continued to grab at her, and her prayers became more fervent.

Merkel, the blabbermouth, sat as quietly as a condemned man on the gallows waiting for the trap door to drop out beneath his feet.

It wasn't long before the Gestapo agent was standing in front of the chatterbox. He presented his ID and stared out the window while the agent examined it. His papers were in order. Merkel let out his breath and thanked the man, before excusing himself and hurrying to the toilet.

Then the agent turned his attention to Erich and Nessa. "Guten Tag."

"Tag," Erich said, handing the man his ID.

The agent studied Erich's papers. "And where are you heading today, Herr Frank?"

"Ulm."

"Is Ulm your final destination?"

"No," Erich said, pointing to Nessa. "From Ulm my wife and I are traveling on to Tengen."

"Tengen? That town on the Swiss border?"

Dear Lord, help us.

"That's correct," Erich said. "My wife's aunt Ingrid passed away and we will be attending her memorial service tomorrow."

The agent's countenance turned from stern to confused. He

tapped Erich's ID on the palm of his hand. "Erich Frank. Tengen," he murmured. He thrust his hand into the pocket of his coat and pulled out a small notebook. He flipped through the pages, finally stopping halfway through the book. "Here it is. Erich Frank. Karlsruhe to Tengen on August 5th of this year." He leveled a cold stare at Erich. "I thought I recognized you, Herr Frank. Since we last met in August, I've transferred from the Karlsruhe-Tengen railway route to this one."

Nessa began to tremble. Dear God, what were the chances of that happening? Life was full of coincidences, not all of them good.

"Herr Frank, you make repeated trips to the Swiss border, it seems. Why is that?"

Erich opened his mouth to speak, but the agent cut him off. "Stand to your feet."

At that moment, the train shunted sharply to the right. The Gestapo agent, with a look of confusion and panic in his eyes, reeled in the aisle before finally managing to grab a railing. Some of the passengers might have enjoyed the look of terror on the agent's face, but they were not afforded the time.

The train's whistle suddenly wailed, and the train decelerated rapidly, its brakes screeching. From the front of the train came the kind of agonizing groan that a mortally wounded dragon would have made after being run through by a Teutonic warrior.

Then came the crash. Passengers screamed in terror as the back of their coach suddenly reared up like a terrified stallion.

The impact was so violent that the Gestapo agent lost his grip on the railing and flew toward the front of the coach, followed by airborne luggage from the overhead racks.

Nessa and Erich were hurled forward onto the floor just as the coach crashed back to earth, skidding sideways along the rails.

When the car finally came to rest, Erich groaned to his feet in search of Nessa, finding her under the seat in front of them. "Are you all right?" he asked, gently helping her back to her feet.

"I'm fine," she said, dusting off her coat. "How about you?"

"I'm okay, but we need to get off this train. It may catch fire."

Cries for help and moans of agony began filling the railway car. Nessa looked down the aisle to see arms and legs and heads poking out from beneath the mounds of luggage that covered them. "We can't leave without helping these people."

She and Erich, along with a few other uninjured passengers, began returning luggage to the overhead racks and helping passengers back into their seats.

And there, three meters away, lay the Gestapo agent under a large trunk, his face and neck a mass of blood. Nessa grabbed the first aid box from the wall and rushed to him, Erich right behind her.

They lifted off the trunk. The man's eyes were open, but his breathing was labored. He still clutched Erich's ID in his left hand. How Nessa wanted to snatch it from him. There would have been nothing the man could have done to prevent her from doing just that. But first, they would help him.

His right hand, red with blood, clawed weakly at his neck. Nessa pulled his fingers gently away. Blood oozed from a jagged laceration on the side of the man's neck and flowed over the front of his uniform jacket, collecting in a pool on the floor. "It looks like he's lost a lot of blood," she said to Erich. She removed a compress from the first aid kit and pressed it firmly onto the wound.

Then she took the man's bloody hand into hers. It was cold and sticky. She drew near his face. "Lie still, you're going to be all right." She had no idea whether he would survive – but weren't those the words you always said to an injured person?

The agent squeezed her hand, then his eyes moved from Nessa to Erich and back to Nessa again. "I'm dying, aren't I?" His voice sounded hoarse and terrified.

"Of course not," Nessa said, squeezing his hand tighter and forcing a smile.

The man released his hand from Nessa's and reached into his uniform jacket. He pulled out a picture and handed it to her. From the photograph, now wet with the man's blood, a young woman and two small girls smiled at her.

The agent pressed a bloody finger onto the picture. "My family." Even the hardest heart turned soft when faced with death.

"They're beautiful," she said, before sliding it back into his pocket. "Now don't move. You'll be with your family soon, I promise."

From behind her, a voice called. "Medical personnel, please clear the way," and a group of medics and a doctor made their way through the train car.

"Doctor," Erich called, "this Gestapo agent's bleeding badly." The word "Gestapo" was enough to compel the doctor into immediate action.

The physician took the blood-soaked compress from Nessa's hand, quickly examined the laceration, and then pressed a fresh bandage onto the wound. "Young lady," he said, "hold this firmly on the wound just as you were doing." The doctor took the agent's blood pressure, and then shone a flashlight into his eyes. "His blood pressure's low and he's lost a lot of blood, but he'll be all right. Let's get him to the hospital," he said to the medics. He placed one hand on the Gestapo agent's shoulder and one on Nessa's. "Sir," he said to the agent, "you can thank this young woman for saving your life. If she hadn't applied the compress when she did, you would have bled to death."

The agent took hold of Nessa's arm. "Thank you. Thank you," he said. "Have a safe trip to Tengen," he added, handing Erich his ID.

The medics lifted the man onto a stretcher and pushed their way through the aisle and out of the train.

Then the doctor asked all uninjured passengers to leave the train. Erich found their bags and they went outside.

Near chaos greeted them. Policemen and railway workers had formed a line around the crash scene, desperately trying to hold back a large crowd of onlookers. It looked as if the entire town of

Heidenheim had come out to gawk at the spectacle. Each time the rescuers pulled the body of a moaning, bleeding passenger from the wreckage, the crowd surged forward like spectators at the circus, craning their necks for a better look.

Medics swarmed around the railway cars, assisting the injured, while railway workers with heavy machinery cleared the wreckage from the tracks, trying to undo the work of devastation that only an instant had wrought.

Erich stopped a conductor hurrying past on the sandy trail that paralleled the tracks. "What can we do to help?"

"Nothing," he said. "Everything's under control now. Just stay out of the way."

"Ach, there you are," a voice called from behind them. It was Robert Merkel. "I see you two survived in one piece."

"As did you," Nessa said, smiling. "Were you hurt?"

"No, but I've been trapped in the toilet ever since the collision," Merkel said. "It took them twenty minutes to get me out. But, no bother. I had a nice conversation with the rescue workers while they were taking apart the toilet compartment to free me."

"Did they tell you what caused the accident?" Erich asked.

"The switcher was either drunk or sleeping on the job. Our train was shunted onto a side-track and we rear-ended a freight train. Our engineer saved our lives. He applied the brakes and slowed the train appreciably before the collision. The police are looking for the switcher as we speak." He pointed up at the telegraph lines, along which dozens of birds perched, craning their heads sideways and to stare down at the frenetic scene below them. "Don't be surprised if you see him hanging from one of those lines before the night is over."

Nessa was about to ask if anyone was killed when Erich made their excuses and led her away. "We need to walk back to the station and phone Josef Eichendorff and tell him we've been delayed. He'll notify our other contacts in Switzerland, Spain and Portugal."

They walked past the baggage car, which had spewed luggage and packages all over the tracks. In one passenger coach the benches had been accordioned together from the impact. Firemen stood near the main tracks in front of the station waving crimson torches to warn approaching trains.

The waiting area in the station house was packed. Nessa and Erich weaved and stumbled their way through the maze of passengers, suitcases and trunks to a group of phone booths near the ticket counter. Long lines had formed in front of each booth and a railway official stood by, making sure that no one spent more than one or two minutes on the phone.

Half an hour later it was Erich's turn and he dropped a few coins into a payphone and dialed Eichendorff's number.

"No answer," he said to Nessa.

He hung up and dialed again. "Still no answer."

"Are you sure you're dialing the right number?" she asked. It's 473 991."

"That's what I'm dialing."

Nessa rubbed her forehead to block out the cacophony of voices in the waiting room. Was it possible that they had both misremembered Eichendorff's number?

"Here, you try," he said, handing her the receiver and some money.

She dropped in the coins and carefully dialed 4-7-3 9-9-1, letting it ring twenty times. "No one's picking up," she said, shaking her head. She hung up. "Erich, what are we going to do now?" *What if Eichendorff's been arrested? It wouldn't be long before they tracked him to Nussbaum and from Nussbaum to us!*

"We'll call him again when we get to Ulm," Erich said. "He probably stepped out for a few minutes. I'm sure..."

A voice behind them interrupted him. "You've already made three phone calls." It was the railway official who was monitoring phone usage. "Now move along and give someone else a chance."

"Let's go outside and wait for the replacement train," Erich said, as they walked away. He glanced at his watch. "It's supposed to be here in an hour."

~

Standing on the platform, Erich saw a faint speck of light appear on the horizon. He looked at his watch. *Right on time.*

The speck grew larger by the second, approaching through a swath that had been cut through the thick carpet of forest that surrounded Heidenheim. Snow-white puffs of smoke shot out of the top of the speck and were instantly whisked away by the wind. The tracks in front of him began to sing in a rhythmic, high-pitched tone. The noise grew louder as the speck finally evolved into a steam locomotive.

Then a voice over the loudspeaker announcing the arrival of the train to Ulm. Suddenly the doors to the waiting room burst open and the noisy, sweaty crowd surged onto the platform.

The train rumbled into the station and they watched the carriages pass: first class, second class, smoking and non-smoking cars rumbling by noisily before coming to an abrupt halt. A mad dash ensued as the passengers, ignoring any sense of German order, exploded into action and pushed, pulled, shoved and squeezed themselves and their luggage onto the train.

Nessa and Erich found two seats together in second class near the front of the train. Erich looked around for Robert Merkel, but didn't see him. In a way, he was relieved that they wouldn't have to listen to him chatter incessantly all the way to Ulm.

A huge man with hunched shoulders and a face not unlike that of a bear, took a seat opposite them at the window. A little man clutching a yellow first-class train ticket came in and took a seat next to him.

"This is an outrage," the first-class traveler spouted. He stopped a conductor hurrying by and held up his ticket. "Conductor, do you know what this is?" he asked.

The conductor looked at the ticket. "I've been working for the railroad for twenty years, *mein Herr*. By now I know exactly what a first-class ticket looks like."

"Then what am I doing sitting in a second-class carriage?" the little man demanded, waving his hand at the rest of the passengers, "with these plebeians?"

"You'll have to answer that question yourself," the conductor said. "You're the one who chose to sit here."

"That's because as soon as the train stopped, the unwashed masses piled into the first-class compartments," he yelled, "and you people did nothing to stop them. Now there's no room there for legitimate first-class ticket holders."

"Sir," the conductor said calmly, "this is an extraordinary situation. An hour ago we were involved in an accident. If you can just be patient, I will make sure you get a first-class seat once we arrive in Ulm." With that he scurried away.

"I'm getting off in Ulm, you idiot," the complainer muttered at the conductor's back. He snorted and then ceremoniously tore up his yellow ticket, letting the pieces waft to the floor. "You see," he said, speaking to no one in particular, "this is what a first-class ticket is worth these days." He sat back in his seat, pouting. "Now I have to spend the next four hours in the company of peasants."

The large, bear-like man at the window had apparently had enough. He turned to the complainer, moving his face very close to his. "Would you rather sit here in second class with the unwashed masses or be dead, your majesty?"

The whiner looked confused and somewhat intimidated.

"Because dead is something all of us nearly were," the bear spat. "Now, shut your trap."

The complainer shot to his feet, waving his forefinger in the bear's face. "How dare you address me in that manner. I have a mind to summon the conductor and have you thrown off this train."

The bear also rose to his feet, his head nearly touching the ceiling as he looked down onto the top of the little man's head. He pointed a large, hairy paw at the man's face and another at the window. "How would you like to go headfirst through this window and wait for the next train? If you're lucky I'll open the window first before I throw you through it."

For a moment the whiner stared up at the bear while the bear glowered down at him.

Erich knew he needed to act. This altercation could not escalate into a brawl. In the aftermath, the police would question him and Nessa about the fight. They didn't need that kind of exposure.

He opened his mouth to speak, but Nessa beat him to it. "Gentlemen, we've all been through a lot today. Don't risk being thrown off the train for fighting. You may have a long wait for the next one and I'm sure you're both very anxious to get home."

The bear pointed at Nessa and then at the complainer.

"Count your blessing, your majesty. This young woman just saved your life." He sat down with a thud and stared out the window.

The little man also took a seat and continued his pout.

Erich smiled at Nessa. "That's twice today you've saved us," he whispered.

She returned his smile. "All in a day's work," she replied, then laced her arm around his and laid her head on his shoulder.

They steamed into Ulm about two hours later than they had originally planned and were finally able to reach Josef Eichendorff and explain the reason for their delay. He promised to meet their train the next evening in Tengen.

Before they boarded the train the next morning, they bought red roses for aunt Ingrid's memorial and then, to look authentic, they slipped black mourning bands over their arms.

The trip to Tengen began smoothly. No questions. No problems.

Halfway there, the train jogged to the left, passed a huddle of houses, and pulled into Ziegenthal for a few minutes to pick up more passengers. Nessa glanced over at Erich. He sat motionless, hands folded in his lap, carefully scrutinizing everyone and everything in the railway car.

Through the window she saw a winding, tree-lined road that looped around a pond. Nearby, an old woman laid a wreath on a grave in a churchyard, a tall stone crucifix with the body of the dying Messiah hovering over her.

Across the street a group of laughing children on bicycles passed under a huge banner that spanned the roadway. The message on the banner said: "This lovely city of Ziegenthal, this glorious spot of earth, was created for Germans and not for Jews. Jews are therefore not welcome here." A sudden feeling of isolation came over her, followed by bitterness. *Don't worry, Ziegenthal, I won't be staying long. In a few minutes, you'll have one less Jew in your midst to worry about.*

When they arrived in Tengen that night, Erich pulled their bags from the overhead rack and Nessa grabbed the roses they had bought for aunt Ingrid's memorial.

As they stepped off the train, a man with white hair and a white beard approached them. Josef Eichendorff. He handed Nessa a single red rose. "I'm so sorry for your loss. May I drive you to the cemetery?"

"Thank you," she said, and they followed him out of the train station.

As they walked across a parking lot, Eichendorff turned to Erich and shook his hand. "It's good to see you again, my friend." He laughed. "I don't know too many people who have survived a train wreck."

"Well, now you know two," Erich said, introducing Nessa.

Eichendorff took Nessa's hand. "It's so nice to finally meet you. Erich can't seem to stop talking about you."

Nessa blushed and shook his hand. "Thank you. Nice to meet you, too."

Eichendorff took the roses from Nessa. "You won't need these any longer. I'll relieve you of your mourning bands as well." They removed them, handing them to the old man, who tossed them into a nearby trash can.

Eichendorff pointed straight ahead. "The car's right over here. You two climb into the back. I'll ride in front."

Erich threw their bags into the back seat, then he and Nessa got in. A man in the driver's seat turned around and nodded.

"This is my brother Rudolf," Eichendorff said. "He'll be taking us to the border. He doesn't talk much."

"Nice to meet you." Nessa said.

Rudolf nodded again, then turned around and stared straight ahead, motionless, silent.

Eichendorff raised an index finger. "Now, here's the plan. We'll drive to within one kilometer of the border. From there we go on foot. Stay down and do *exactly* what I say as we approach the border. Is that clear?" He turned the rearview mirror to see them nod. "Now, before we go, I need to check your travel documents for accuracy."

They handed him their papers.

"Your man, Konrad, always supplies immaculate papers, but I always do a final check before we go over the border." He scanned the papers with a flashlight. "Excellent, excellent," he murmured, before returning them. "You should have no problems."

They drove for a few minutes, turned onto a forest trail, and then stopped in a clearing. Eichendorff opened his door. "From here we walk. Rudolf, meet me back here in two hours." Rudolf looked straight ahead and nodded.

Erich grabbed their things and they followed Eichendorff. After a minute, their eyes became accustomed to the dark. Ten minutes later Eichendorff signaled for them to stop. "We're just a few meters from the border," he whispered. "There's no actual fence, so we won't have to worry about that. Luckily, tonight's a new moon, so we won't have moonlight illuminating the entire landscape. Now, stay close behind me."

They walked for another thirty seconds, before Eichendorff stopped again. "Listen," he whispered. "Those voices you hear are the German border guards. It's ten o'clock. Shift change. This is the perfect time to cross, because the two shifts always visit for a few minutes before going their separate ways. Follow me and stay close to the ground."

They hunched over and went a few more meters. Nessa could hear the guards talking and laughing. Then her foot found a hole, and she went down with a thud. Eichendorff and Erich dropped instinctively to the ground.

The guards' voices stopped. Nessa could feel a group of eyes looking in their direction, straining to determine the source of the noise. Her heart began to pound, and she clasped her hand to her mouth to keep from crying out in terror.

Suddenly a flashlight began scanning the area where they were hiding. Then Nessa heard one of the guards call out, "Stay here, I'll check it out. It's probably nothing."

The guards resumed their chatting, while a single beam of light worked its way toward them. The guard's footsteps moved closer, rustling in the grass nearby. Then a blast of light focused directly on Nessa's face. She stared into the light in terror and gasped under her cupped hand. Her heart was racing so fast she was certain the guard could hear it pounding. *Dear God, no.* The beam of light left her and drifted over to Eichendorff. It rested on him for a few seconds, then moved on to Erich.

At last the guard called out to his colleagues. "I don't see anything here. Must have been a deer." He turned and moved away.

As they lay on the ground Nessa heard the guards wishing one another good night. The sound of footsteps crunching on gravel drifted away and then all was silent.

"Let's go," Eichendorff whispered. "We crawl from here."

They belly-crawled through some tall grass, then into a ditch, over a road and through another ditch on the other side of the road.

"It's safe to get up now," Eichendorff said, rising to his feet. "We're in Switzerland."

They dusted themselves off, then scurried another fifty meters toward a stand of trees. Nessa stumbled along, trembling almost uncontrollably, while Erich guided her.

"There's Kurt with the car. He'll be taking you to Zurich. From there you'll travel on to Lisbon. As I said, your papers are in order, so you should encounter no problems during the rest of your journey."

When they got to the car, Eichendorff shook their hands. "Have a save trip, you two."

"Thanks so much," Erich said.

Nessa could stand it no longer. "Why didn't that German border guard arrest us?" she demanded, still trembling.

Eichendorff laid his hand on her shoulder and laughed. "That was Gustav Freytag. We pay him well to look the other way."

CHAPTER EIGHTEEN

Their journey went smoothly from Switzerland, through Southern France and from Spain to Portugal.

It was evening. The train was approaching Lisbon when a man in uniform entered their railway car and began working his way down the aisle checking travel documents and after a few minutes he was standing next to Erich and Nessa. He extended his hand toward them and addressed them in Portuguese.

"We're from Germany," Erich said in German.

The man bowed and repeated his request in German. "Customs Inspector. May I see your travel documents, please?" His hand still hovered in the air.

They complied.

"You are Erich and Anastasia Frank? A married couple?"

"That's correct."

"Anastasia. What an interesting name."

"I was named after my great-grandmother. I go by Nessa." She squirmed in her seat and tensed. Never share information that isn't requested, Erich had warned her.

"I see that you sail tomorrow from Lisbon to New York."

"Yes." She resisted the urge to elaborate and stared out the window while the inspector leafed through her documents. In the window's reflection she saw him look at her and then at her passport and then back at her. *Dear God, please protect us.*

The man handed back her documents and turned his attention to Erich. "And you are returning to Berlin? Why would you not accompany your wife to America?"

"I plan to join her after I conclude the sale of the family business," he lied.

Nessa still watched the official in the reflection of the window. The cruelty she had seen in Schmutze's face was absent in this man. Empathy, not brutality, etched his features.

The inspector returned Erich's papers and bowed. "I wish you both Godspeed," he said, then moved down the aisle.

The short man with large brown eyes and a wide mustache bore an expression of perpetual surprise. Nessa recognized him as their Lisbon contact from the photograph Erich had shown her.

"Alfredo do Carmo," the man said." He bowed, revealing a generous bald spot on the top of his head. "I saw you get off the train," he said, his German almost flawless. "Please follow me," he added, gesturing to the left. "My car is just through that door."

"Your German is excellent." Nessa commended, as they walked along.

"Before the war I spent ten years working in a hotel in Munich." He chuckled. "The birthplace of the Nazi Party, you know."

As they exited the station, Nessa was nearly overcome by the dazzle of neon lights flashing and blinking from the marquees of dozens of cinemas and restaurants and hotels, shouting out their exciting, chaotic messages in every color of the rainbow.

The little man noticed her astonishment and laughed. "I know. At night German cities are as dark as the far side of the moon to make it difficult for the Allied bombers to find them. Yet Lisbon is ablaze with light." He pointed to his left. "Here's the car. Let me help you with your bags." Their host put their luggage in the trunk, then settled them in the back seat. He started the car and plunged into the busy traffic. "You could call Lisbon a city on a hill," he said, "and you know what they say about a city on a hill."

Nessa smiled. "You are the light of the world," she said. "A city set on a hill cannot be hidden."

"That's correct and Lisbon is built on seven hills, just like Rome," said do Carmo. "Except Fascist bullies don't run our city. In German cities, your nights are full of darkness and death and oppression. Here in Portugal we shout: 'Light. Life. Freedom!'"

They rounded a corner and raced down a street barely wide enough for their car. Pedestrians scattered and ducked into doorways as the car sped past them.

"Even though Portugal is a neutral country, we are still engaged in the struggle against the Nazis," do Carmo said. "Thousands of refugees displaced by the war make their way to Lisbon and we help them escape to America." He laughed. "And yet in Portugal's war effort against Germany, not a shot has been fired!"

Labyrinthine streets and alleys flashed past as their host sped through the city before finally pulling into a courtyard at the top of a hill. Before them stood a three-story, pastel-tinted building. "Welcome to my humble establishment. Hotel Rio Tejo."

Their footsteps echoed in the cool night air as their host led them across the courtyard, its perimeter lined with palm trees.

Once inside, Alfredo do Carmo escorted them to a room on the third floor, throwing open the door and switching on the lights. Nessa bolted to the switch and turned them off.

The little man whirled around and let out a laugh. "As I said before, we don't have to worry about leaving the lights on in Lisbon, dear one," he declared, putting his hand on her shoulder. "There will be no air raids here tonight," he added, turning the lights back on.

Of course. She was no longer in Germany. She was free and bathed in light. Such luxury!

The double doors leading to the balcony were open, revealing a stunning view of a shimmering golden city that sloped down to a river. Their host led them out onto the balcony, where the tang of salt air assaulted Nessa's senses.

"That's the Rio Tejo down there. I named my hotel after the river. For you, it will be the river of life." He pointed to the right. "The river flows that way into the sea. Tomorrow, the sea will bear you in her arms to freedom, to America. In fact, down at the water's edge, many, many years ago, we celebrated the return of Vasco da Gama from the New World."

"Is that Nessa's ship in the harbor?" Erich asked.

"Indeed. I'll drive you down there tomorrow."

A bright yellow streetcar below them wound its way along the cobblestoned, tree-lined street, descending toward the harbor. Mist and fog from the river had begun to roll in, drifting through the winding streets and over the whitewashed buildings.

Do Carmo beckoned to two chairs and a table on the balcony. "Please, have a seat and relax. You've had a long journey."

Erich pulled out a chair for Nessa and sat down next to her.

"Is that a restaurant?" she asked, pointing to a small patio just below their balcony where a handful of people sat. Half a dozen round tables draped in white linens stood in a small circle. On each table a candelabrum with two snow-white candles bathed the occupants in a soft glow.

"Yes, generations of Lisboêtas have gathered on that very patio to exchange gossip and enjoy fresh bread and wine. You probably..."

The chords of a classical guitar wafted up to them, interrupting do Carmo. Their host winked and put his finger to his lips. Below them a woman in a flowing black dress emerged from the shadows and began to glide among the guests. She stopped in the middle of the ring of tables and began singing a mournful, somber melody.

"*Fado* music," do Carmo said. "It's full of longing and nostalgia. It speaks of a yearning that cannot be satisfied."

Their host translated:

"Why did you leave me? Where did you go?

I wander the streets searching for you,

You sailed out to sea and never returned."

Do Carmo seemed transfixed by the music, his eyes focused on a point far beyond the horizon. "Very sad, isn't it?" he finally said. "A *fado* performance isn't considered a success unless the listeners are moved to tears." He turned to his guests and bowed. "I'll leave you in peace now. Please feel free to come down and dine in my restaurant." A moment later he was gone.

Nessa put her elbow on the table and cupped her face in her hand, staring down toward the harbor. Although she was trying not to cry, a tear escaped to work its way down her check.

Erich took her hand. "Don't worry, *Liebling*. I'll cross this sea and come to you. Nothing will be able to hold me back."

The singer concluded her lament, and the band began playing a slow tango. Erich stood, drew Nessa to her feet, and took her into his arms. She relaxed as he led her back and forth across the balcony. Ever since that first tango with Erich years before, the steps had become engrained in her mind and she followed his lead instinctively.

How she wished this night would never end. Her thoughts moved in a thousand different directions. She imagined the two of them dancing in Ohio under the light of the moon. They were in in a cherry orchard in full spring bloom, far from the insanity of Europe. In her imagination she saw the blossoms falling from the trees and swirling around them like snowflakes in moonlight.

Then she saw herself back on the balcony in Lisbon, dancing with Erich and refusing to stop until the war was over. How she wished that, as they danced, news would arrive from Germany that

Hitler had died or that the German Army had laid down its weapons, refusing to participate any longer in the slaughter of Europe. They could return home to Germany, marry, raise their children, and then help rebuild their country.

~

Early the next afternoon, do Carmo chauffeured them down to the harbor. He dropped them off at the dock, promising to return and fetch Erich once the ship had sailed.

They watched dock workers load provisions onto the ship, while tall cranes swung large crates on board which disappeared into the bowels of the vessel. Passengers were already cuing up at the gangplank where ship's personnel checked their passports and travel documents.

"You can send letters to the address I gave you here in Lisbon," Erich reminded Nessa. "Our underground contacts will forward them to me in Berlin."

She smiled at him. "That's the third time you've told me that in two days."

"I know. I just wanted to be sure."

They walked along the dock arm-in-arm until the final boarding call sounded. Then Erich led her to the gangplank.

"Promise you'll come to me. Tell me once again," she begged, searching his face as though memorizing every feature.

"I'll see you in America soon, very soon. I promise."

Nessa smiled, although her eyes somehow couldn't. She leaned her head into the crook of his shoulder, which was just right for leaning on. "And promise me you'll be careful," she said into his shoulder. "I don't want to get a letter from Nussbaum saying that the Gestapo has arrested you."

"I will come to you," Erich reassured her. "Wait for me." He pulled her closer and kissed her. "I love the fragrance of roses on your skin," he said. "For the rest of my life I'll think of you when I smell roses."

She wished he hadn't said those words as if they would never meet again. She touched his cheek, then turned and hurried on board. She stood at the ship's railing, arms outstretched toward him, while he stood on the dock reaching out to her, drinking in their last few shared moments in Europe. Already a great ocean seemed to separate them.

With one more whistle blare, the ship began pulling away.

Nessa waved until Erich was out of sight. She stood at the railing for a few more heartbeats, then descended to her cabin and remained there, unable to watch Europe disappear from sight. At that moment all she knew was loss, all she felt was pain.

After a few hours Nessa forced herself to venture out on deck. Clinging to the railing, she worked her way to the bow and stood there for a long time as the ship pitched and rocked its way toward the setting sun. On the western horizon the clouds were ablaze with reds and purples, interwoven with orange.

She turned and looked back toward Europe, which had long since disappeared, and watched a tiny sliver of moon inch its way above the eastern horizon. That moon hovered over her past life, just as the setting sun behind her hovered over her future.

She hadn't thought the journey from Germany to freedom would be so overwhelming. She had spent her entire life in Berlin. Then, in the space of a few days, she had traveled through five countries and was now making her way across an immense ocean to the Promised Land.

Tears moved down her cheeks before being blown away on the wind. A thousand regrets and fears accompanied her as the ship pushed through the waves. Should she have stayed in Germany with Erich? Would he make it safely back to Berlin? Or would he be arrested and sent to a work camp in Poland or Czechoslovakia – or worse?

She returned to her cabin. It was almost dark, but she didn't bother switching on the light. Through the porthole she could see the river of stars that stretched over the Atlantic, the same stars that were shining on Erich.

She laid down on the bed and took the locket from her neck and opened it to see Erich smiling at her in the dim light. She kissed his picture and held the locket to her heart. The steady rocking of the ship, intermingled with its creaking and groaning, relaxed her; soon she drifted into sleep.

In dreams she saw the ship slipping into New York harbor, the Statue of Liberty sliding past on the left, while sea gulls shrieked overhead. She looked in amazement at the huge buildings that rose out of the earth and reached up into the heavens.

When the ship docked, a familiar figure waved to her from the pier below. It was Erich. A moment later they were walking arm-in-arm through the rolling hills of Ohio. In the distance flashes of lighting and rumblings of thunder warned them to take shelter. They walked past an ancient stone fence blanketed in moss, then turned onto a flagstone walkway that led to a small red brick cottage.

Nessa looked down into a valley where a handful of sheep grazed beneath a group of cherry trees that were alive with pink blossoms. The air was rich with the droning of insects and the scent of clover. Erich led her through the front door of the cottage and into a room bathed in shadows. It felt warm and secure, the dim light, soothing. He took her into his arms and kissed her. "You're home now," he whispered. "We're safe."

A thud from somewhere in the ship brought Nessa back from Erich and Ohio to her cabin. Her eyes fluttered open. Gradually, surrounded by a sea of darkness, she remembered where she was as the dim contours of the room began to come into focus. She rose, walked over to the writing desk, and turned on the lamp. She sat down, slid open a drawer, took out some paper and a pen, and began to write.

My Darling,

I pray that you made it safely back to Berlin. I love you. I pray that you made it safely back to Berlin. I love you and miss you so much already. I can still see you waving goodbye in Lisbon. What I would give to have been able to spend just a few more minutes with you before I left.

You won't believe this, but the two of us were just walking in my dreams in Ohio. The air was clean and fresh, full of the scents and sounds of springtime. I remember hearing distant thunder, but it wasn't the thunder of cannons and bombs. It was the sound of nature preparing to drench the earth with rain. And then you led me into our new home where you held me and told me that I was no longer in danger.

I pray that this war will be over soon. Hurry to me, for my life will be suspended until we're together again.

Yours forever,

Nessa.

With tears in her eyes, she found an envelope in the desk, sprinkled some of her precious rose-scented cologne on the letter, then folded it and slid it into the envelope. She knew her tears would not dry until long after she had arrived in the New World.

An hour earlier the ocean had been perfectly calm, like an immense, peaceful pond. Now huge breakers, crowned with white froth, hurtled through the Atlantic, smashing into the side of the ship, chasing everyone from the promenade.

Nessa sat at a table in the dining room and looked out at the aggressive sea, then glanced back at her newspaper. "Staggering Carnage in Stalingrad," the headline said. Before the war, Stalingrad had been to her no more than a name on the map. Now

German troops had reached the outskirts of the city. According to the paper, a Russian general had vowed to defeat the invading army or die trying. Nessa wondered if Frau Sturm's two remaining sons were among those German troops.

She hated reading about what was happening in Europe. And yet, though it disturbed her, she felt compelled to seek out any and all news, for the question always at the front of her mind was how the events in Europe were affecting Erich.

The waiter appeared and asked if he could remove her plate. "Yes, thank you," she said, even though she'd only picked at the roast mutton, baked jacket potatoes, and biscuits.

The elevator at the end of the dining room opened and spilled out a dozen passengers chattering in German. A few of them staggered in Nessa's direction while the ship rolled and pitched under their feet. A tall man with dark, swept-back hair sat down with a young girl at the table next to Nessa. The girl wore a frilly polka dot dress and clung to a one-eyed cloth doll.

An older woman, wearing a gray tilt bowler crowned with a plume of black feathers, asked in German if she could join Nessa.

"*Natürlich*," Nessa said, gesturing to the chair next to hers.

"Quite a wild ride," the woman commented. "Is this your first time traveling at sea, dear?"

"Yes, it is."

"Mine, too. I wonder if German U-Boats patrol these waters."

Nessa cast an irritated glance at the woman and then at the frantic waves. *Where on earth had that remark come from?* She could almost see their ship going down after a torpedo attack while she clung to a lifeboat in twenty-meter swells.

The woman noticed Nessa's glower and then put her hand to her mouth. "I'm sorry, dear. My husband always told me to think before opening my mouth, God rest his soul." She reached out to shake Nessa's hand. "*Ich heisse Siglinde Bachmann.*"

"Nessa Baumgartner. *Freut mich.*"

"Glad to meet you, too. I'm returning to America from visiting my sister in Zurich. Where are you from?"

"Berlin."

"It's unusual to see a young woman traveling alone."

"My fiancé will be joining me soon in America."

"He stayed behind in Berlin? That's odd. Why on earth would he leave Germany without you?"

"He's working," Nessa said bluntly, resisting the old woman's prodding.

"He's not in the army?"

The band in the adjoining lounge began playing a waltz.

"Excuse me," said a man from the next table, smiling at Nessa. "Would you care to dance?"

"Of course," she said, anxious to escape Frau Bachmann's prying.

"Stay here, Brigitta," the man said to his daughter. "I'll be right back."

"I'll keep an eye on her," Frau Bachmann offered.

Nessa and the man slipped into the lounge and danced quietly for a minute before she broke the silence. "My name is Nessa."

"Theodor," the man said, stepping on her foot. "Sorry, I'm not much of a dancer."

Her thoughts went back to the evening Erich had taught her to tango, wishing her arms were holding him instead. "Neither am I. Where are you headed?"

"Wisconsin. My wife died several months ago. My daughter and I are making a fresh start in America."

Nessa had recognized the accent when Theodor had asked her to dance. "What part of Switzerland are you from?"

"Is my accent that obvious?"

Nessa smiled and nodded.

"We're from Bern. My brother in Milwaukee is going to put us up until I find work."

The dance ended and they strolled back to the dining hall.

"Did you behave for the nice lady?" Theodore asked his daughter.

"She was an angel," said Frau Bachmann.

Theodor coaxed Nessa over to his table and introduced her to the child.

"Nice to meet you, Brigitta. My name is Nessa."

Brigitta smiled and searched Nessa's face with her big brown eyes, then turned to her father. "Papa, is Nessa going to be my new mommy?"

The man stared at his daughter, dumbfounded.

"Papa says we're going to America to find a new mommy," Brigitta continued, looking hopefully at Nessa.

"Brigitta, that's enough." He turned to Nessa. "I'm so sorry."

"Don't worry about it," Nessa said. "Children aren't afraid to say what's on their mind."

Theodor took a seat at his table and Nessa returned to hers. Frau Bachmann leaned over toward Nessa. "What a nice man that Theodore is. And what a beautiful daughter he has. You could do worse."

Frau Bachmann's husband had been right. His wife should think before speaking. "I'm already engaged," Nessa reminded her stiffly.

"Madam, what can I get you?" The waiter had returned and was hovering over Frau Bachmann with a note pad and pen in his hand.

She pointed to the menu. "I'll take the spaghetti au gratin and an apple tart. To drink, coffee. Black."

The waiter recorded her order, nodded, and withdrew.

"Nessa, I have to honest with you," Frau Bachmann said. "There aren't too many young men in Berlin these days who are simply working. Most of them have been drafted into the army."

Nessa remained silent, staring out the window at the huge gray waves swirling past the ship. She returned her gaze to the dining room, watching the chandeliers sway in rhythm with the waves.

"I don't believe in prying," Frau Bachmann said in a low voice.

"I know your young man had a good reason to stay behind in Berlin. I'm guessing he's with the underground. I really admire that."

"Thank you."

"But, my dear, consider the odds of him surviving. If he gets picked up by the Gestapo, you'll never see him again. The Allies have increased their bombing raids on Germany. Berlin's got to be at the top of their list. They won't stop until they've leveled the city."

Nessa's eyes began to well up. She was furious and terrified at the same time.

Frau Bachmann laid her hand on Nessa's. "I'm not trying to upset you, dear. I'm just advising you to count your losses. I waited four long years for my husband to return from the Great War. He never did. I don't even know how he died or where he's buried."

Nessa rose from her seat. She wanted to scream at the woman, tell her to mind her own business, to find some other poor soul to torture with her dreadful predictions. Instead, she forced herself to be polite. "He's *not* dead yet," she said firmly, then left the dining room.

"But he will be." Nessa could almost hear Frau Bachmann say those words.

No, he won't. God will protect him. She believed that. She had to. Otherwise she would go mad.

September 17, 1942.

"We're almost home, Nessa." Greta, Erich's mother, patted her hand. Shafts of sunlight poured through the windows of the train, highlighting swirls of dust particles.

She smiled at Greta and then at Erich's father, Franz, who sat across the aisle. Then she turned her attention back to the Ohio countryside. They'd been traveling for twelve hours, but it felt like twelve days. Her arrival in New York seemed years ago, and her old life in Germany centuries removed.

A childhood friend had once told her that America west of New York was still inhabited by Indians who attacked trains on horseback, robbing their occupants before riding off into the hills. But outside her window Nessa saw only huddles of houses, roads lined with street lamps, garden patches, a church steeple with a shimmering cross, a schoolyard full of children, and women sweeping their front porches. This could have been Europe, except people weren't shooting at one another. And not an Indian in sight.

A man a few rows up from them sat reading in his newspaper. Nessa had studied some English in school and could decipher a few of the headlines. The German Army was in serious trouble in Stalingrad. A Japanese plane had dropped bombs in Oregon. She wasn't sure where that was and hoped it was very far from Ohio. The Royal Air Force had dropped seven hundred tons of bombs on Düsseldorf. She knew exactly where that was.

Sometimes she found herself conflicted, daydreaming about, even praying for the defeat of her own homeland. How many more Russians and Germans would have to die before that would happen? She recalled Erich standing in the bookstore shortly after they had first met, reading her a quote by Heinrich Heine, a Jew. "If it should happen, God forbid, that freedom has disappeared from the world, a German dreamer will once again discover it in his dreams." When had her people stopped dreaming? Would they ever dream again?

Franz began a conversation with a young soldier sitting next to him, who had dark hair and an intelligent-looking face. Nessa studied the man's uniform. His brown jacket had an insignia depicting a pair of golden wings above a white and blue star. The name tag on his jacket said "Smith." One of his pant legs was neatly tucked under the stump of a missing leg. Crutches leaned against the seat next to him. Whenever the train jogged, he winced and closed his eyes, rubbing the end of the stump.

Nessa strained to understand the conversation, catching a few English words: Army Air Corps, German-occupied Holland, July.

Franz shook the soldier's hand and said, "thank you for your sacrifice." Then he leaned in toward Nessa. "He's with the Army Air Corps. He lost his leg in July when the Germans shot down his plane over Holland. The Dutch Underground rescued him and three other crew members and hid them until they could smuggle them over to England."

Nessa held her breath while Franz spoke, praying that no one would notice that he was speaking German. A man two rows up turned around and stared in their direction. What was he thinking? That they were German spies? That the world would be a perfect place if every stinking kraut were dead?

Nessa wanted to tell the soldier with the missing leg that she was sorry for what Germany had taken from him. She wanted to get up and walk through the train cars, embrace every stranger, and beg for forgiveness for the sins of her homeland. She wanted to beg forgiveness in advance for every American son and daughter and father who would yet die in the war, who would be returning to America in a casket. But would these Americans be inclined to forgive her once they heard her broken English wrapped in a German accent?

The brakes squealed as the train leaned into a turn. On her left, Nessa saw a sign announcing their arrival in Cambridge, Ohio.

"I see Karl on the platform," Franz said to Greta.

Nessa, looking through the window, gave a start. Karl's hair was darker, and he was a bit taller, but his resemblance to Erich was startling. She felt pressure in her chest and found it suddenly hard to breath, the gaping wound in her heart caused by losing Erich oozing. Where was he right now? Safe in Berlin? Lying in a cell at Gestapo Headquarters, broken and bleeding?

The train came to a stop. They stood up and Nessa and the Reinholds took their bags from the overhead racks and followed the crowd to the exits.

"Mother. Father," a husky voice called as Franz and Greta exited the train. Karl helped his parents onto the platform, embracing them, while Nessa waited on the top step of the coach. Then Karl turned to face her. His gaze seemed to penetrate her. He reached up and took her hand. His was firm and warm and strong; his facial expression seemed to coax her to jump from the train into his arms.

Nessa hesitated for an instant, dropped his hand, and took a small step backward.

He reached out again and laughed. "Don't be afraid. Trust me, I won't let you fall."

Why did he have to look so much like Erich? Her heart stuttered, for seeing Karl made every memory of Erich come alive. But he wasn't Erich, and she could never feel for him what she felt for his brother.

She wished she'd never let Erich talk her into leaving. There were no bombs falling on Ohio, but here was danger of a different kind.

She lifted her suitcase and handed it to Karl, then descended the steps before he could touch her again. She slipped over to Franz and laced her arm through his as they walked to the car.

CHAPTER NINETEEN

Mid-December, 1942.

Nessa made her way along Wheeling Avenue, shivering against the cold night air. A light frost covered parked cars, fire hydrants, and sidewalks. Fat, blinking Christmas lights in rainbow colors spiraled up the lampposts, stretching from one side of the street to the other. On the corner stood an enormous Christmas tree, white lights clinging to its branches, plastic candy canes dangling from its boughs.

Snowflakes tumbled all around her, streaming onto her face, catching on her hair and lashes, dissolving against her skin. She remembered walking to church in the snow with her family on Christmas Eve to sing and pray, carrying flaming candles to symbolize the advent of the Light of the World. Papa had always said that the best part of winter was Christmas.

Store windows cast rectangles of light onto the slippery sidewalks. Nessa stopped at the window of a toy store where a boy and his father stood watching a model train race along tracks suspended from the ceiling. The boy pointed at the train. "Papa, can I have that train for Christmas?"

"We don't have a lot of money this year, Billy."

"Maybe after the war?"

"Maybe after the war, son," the man muttered, leading the boy away.

Nessa watched a gaggle of noisy children race by in the middle of the street until a car behind them honked them off the road.

To her left she heard a crunching sound she couldn't quite identify. She turned to see a young man on crutches moving in her direction. It was the disabled airman she'd seen on the train when she'd arrived in September.

Nessa smiled at him. "Hello."

He stopped a few feet from her, returning her smile. "Hello. Have we met?"

"Your last name is Smith, right?"

"That's right." He knitted his brow. "How on earth did you know?"

She moved to where the man stood. "I saw you on the train when I arrived in Cambridge a couple of months ago." She hoped her English wasn't too horrible.

"I don't remember meeting you. Did we talk then?"

"No, my father-in-law spoke with you for a while. We'll, Franz Reinhold isn't my father-in-law yet..."

"So, you're getting married? Congratulations."

"Thank you."

"Is it anyone I know?" He looked embarrassed for a moment. "I mean, I know just about everyone in town."

"You couldn't know my fiancé. He's never been to America."

"Oh? Where does he live?"

"In Germany."

"So that's where you're from. I thought I recognized that accent."

She tensed. *You mean the accent of the enemy?* She searched his eyes, and seeing no sign of revulsion, she relaxed. "I studied English in school in Germany, but I've forgotten a lot."

The man on crutches smiled. "I think your English is very

good." After a moment's silence he cleared his throat. "Say, it's awfully cold out here." He darted a look down the street and pointed with a crutch. "Kennedy's is still open. How about a cup of coffee to warm us up?"

She thought for a moment. He seemed nice enough and his casual friendliness made a nice break from Karl's constant attention. "Sure."

He held out a gloved hand. "My name's Paul. I'd love to hear more about Germany."

Nessa wrapped her mittened hand around his. "Nessa Baumgartner."

At Kennedy's bakery, a display case in the front window showed off cakes, pies and breads. Nessa opened the door for Paul, and he hobbled past her inside. Behind the counter stood a man in a baker's apron who had a dusting of flour on his face and arms. Along the front window, next to the display case, chairs huddled around Formica-topped tables standing in a long line.

Paul motioned again with his crutch. "Go ahead and grab a table. How do you like your coffee?"

"With just a little cream."

Nessa walked to the end of the window and pulled out a chair, the sound of its metal legs scraping across the linoleum floor like fingernails on a chalkboard. She sat down and huddled into her coat. The inside of the bakery was nearly as cold as the air outside.

Half a minute later Paul was back. He laid a napkin on his forearm and gave a curt bow, as if he were her maître de. "Mr. Kennedy will be right over with your coffee, ma'am."

Nessa smiled up at him. "Thank you."

He leaned his crutches against the window and lowered himself onto his chair, then rubbed the stump of his missing leg.

Nessa's smile crumbled. She looked out the window at gleaming snowflakes passing through the circle of light cast by the streetlamp on the corner, then returned her gaze to Paul. "I'm so sorry about your leg."

"Don't be. I'm getting used to the new me."

"If only Hitler..."

"Don't apologize. The war's not your fault." He patted his stump and grinned. "I'm looking forward to saving a ton of money on shoes."

Nessa couldn't help laughing.

"So what did you do in Germany?" Paul asked. "You had a job, didn't you?"

"I wanted to be a nurse, but my career was cut short before it even started."

"The war?"

"No, Hitler. I grew up Lutheran, but about ten years ago the Nazis passed a law reclassifying me as Jewish."

"Too much Jewish blood?"

"Right."

"I heard about that law. So, Jews weren't allowed to attend nursing school, I assume."

"Right again."

"So what did you end up doing?"

"Working in the underground. We smuggled Jews out of Germany."

"Wow," Paul said. "Dangerous work. You're very brave."

"Not really."

"I almost got to Germany this past summer, you know," he said.

"Really?" Why would anyone want to go to Germany these days?

"Well, my bomber went down over Holland on the way to Germany. Dutch partisans pulled me and my parachute out of a tree before the Germans found me. The doctors couldn't save my leg, though. It shattered when I landed in the tree."

She cringed at the word "bomber," remembering that the Allies had begun bombing Germany. It wouldn't be long until they erased Berlin from the map. And Erich from her life.

Paul seemed to read her change in mood. He touched her hand. "I'm sorry, Nessa. Did I say something to upset you?"

She exhaled. "Erich, my fiancé, lives in Berlin. If any German city gets bombed out of existence, it'll be Berlin."

"Oh, my. Is there any way to get him out?"

Nessa shook her head. Despair flared inside her. "He works in the underground. He wouldn't leave Germany even if you offered him a first-class ticket to America."

"He sounds like the kind of man we need in the underground. Faithful to his cause. Dauntless."

Mr. Kennedy arrived at their table with a tray. He unloaded two cups of coffee, two forks and two servings of *Bienenstich*.

Nessa poked her fork absentmindedly into the pastry and forced a smile. "It's funny. Last summer Erich and I had *Bienenstich* in Berlin right before I came to America." She shook her head. Now she had arrived in her safe harbor, but it was quite possible Erich would never join her.

"*Woran denkst du*?" Paul asked. Compassion etched his face.

Nessa gave a start. "You speak German?"

"Not much. My grandmother was German. Jewish actually. She taught me a few expressions."

"I was just thinking about Erich," Nessa said, "praying that he's all right. He brought me to Lisbon last September, then put me on the boat before he went back to Germany. Nothing I could say could convince him to come with me."

"I can understand why he stayed behind," Paul said. "Working in the underground means saving lives."

And maybe losing your own. "You're right," Nessa said, looking at the floor.

"Anyway, I think the war will be over soon," Paul speculated. "The Russian winters will stop the German Army in its tracks long before the Russians do." He pointed his fork at her *Bienenstich*. "Try the pastry."

She sliced off a corner and put it in her mouth. It was just as tasty as the German version. Good thing she wasn't on a diet.

"Is it as good as what you had in Berlin?"

"Yes, it's very good. Do you know what *Bienenstich* means in English?"

"It has something to do with bees, I think."

"It means 'bee sting.'"

"Ouch," Paul said, putting a finger on his lips. "A bee sting in your mouth could be dangerous."

"My mother told me that the baker who invented the pastry was stung when a bee was attracted to the honey in it."

"A prickly name for something so delicious," Paul said, finishing his piece. He laid his fork on the table. "So, what brings you to the big city?"

"Christmas shopping."

"Me, too." He chuckled. "Although, it looks like we've gotten a little sidetracked."

Nessa smiled. "Yes, it does." She took a sip of coffee, savoring the warmth and the flavor. "Real coffee is so much better than ersatz coffee," she said.

He smiled. "You should taste the coffee they serve in the military mess halls. I think they make it with dish water."

She laughed. When was the last time she had done that? She honestly couldn't remember. "So, Paul, did you grow up here in Cambridge?" she asked.

"No, in Berlin."

Nessa's eyes widened. "Berlin?"

He laughed. "I was born in Berlin, Ohio. It's on the other side of the state. Anyway, I still call it Berlin. During the last war Germans weren't too popular around here and the people of Berlin changed the name of the town to Fort Loramie."

Nessa blushed with guilt.

"A lot of German words disappeared from English during the last war, you know," Paul said. "They changed sauerkraut to 'liberty cabbage' and German measles to 'liberty measles.'" He leaned toward her as if to reveal a secret. "We even had to hide Nellie," he said in a soft voice.

"Nellie?"

"Our dachshund." Paul rolled his eyes and smacked his forehead with his palm. "Oh, I mean, our 'liberty pup.' We had to walk her at night so the neighborhood kids wouldn't throw rocks at her. Someone even phoned our home once and threatened her."

Nessa shook her head in disbelief.

"It's the truth," Paul said. "Our German dog got death threats!" He touched Nessa's sleeve and laughed. "After that we didn't let Nellie answer the phone anymore."

Nessa laughed again. Behind the counter Mr. Kennedy smiled, although he surely had no idea why she was laughing.

"My last name was originally German," Paul said. "My parents changed it from Schmidt to Smith. After that I didn't get involved in as many fights on the school playground. Germans against the Americans, you know."

Nessa smiled and finished her coffee.

"Do you miss Germany?" Paul wanted to know.

"Yes, but not what it's become. In America, I'm Lutheran, in Germany, Jewish, so I'm no longer welcome in my homeland."

"Then we have something in common."

"What's that?"

"If the Germans had captured me when my bomber went down, I wouldn't have been very welcome either. They would have hung me as a terrorist."

Nessa nodded and looked at the clock over the front door. Almost six. "I need to get going. Franz is picking me up in an hour and I haven't bought a thing." She stood and held out her hand. "Thanks for the coffee and pastry."

Paul struggled to his feet and took her hand. "The pleasure was all mine. Maybe we'll run into one other again sometime."

"I hope so. Good luck with your shopping."

She stepped out into the cold. She wasn't looking forward to returning home. Her life was wearing on her – the strain of missing Erich and of keeping from his parents the full details of what he was doing. She just didn't want to worry them with the truth. But knowing what she did, she worried enough for all of them.

At the corner, under a streetlamp, a group of carolers sang. The melody was familiar, but not the words. Although Cambridge was a peaceful town, Nessa was sure that the nights in Germany were anything but silent, calm, and bright. And the bombers would make sure that her homeland sank ever deeper into the dark, cold, restless night that had engulfed it.

She felt weary and burdened, as though despair was stalking her. She knew she had to believe that God knew what He was doing. But sometimes she found it almost impossibly hard to trust Him.

～

January, 1943.

The sun dipped below the horizon on a frigid Tuesday as Erich returned home from a supply run. He saw a crowd, faces somber, gathered in front of the public kiosk, where daily newspapers were always displayed. He drew closer and read the news from the Russian front. "Undying Honor of the Stalingrad Fighters." "Comrades in Death to the Last Bullet."

"Is anyone fooled by this crap?" a man next to him mumbled. "Even an imbecile can read between the lines."

Erich had to agree. The media was trying to spin straw into gold. All was not well in the New Germany, nor on the Russian Front. Surely all of Germany recognized the hollow bravado behind the newspaper headlines. Thousands of German soldiers had perished in battle and were lying in mass graves beneath the frozen Russian soil – and still the Führer sent more of them into battle.

The man next to Erich looked him up and down. "You look young and healthy. Why aren't you in the army?"

"I have a heart condition," he lied. At least that was what his forged papers said. "As a child I had rheumatic fever. The doctors never expected me to live this long."

He wondered how much longer he'd be able to pass himself off as unfit for military service. Eventually a policeman would doubt his story and haul him to a heart doctor for testing. Then he, too, would end up on the Russian front – or standing in front of a firing squad. But so far, the ruse was working.

"Rheumatic fever, eh?" The man pursed his lips and studied Erich's face. "Well, you're one of the fortunate ones," he said, moving away.

Erich closed his eyes and breathed a sigh of relief. Speaking to any member of the Volk was dangerous for him. An entire nation of men, women and even children spent much of their time informing on their neighbors to gain favor with the Nazi regime.

He turned away from the kiosk and continued toward home. His thoughts flew to Nessa as they did a hundred times a day. Thinking of her produced a comfort that chased away much of his despair at the senseless loss of so many of his fellow Germans in bombings and in battle.

That night he and Frau Sturm and her other illegal guests listened to the forbidden BBC. "The situation for Germany is desperate," the announcer told them. "The German Sixth Army in Stalingrad is surrounded by Red Army Forces with no hope of escape. The Führer has said that the German Army will never leave Stalingrad. People of Germany, your Führer is right. The German Army will never leave Stalingrad *alive*."

"Let's hear what Radio Berlin has to say," Erich suggested.

The radio speaker crackled and squealed as Nussbaum turned the dial. The German announcer's voice was unusually somber. "Let us turn our thoughts to those who have sacrificed their lives for Volk, Führer, and Fatherland in Stalingrad. An eternal bond exists between those who have died for Germany and the grieving survivors on the home front. Our warriors have not died in vain. They are still with us. Yes, individuals die, but the Volk live on. The living Volk will forge the victory in concert with our fallen heroes, who even now march at our side in spirit."

"Why is it that those who talk so much about dying for the Fatherland are in no great hurry to make the sacrifice?" Frau Sturm demanded bitterly. "It's always someone else's son who gets chosen to do the dying." She had taken the pictures of her husband and her four sons from the lamp table next to her. She held them in her lap and began to weep. Erich moved over and knelt at her chair and put his arm around her, but she was inconsolable. "These wretched wars have robbed me of my family," she wailed, her tears falling in her lap. "Soon my two remaining sons will be taken from me. They'll bury them somewhere in Russia alongside thousands of other German sons. I can't stand anymore. I just can't."

Erich wished he could find words to ease her heartache. But he couldn't. He wished he could write a newspaper headline that would speak comfort and solace to the multitudes of German mothers whose sons would never return. But he couldn't. Only two facts remained. The war was lost already. And German sons continued to perish for no good reason.

Early February, 1943.

Nessa hung up the phone. "Paul just asked me to the USO dance at church tonight," she told Greta.

"What did you tell him?"

"I said yes. I don't think Erich would mind."

"Absolutely not. Paul knows you're engaged, doesn't he?"

"Of course."

"Then go. Karl won't be home from Pittsburgh until tomorrow."

Nessa frowned. "What do you mean by that?" Why on earth would she need Karl's permission to attend a dance? Or to do anything, for that matter?

Greta let her needlework slip to her lap. "Nessa, even a blind man can see that Karl's in love with you. Go to the dance and enjoy yourself. What Karl doesn't know won't bother him."

Nessa thought she was the only one who had noticed Karl's overtures, but, of course, they must have been quite obvious to her entire family. He brought her gifts from Pittsburgh, invited her on long walks, touched her hand or her arm when they talked. She talked of Erich whenever they were together, spoke of their engagement, yet Karl behaved as if he never heard a word she was saying.

Franz glanced at his watch. "What time's the dance?"

"Seven. Paul's picking me up at six-thirty. And I don't have a thing to wear."

Franz laughed and looked at Greta. "Does every woman in the world use that line?"

Greta smiled, but didn't answer. She rose from the couch and put her arm around Nessa. "Come on. Let's see what we can find you to wear, dear."

"Any of my clothes are up for grabs," Franz teased as they left the room.

By the time Paul arrived and started hobbling up the walk on his crutches, she was ready to go.

Nessa ran down the path to meet him.

"You look great," he said.

She thought so, too. Greta had found a light-blue flowing party dress with matching belt that she had purchased the year before. Pleated above the waist, smooth and flowing below, it required only a bit of hemming.

"Yes, thanks to my future mother-in law. But I'm afraid my wardrobe's still a little limited."

Paul walked her to the passenger's side of the car and opened the door for her.

Then Nessa watched him hobble back around the car on his crutches to the driver's side. He opened the back door and tossed them in, then hopped behind the wheel.

"I could have opened my own door," Nessa insisted.

He smiled and shook his head. "Nonsense, I'm not totally helpless, you know. Don't be self-conscious about my missing leg. I'm not." He touched her on the shoulder and grinned. "Besides, in heaven I'll have two legs again."

He started the car, put it in gear, and pounded his right foot on the gas, throwing Nessa back against her seat.

"I used to love driving a manual shift," he said. Unfortunately, what's left of my left leg won't reach the clutch. Thank goodness for automatic transmissions. You only need one foot to drive."

They flew along Wheeling Avenue, then screeched right onto Eighth, sending Nessa scooting across the seat against Paul. "They won't start without us," she said, moving back to her side of the car.

He took his foot off the gas and moved it to the brake pedal. "Sorry. I guess I'm used to flying airplanes."

Once they pulled up in front of First Presbyterian, Nessa jumped out of the car before he could hobble around the vehicle to her door.

"I could have come around and opened the door for you," he said.

"I know, but I'm not helpless either," she answered with a smile.

Since they had first met in December, Nessa and Paul had run into one another often.

They had both started attending services at First Presbyterian and volunteered time wrapping bandages for wounded soldiers. Nessa had spent many hours a week at other USO events, serving coffee and doughnuts to broken soldiers returning home from Europe and the Pacific – men like Paul with their arms and legs torn off – and lending an ear to their tales of heartbreak, loneliness, and fear.

Paul was an inspiration to her. If anyone had a reason to be bitter, it was him. Her heart nearly broke every time she watched him struggle to his feet onto his crutches, and yet he never complained. On the contrary – he always had a smile to share and an encouraging word for the other crippled servicemen who showed up at USO functions. His love for life and his trust and joy in God were infectious.

The dance had indeed started without them. Jitterbug music blared from the makeshift stage in the church basement. Behind the band a huge American flag dominated the wall. Red, white, and blue streamers festooned across the ceiling. Mountains of dough-nuts and cookies and gallons of coffee and Coca-Cola sat on a long table near the stage. Two dozen round tables, each surrounded by folding chairs, were draped in white linen and crowned with candles.

A couple dozen soldiers milled around the edges of the dance floor. A handful of the guests acted as chaperones, some of them dancing. A few older women chaperones danced with other women.

Paul and Nessa had just settled in at a table next to the stage, when the band began playing a fast waltz. He stood and leaned on his crutches. A smile touched his lips as he reached out his hand. "Come on," he said, "let's dance. Not many girls get to waltz with a three-legged soldier."

Nessa rose and took his hand. She placed one hand on each of his shoulders, and he led the way.

But dancing with Paul turned out to be nearly disastrous. He had mastered the art of walking on crutches, but dancing with them was another matter. Nessa finally resorted to hanging on to his crutches right along with him, all the while dodging his remaining foot.

"You should see me jitterbug," he joked after they almost lost their balance and fell.

Two minutes later the music stopped, and they started toward their seats.

The band began playing the introduction to "Somewhere Over the Rainbow," in a leisurely tempo, and a band member stepped up to the microphone and began singing.

"I love this song," Paul said, pulling gently at Nessa's arm. "Let's try again."

The song was slow enough that the two of them could sway together in a small corner of the dance floor without endangering themselves of others.

Nessa recalled seeing "The Wizard of Oz" a few weeks earlier for perhaps the fourth time. She always cried and thought of Erich when Dorothy began musing about an elusive place where there were no troubles. She still remembered Dorothy's exact words. "Do you suppose there is such a place? There must be. It's not a place you can get to by a boat or a train. It's far, far away. Behind the moon, beyond the rain ..."

She laid her head on Paul's shoulder and wept.

"Nessa, what is it?" he whispered in her ear.

She shook her head. "Nothing," she lied, hiding her pain behind a smile. "Everything's fine."

He stopped dancing, swiping away her tears with the back of his fingers. "You're crying on my shoulder and everything's fine?" He nudged her toward their table. "Come on, we better sit down."

By the time they reached the table and sat down the happy little bluebirds in the song had disappeared over the rainbow, and the songstress had backed away from the microphone. The bandleader announced an intermission, and the musicians vacated the stage.

"What's troubling you, Nessa? You can tell me," Paul urged.

"It's just that I miss Erich." *And I'm terrified that I'll never see him again.* It was easier to tell the partial truth than the whole truth. Anyway, she didn't want to fall apart in front of a roomful of people.

Paul put an arm around her, solicitously.

"Listen, I know you're afraid for Erich. God will protect him, I'm sure of it."

Paul was right. God wasn't going to abandon her or Erich. If Paul could still believe in Him after losing his leg, she could still believe when she had lost nothing, really.

Yet.

"What's going on here?" a man's voice demanded.

Nessa gave a start, then looked up to see Karl hovering over them, scowling. "Karl, I didn't think you were coming back until tomorrow."

He balled his fists, staring down at Paul. "Obviously."

"Karl, this is my friend Paul. Paul, this is Erich's brother."

Paul struggled onto his crutches and held out his hand.

Karl ignored him. "Nessa, you need to come home."

"Is there a problem at home?"

Karl's expression grew more violent. "No, there's a problem *here*. What are you doing out with another man?"

Now she too was scowling. "You don't own me, Karl. And I'm not going anywhere."

She could see that Karl wasn't used to being defied, for his brows drew even more fiercely together. "And not that it's any of your business, but Paul is just a friend. As are you."

"It's not proper for you to be out with another man when you're engaged," he snapped.

"It's also not proper for you to look at me the way you do, so I'll thank you not to lecture me on what's proper," she shot back.

Karl's countenance fell. He turned on his heel and stormed out of the building.

"I'm sorry to have caused a problem," Paul said.

"Don't be. The problem is his."

They stayed for a few more dances but Nessa's heart was no longer in it and Paul suggested they head home.

When they stepped outside it was snowing. Someone was

burning coal to heat their home and coal dust drizzled down among the snowflakes. The scent transported her memories back to winters in Berlin when the air was full of coal dust. To ice-skating through snowy streets. To returning home frozen to the bone to find Papa building a fire in the fireplace and Mama making mulled wine.

The ride home was silent. Paul drove slowly through the blanket of snow and ice that covered the city. Nessa laid her head back against the seat and closed her eyes. She was exhausted.

When they arrived home, she gave Paul a quick hug and went inside.

Franz and Greta were in the living room with Opa and Oma Schulz, listening to the radio.

"You're back early," Greta observed. "Did Karl find you?"

"Yes, he did," Nessa said. Then before anyone could ask about her evening, she claimed a headache, kissed them all and went to bed. The last thing she wanted was to relive her evening. She was too angry with Karl.

How dare he insinuate she was being disloyal to Erich! There was no other man for her and there never would be. Oh, when would this horrible war end? When would they be together again?

Would they ever be together again?

"We will," she muttered fiercely. "We will."

By the fall of 1943 only a fraction of the 160,000 Jews who had lived in Berlin before the war still lived there. This was a plus for the Berliners who had chosen to remain in the city. Thousands of German homes had been destroyed in bombing attacks and the apartments and homes of displaced Jews provided much needed housing for homeless members of the Volk.

And although Germany's Minister of Propaganda, Joseph Goebbels, had declared that Berlin was now "judenrein" – cleansed of Jews, a remnant of God's Chosen People – about 7,000 in all – lived in the shadows, having become self-styled "U-Boats." The new term had been coined to describe people who disappeared underground, those who submerged illegally below the surface of everyday life.

And the number of U-Boats who so desperately wanted to flee Germany was increasing so quickly that Operation Nussbaum and the other underground groups could barely keep up with the demand. They had their fingers in the dike, trying to handle the flood of people desperate to leave the country, but Erich feared that very soon they would run out of fingers.

The sign on the subway tunnel wall said "Zoologischer Garten." Konrad elbowed Erich. "It's past dinner time – I'm hungry. Let's get off at this station and grab something to eat before we head home."

They had spent much of the day delivering the forged ration cards they had produced to other underground groups and Erich was ready to eat as well.

"At least some of the subways are still running," Erich remarked, as they reached street level and exited the station.

"For the moment anyway. The next air raid may change all that."

They crossed the street, weaving their way around passing cars, trucks, and bicycles. "Have you heard of Café Roland?" Konrad pointed down the street to the right. "It's down there opposite the Kaiser Wilhelm Memorial Church. They serve the best *Schwarzwaldkirschtorte*. It's made entirely of black-market ingredients."

"Black Forest Cherry Cake sounds tempting, but I'd rather have an actual meal, not dessert."

"They serve sandwiches, too. You can order a couple and watch me eat my cake."

Many Berliners had already lowered their shades for the night. "It's odd to see the city practically pitch black every night," Erich said. All his life Berlin has been a city of lights. Now it was as dark as a tomb.

"I guess we could leave the lights on at night," Konrad joked. "That way the Allied bombers would have an easier time finding us."

They crossed the street to the cathedral square. A streetcar with a masked headlight rumbled in their direction, screaming a warning whistle at them, before screeching on the rails as it looped into a curve.

"Isn't this the church your family used to attend?" Konrad asked, as they walked by the Memorial Church.

"Every Sunday, rain or shine."

"Or bombs," Konrad quipped.

"Konrad, does everything have to be a joke?"

"Actually, it does. It's the only thing that keeps me sane." He pointed straight ahead. "There's the café. It's not as nice as Café Nola, but I think you'll like it."

A metal sign on a post in front of the café greeted them. "*No Jews.*"

They looked at one another, smiled, and went in.

They worked their way to the back of the candle-lit café and sat at a table with a clear view of the front door and an unobstructed path to the back exit. Just in case.

Konrad chuckled. "I can't help laughing when I see one of those signs telling Jews to stay out," he said in a low voice. "The café owner should take the sign down. Hasn't he heard that there are no more Jews left in Berlin?"

"Out of sight, out of mind," Erich said.

Konrad nudged his friend. "Thanks to my brilliant craftsmanship, vermin like you are still walking the streets of Berlin, hidden, yet in plain sight."

Erich nodded. "Indeed. You can't tell your forged ID's from the real thing. But I still feel a bit nervous walking around so blatantly in public. If someone finds a flaw in your artistry, they'll discover we're U-Boats and then we're sunk. No pun intended."

"You worry too much," Konrad said. "The best place to hide is out in the open, where the Nazis least expect to see you."

Erich did worry. How long could he hide in plain sight? Yes, he looked like a full-blooded Aryan, but both he and Konrad also looked like young men who should have been drafted into the army long ago. His ID card claimed that he had a heart condition, making him unfit to serve the Führer. But he was also a wanted man. He knew that neither Gerhardt Schmutze nor Martin Schneider would rest until they tracked him down.

He turned and waved to the waiter. "*Herr Ober!*"

The man smiled and headed their way. "What can I ...?" At that moment the air raid siren blared. The waiter dropped his order pad and pencil to the floor and fled through the front door.

Konrad looked at Erich. "I wouldn't give this place very high marks for customer service."

CHAPTER TWENTY

Erich and Konrad hurried outside, joining the throng running past the Memorial Church and toward the subway station. A handful of air raid wardens stood at the entrance to the station, repeating the same mantra over and over: "*Ruhe bewahren! Ruhe bewahren!*"

"How can they tell us to keep calm when we're about to be blown to pieces?" Konrad snapped as they ran down the stairs.

Erich pointed to his right when they reached the station platform. "Let's sit over there in the corner."

They worked their way through the crowd, squeezed into the corner and sat down. At a distance Erich heard muffled explosions. The earth shuddered beneath them.

"Bombs falling on the just and the unjust," Konrad muttered.

This time it looked like Erich's friend wasn't making a joke. His face was ashen and his hands trembled.

The pounding of the bombs crept closer and closer. Then it seemed as if the *Götterdämmerung* – the end time cataclysm – were taking place directly over their heads. High above them, a city forsaken by its inhabitants seemed to groan in agony. Down below, the tunnel echoed with cries of terror from the men, women, and children cowering in it.

A woman next to Erich threw her hands over her face. "God save us!"

"Why should He save us?" the man next to her sneered. "For years we've done nothing but attack and kill our neighbors. And now you're surprised they're retaliating?"

"We're civilians, we had nothing to do with any of that," objected another man.

"Whether that's true or not," the first man retorted, "our enemies think every German has been a party to the invasions and the bloodshed."

Above them the pounding continued. The tunnel swayed like a ship at sea, threatening to collapse. Then the lights went out. The screams and wails of the Volk intensified for a moment, then subsided when the air raid wardens switched on their flashlights.

The mantra began again. "*Ruhe bewahren. Bitte Ruhe bewahren.*" This time the voices of the wardens were hoarse and trembling.

After what seemed an eternity, the bombing subsided and finally stopped. In the semi-darkness adults whimpered and children wept.

Another eternity passed before the lights flickered on.

At long last came the all-clear siren. Those who were sitting on the platform groaned to their feet.

"I can hardly get my feet under me," Konrad said, hugging the wall.

"Sometimes I'm almost disappointed to have survived another attack," a man next to Erich lamented.

"Why's that?" he asked.

The man shuddered. "Because very soon those bombers will be back, and we'll have to go through this again. If I had been killed tonight, I'd be spared all that misery." He gave a sad laugh and walked away.

"Ladies and gentlemen," a warden called out. "We've just received word that the subway lines serving this station will be running again in a few minutes."

"Let's go home," Erich said to Konrad. "We can try Café Roland tomorrow. If it's still there."

~

The next day Erich and Konrad took the same subway line they had taken the previous evening, once again getting off the train at Zoologischer Garten. Based on the destruction left behind by previous bombings, they weren't surprised by what they saw at street level. Nearly every building as far as they could see was either gutted or obliterated. Men with heavy machinery strained to clear piles of rubble from the streets.

The smell of something burning permeated the air. A huge smoke cloud hung over the city and from it a caustic mixture of dust, soot, and ashes rained down, settling on buildings and people alike. Berliners hurried by, clutching handkerchiefs to their faces to protect their lungs from the acrid dust and smoke. Erich and Konrad copied their example.

Konrad pointed down the street. "Erich, the church ..."

Erich stopped in his tracks. "Dear Lord!" The main steeple of the Kaiser Wilhelm Memorial Church looked like a jagged, hollow tooth, almost as if a giant hand had reached down from the sky, snapped off its top and discarded it. There wasn't much left of the smaller steeples, either.

They continued on, picking their way through the debris littering the sidewalks and streets until they reached the church. It was a blackened, smoldering ruin. The entire square around the church was littered with pieces of the shattered church.

"We stood on this spot not twenty-four hours ago," Erich gasped, shaking his head. He looked up at the church, attempting to mentally reconstruct what it had looked like before the bombing raid, but his mind's eye wouldn't cooperate.

"Come on, Erich," Konrad said after another minute, "let's go."

They moved on and turned a corner to find a huge crater where

Café Roland had been. "It's as if it never existed," Konrad whispered.

"One thing survived," Erich observed, pointing to a scorched metal sign lying in the debris. The words were faint, but still legible: "No Jews."

Next door to where the café had been, stood the scorched skeleton of a burnt-out apartment building, looking more like an abandoned warehouse than a place that had housed a hundred families not twenty-four hours earlier. On the doorway someone had scrawled messages in chalk, like notes on a classroom blackboard: "The Bergengrün Family has relocated to the town of Ludwigsfelde, König Strasse, Number 67." "The Breuer Family perished in the bombing of November 22nd."

They turned to head back to the subway station, but stopped in their tracks, staring down the street in numb disbelief. At the end of it, scores of bodies had been stacked against a wall like cordwood. On top of the stack, the blackened corpse of a young boy clung in death to the charred, lifeless body of an air raid warden.

Erich's stomach tightened at the sight, but he managed to suppress the bile that threatened to rise in his throat. War, and the angel of death were no respecters of age. But he knew the carnage was just beginning. The bombers would keep coming and soon there would be nowhere in Berlin that was safe. If the Gestapo didn't get him, the bombs eventually would.

After a minute they moved on. On some blocks it seemed as if an enormous claw had moved down the street and crushed every building, leaving behind only a maze of bricks, beams and scattered roof tiles. On other blocks the buildings were still standing but they were no more than charred walls without windows and doors.

Erich and Konrad joined the army of Berliners who were once again digging themselves out from under the devastation left behind by bombers. They worked their way down a street, helping several families salvage food and clothing from what was left of their homes. On another street they helped a homeless man erect a temporary shelter. No one asked whether they were Aryans or Jews or *Mischlings*. No one cared.

～

Late that evening Erich and Konrad once again started toward the subway station to return home. On every street Berliners had drawn their window shades in anticipation of another air raid. A few bombed out buildings were still smoldering, feeble flames weakly illuminating their charred interiors.

Near the station a petroleum lantern in an apartment house window cast a swath of light over the street, while an air raid warden stood on the sidewalk squabbling with a man leaning out of the window.

"Extinguish that lamp immediately," the warden shouted at the man, the veins in his neck bulging in his shirt collar. "Are you trying to show the bombers exactly where we are?"

"The Allies will have no trouble finding Berlin," the man shot back, swilling from a bottle of wine. "Half the city is still on fire from last night's bombing." He pointed at his lamp with his bottle. "What difference will one more speck of light make?"

"Put out that lantern or I'll call the Gestapo."

"The Gestapo?" The man in the window laughed, his voice echoing in the street. "Good luck finding them. They hide safe and sound in their underground bunkers while the rest of us get blown to pieces up here." The man belched, looking bleary-eyed at his wine bottle. It was almost empty. He took another swig, then threw it at the feet of the warden, sending shards of glass and leftover wine scampering up the man's uniform trousers. "Tell the Gestapo to suck on that," the drunk slurred.

The veins in the warden's neck threatened to explode. He brushed the wine and glass from his legs, then raised a fist toward his adversary. "I'll be back with the Gestapo, you swine."

The drunk wasn't listening. He stood in the window, trying to impale a corkscrew into the cork of another bottle.

"What are you two looking at?" the warden screamed.

Erich and Konrad jumped.

The warden pointed down the street. "Move along, both of you."

They moved.

Once in the subway car they sat without speaking as it rattled and lurched through the dark underground tunnels.

Erich cupped his head in his hand and closed his eyes.

He recalled Hitler's dream of tearing down entire sections of Berlin, so he could transform his capital into a city worthy of the New Germany. Erich smiled sadly. Allied bombers were flattening the city, saving Hitler the trouble. If peace ever returned, Berlin would be leveled and ready for the Führer's great transformation.

Frau Sturm's neighborhood had been ignored by the bombers and Erich and Konrad arrived home to find her and Nussbaum in the living room, talking. Erich joined them, but Konrad went off to bed.

The window shades in the room had been drawn because of the bombing raids, although Frau Sturm had kept them drawn as a precaution against prying eyes ever since her U-Boats had come to live with her.

"My parents moved to Berlin in 1881 from Saint Petersburg after the Tsar was assassinated," Nussbaum was saying. "The Russians blamed his murder on the Jews and mobs burnt dozens of Jewish businesses to the ground, including my father's. That wasn't the first time the Russians had attacked the Jewish community. My mother always called those pogroms 'birth pangs of the Messiah.' She expected the Messiah-deliverer to come any day to rescue His people and at every evening meal she set a place at the table for Him."

Frau Sturm reached over and laid a hand on her friend's arm.

"God has protected you so far. I see no reason why He won't continue to do so."

Nussbaum took a sip of ersatz coffee. "Yes, but so many of my friends have vanished. God didn't protect Dieter or Roland or Sybille. Dear Lord, what's become of them? Will they ever return?" He dabbed his eyes with his handkerchief. "And here I sit trying to escape the collective fate of my people."

"Sometimes it seems like God is sitting on His hands," Erich complained, looking into his coffee cup. "You wonder if He cares about us at all."

"He does," Frau Sturm assured him. "Even if it doesn't look like it sometimes. She reached over and took Erich's hand. "We are God's hands and feet. He expects us to stand against the monsters who have taken over our country."

She was right, of course, but sometimes Erich felt very alone, almost deserted, knowing that he and Konrad and Nussbaum were among the vanishing number of fugitives left in Berlin. The Nazi agenda seemed unstoppable, which aggravated his sense of hopelessness. Where was God? How could He sit by and watch what was happening and not intervene? In his heart Erich knew that God had a purpose for allowing Germany to wallow in despair. But what was it?

He studied his friend, Nussbaum. *Jesus probably looked much like this man.* He would have had the same olive skin and dark eyes, a far cry from the sandy-haired, blue-eyed, Aryan Jesus one saw in the paintings in German art galleries and churches. And if the Messiah had lived in Germany during this Nazi era, he'd have been loaded onto an eastbound cattle car by now.

CHAPTER TWENTY-ONE

December, 1943.

"There's the postman," Frau Sturm said to Erich. "He's running late today." She rose to meet him at the door. "I might be a minute or two. Herr Brandt loves to talk."

Erich leaned out from the dark corner he had settled into and peeked toward the window. In the dim light he saw the postman climbing the front steps, in his hand a khaki colored *Feldpost* letter. He paused almost imperceptibly on the stairs as though contemplating whether to deliver it. He extended his index finger to ring the doorbell and then withdrew it. He was about to slip the letter into the post box on the wall when Frau Sturm opened the door. "*Guten Abend, Herr Brandt!*"

Brandt gave a start and the letter fluttered out of his grasp. He bent down to retrieve it and placed it into Frau Sturm's outstretched hand. "*Abend, Frau Sturm, Post für Sie.*" He turned and retreated down the stairs.

Oh, no, this can't be good news, Erich thought.

"*Danke. Wiedersehen, Herr Brandt,*" Frau Sturm called after him as she closed the door. A smile lit her face as she entered the room. "A letter from Horst! Even in these hard times the Military Mail

Service is still functioning." Then her brows knit. "That's funny, the name of Horst's regiment is on the letter, but this is not Horst's handwriting."

She tore open the letter and began to read. Erich watched her eyes move over each line. Then with a shriek, she sank onto the sofa; the letter fell to floor, landing face down on the carpet.

"Frau Sturm, what is it?" Erich rushed across the room and put his arm around her. But he already knew what was wrong. He reached down and picked up the letter and read it.

Dear Frau Sturm,

It is with a heavy heart that I must inform you that your son, Horst, died a hero's death on November 18th near the Don River in Russia. His noble sacrifice for Führer and Fatherland has spared many other German mothers the agony of losing their sons. We buried him beside other fallen comrades on a hill overlooking the river with a view to the west, toward Germany. We share the grief that you feel at this loss. You can be proud that your son died to protect and save our Reich. We, his friends and comrades, greet you in deepest sympathy.

Friedrich Martinsohn,

First Lieutenant, Fourth Panzer Army

Frau Sturm's raw, overworked hands covered her face, trembling as she sobbed. "*Lieber Gott, nein, nein, nein!*"

Erich put his arms around the grieving woman until she let her hands drop from her face. She began to stroke the sofa she was sitting on like she would a cherished child's head. "When he was home on leave last year, he sat on this very sofa." Tears made their way down her cheeks and fell in her lap. She gestured toward the open bedroom door. "He slept in that bed."

"Frau Sturm, I'm so very sorry," Erich said. He, too, wanted to cry.

"I thought that after my Thomas and Norbert died, I would end it all. But then I told myself, 'No, you have to stay strong for your remaining sons.' And now another one is gone. I don't even have graves to visit. They're buried in some God-forsaken plot of earth in a frozen land. I'll never see Horst again. I will never see Thomas or Norbert." With the mention of each name her voice grew more shrill. "And I will likely never see my Hans again, either."

She was probably right, Erich thought.

CHAPTER TWENTY-TWO

January, 1944.

Snowflakes, not bombs, were descending on Berlin, and the entire city – the streets, the buildings, and the ruins – lay buried under a garment of white, almost as if the heavens were trying to conceal all of the guilt and pain and terror that had victimized the city under a spotless, snowy blanket.

On this frigid night Erich had succumbed to the urge to surface for a few hours to enjoy a walk in the wintry silence. Few Berliners passed him as he made his way through the narrow streets near the Spree River. He had wandered this quarter many times before and knew every house, every window, every doorway. Faint, flickering streams of candlelight shone through the gaps in the window shutters, casting weak glimmers on the snowy streets.

He shivered as the cold wind blew puffy snowflakes into his face, light from the full moon transforming each one into a glistening piece of silver. He reached up and pulled his scarf tighter around his neck. His footsteps muffled, he walked nearly soundlessly in the moonlight.

Tonight, an ocean away, when evening came to Ohio, the same moon would shine on Nessa. How she had loved to sit with him in the evening on the banks of the Spree, watching the lunar disk ripple a path across the water.

It was afternoon in America. What was she doing right now? He imagined her helping his mother prepare dinner. Or perhaps she sat by a window, writing him a letter. Or maybe she waited at the front door for the postman to come strolling up the walkway with a letter from him.

Turning a corner, he buried his hands deeper into his coat pockets. The smell of burning coal hung in the air. A cat darted out of the rubble that was once someone's home and crossed his path, leaving in its wake a zigzag of paw prints and Erich hesitated for a moment, startled by the sudden movement. He stood in the snow in the middle of the street, and watched the animal disappear between two houses.

And at that moment he saw it in a doorway a few meters away – the round, golden glow of the tip of a cigarette. As the smoker drew the smoke into his lungs, the illumination from the cigarette painted his face in a crimson glow. Erich's heart rate quickened. That face was all too familiar.

Erich had managed to elude Schmutze and the Gestapo for nearly three years. Until now.

He began to back up, willing the other man not to see him. But it was too late. It was as if some lethal spark flashed between them. Schmutze hurled his cigarette to the ground and shot across the street. Erich turned and ran, but after a few steps his feet slid out from under him and he suddenly lay sprawled in the street, listening to the crunch of snow as Schmutze closed in on him.

Then he heard a click and looked up to see the faint outline of a gun muzzle aimed between his eyes. His heart hammered in his chest. *Oh, God. Is this the end of me?*

"Did you hear that, Reinhold? This gun is now ready to send you into the next world."

Erich pulled himself up to a sitting position. "Go ahead," he taunted, lifting his hands to shoulder level. "What's one more death on your conscience? Oh, but yours is seared, isn't it? As dead as all the innocent people you've sent to their doom."

"Shut up," Schmutze snapped, then winced and looked away. He waved his pistol to the right. "Get up and move over there into that doorway."

Erich struggled to his feet. The temperature had dipped below freezing, but he was sweating like a pig. His galloping heart was apparently demanding more oxygen, for his lungs began to expel great puffs of mist into the air.

As he walked, he knew he'd never see Nessa again. Nor his family. They'd never know what happened to him. Maybe that was just as well. He wouldn't want them to know he'd been shot down in the street like a dog.

When they reached the shelter of the doorway, Schmutze began to speak again. "My father used this pistol during the Great War," he said, waving the weapon in the air. "Who knows how many Frenchmen are lying dead at Verdun because of it."

Something was wrong. Schmutze's voice has lost its coarseness. The hate seemed to be gone. What was he up to?

"I've been tracking you for some time," Schmutze went on, his voice weak. "A U-Boat shouldn't become a man of habit. A U-Boat should vary his route. You were foolish. You kept wandering through these same streets. You made it easy for me to find you."

Schmutze was right. He'd become careless, almost reckless. In a normal society foolishness could be forgiven, but not in Hitler's Germany. How often had he caught himself lost in thought while walking the streets, paying no attention to his surroundings? How often had he caught himself failing to check the reflection in every shop window he passed, to make sure no one was following him? And now his carelessness was going to cost him his life.

He stared at the gun. "Well, now you've found me," he said, resigned to his fate. "Sad, isn't it? Two boys who once played together as friends grew up to be enemies, simply because a mad man told them they should hate one another."

Schmutze stared at Erich, a faraway look in his eyes. "Did you know that my father died a few weeks ago?"

"I'm so sorry to hear that, Gerhardt. I always liked him."

"Now I'm alone. Both of my parents are gone. My brothers are lying dead somewhere in Russia."

Thousands of German soldiers are lying dead in Russia. Why is he telling me all this? Why doesn't he just shoot me and get it over with?

"On his deathbed my father told me something that might interest you." Schmutze stopped, silent at the edge of some confession.

"What did he tell you?" Erich prompted.

"My parents bribed a government official years ago to falsify my mother's heritage. Both of her parents were Jewish. She was Jewish."

Erich's mouth dropped open.

Schmutze laughed morosely. The hand holding the gun fell to his side. "That means I'm a *Mischling*, a mongrel, same as you. If the Gestapo found out, they'd execute me on the spot."

"There's nothing wrong with being Jewish. It doesn't make you any less human."

Schmutze shook his head as though struggling with an inner demon. "Who knows how many of my own Jewish relatives ended up in work camps in the East because of me?"

A man in a wool coat passed their doorway and stared curiously at them. When he saw the glint of Schmutze's gun, he quickened his steps and vanished into the night.

Schmutze raised his right hand and waved the pistol weakly. "Reinhold, I want to be alone now. Get out of here before I have to shoot you."

Erich put his hand on Schmutze's shoulder for a moment, then slipped out of the doorway, leaving him weeping in the dark. He'd only gone a few meters when he heard the gunshot.

Once home at Frau Sturm's, Erich headed directly for the basement, his legs still shaking from his close encounter.

"How was your walk?" Konrad called to him, stoking the fire in the stove.

"I ran into Schmutze tonight."

"And you're not dead?"

"He won't give us any more trouble."

Konrad's eyes widened. "So you killed *him*?"

"Didn't need to. You know, he told me he'd been tracking me for some time. I walk those same streets by the Spree far too often. I should never have been so careless."

"What happened?" Konrad settled onto the couch and pulled a blanket around his shoulders. "How did you manage to get away?"

"I was walking near the river when he stepped out of a doorway and got the drop on me. He had a gun. I was sure he was going to kill me." Erich shuddered at the memory, holding his cold hands to the fire.

"Well, go on."

"That's when he confessed that his mother was Jewish. All these years the family had managed to conceal the secret. His father told him on his deathbed."

"Being Jewish is not good for career advancement in the Gestapo," Konrad joked. "So, he just let you go?"

"Yes. I guess he finally found his conscience. I told him being Jewish was nothing to be ashamed of, and I wanted to tell him more."

"Such as?"

"I wanted to tell him that his life wasn't over. That all the horrible things he'd done were in the past and he should embrace the present. Does that sound foolish and idealistic?"

"Maybe a little," Konrad conceded. "He'd just discovered that he was related to all of the people he'd been helping to kill and deport. One of his first victims was your own grandfather. Can you forgive him for that?"

Erich bowed his head, struggling with Konrad's question. "I'm going to have to. He spared my life tonight."

Konrad shrugged. "He has to live with the things he's done for the rest of his life."

"There'll be no chance for that. He's dead."

"Then you *did* kill him!"

Erich shook his head. "His own guilt and shame did that."

CHAPTER TWENTY-THREE

March, 1944.

Dear Nessa,

Your letter came just this morning. News from you sustains me.

Just a few lines before I leave on another business trip.

I'm sure you're aware of the situation here, so I won't sugarcoat it. The bombings are turning Berlin into a wasteland. The government tells us not to give up, that the Führer is still at his post and we have nothing to fear. But that doesn't stop the bombing raids.Thousands of homeless are sleeping in the subway tunnels. Many of those who still have homes refuse to leave Berlin, insisting on staying in the city to protect what they have from looters.

I'm praying this war will end soon and that we'll finally be together. I don't think Germany can last much longer.

Give my love to my family. I think about you every moment of the day.

I'll love you always,

Erich

Nessa touched her lips to the letter and placed it, along with Erich's other letters, in a small wooden trinket box on which she had painted pink roses. She tied the box shut with twine that she had dyed blue, Erich's favorite color, and placed it on her bedroom dresser.

The days without him had stretched into weeks and the weeks into months until almost two years had dragged by. She opened the locket around her neck and savored Erich's image. But within moments she flinched in fear.

Earlier that day she'd fled the living room in tears when a voice on the radio reported another bombing raid on Berlin. American and British bombers flocked across the English Channel nightly to incinerate everyone and everything in her homeland, including, if need be, anyone who worked in the underground against Hitler.

She had decorated her bedroom in blue in memory of Erich, a color she found soothing. But her cozy room could offer little solace from what she knew was happening in Germany. Its four walls seemed like a prison cell, where she counted the days until she and Erich would be together again. The trouble was, she had no idea how long she'd have to keep counting until that day came.

She closed the locket and stood up, looking out the window. Cambridge was sleeping its winter sleep under a blanket of snow. Two deer – a buck and a doe – strolled under the slumbering fruit trees in the orchard, leaving behind a jagged line of tracks. Soon the snow would melt and spring would come. She pleaded with God to allow the hope that always came with spring to bring peace to Europe.

June, 1944. Dusk.

Erich walked up the steps of the Hotel Schwarzwald and stopped, looking through the front door glass and scanning the lobby. Three older women sat on a couch, drinking coffee, and chatting. In a corner a man sat hidden behind a newspaper. His legs were crossed, and his hat sat on an end table next to him. He wore a blue suit. Gestapo? Probably not. They usually traveled in pairs.

Erich removed a picture from his pocket. The Braunschweiger family stared at him from the photo. He was there to accompany them from the hotel to the safe house near the Anhalter Train Station. In a few days, after Konrad had forged their IDs and travel documents, Erich would "conduct" them to southern Germany, where his colleagues in Tengen would spirit them over the border into Switzerland. The trip to Tengen would take a little longer than it had in the past. Allied bombing of major railway stations in Germany meant delayed train, but with rerouting it was still possible to reach most destinations.

Erich scanned the lobby again and checked the hallway leading to the guest rooms. Nothing suspicious. But he knew he couldn't be too careful. In the past month, the Gestapo had apprehended half a dozen Jewish families at hotels such as this. He had no desire to join them in a concentration camp.

He opened the door and stepped inside. The lobby smelled of beeswax and old furniture. He crossed to the front desk. Where was Wolfgang? His contact was normally at his post behind the reception desk. Erich drummed his fingers on the counter and checked the lobby again. Nothing had changed. The three ladies sat talking about their grandchildren. The blue suit was still engrossed in his newspaper.

Wolfgang finally emerged from a back room and Erich launched into his script. "Could I see a price list for your rooms?" He could almost feel the man with the newspaper staring holes in his back.

"*Jawohl, mein Herr.*" Wolfgang reached under the counter and laid a piece of paper on the counter, motioning with his eyes toward the man in the blue suit.

Erich bent over to read. No room prices. Instead five words: "Braunschweigers arrested ten minutes ago."

Erich drummed his fingers on the counter again. "May I keep this?"

"Certainly, sir."

Erich folded the paper and stuffed it into the bag slung across his shoulder. "Would you mind if I use your toilet?"

Wolfgang pointed down the hallway. "Of course. Third door on the left."

Erich strolled down the hall and paused at the door to the restroom, looking back at the blue suit in the corner. The man had lowered his newspaper and sat watching him.

Erich slipped into the restroom and locked the door behind him. As he threw open the window, he heard footsteps outside the door, then someone fumbling with the doorknob.

"Are you all right in there?" the voice called. Fumbling with the doorknob turned into pounding on the door. "Gestapo, open up at once!"

Erich climbed out the window into the alley and ran for his life.

He had known for a long time that this day would arrive – the day they finally caught up to him. He wasn't surprised. Any young man walking the streets of Berlin who wasn't in the army naturally aroused suspicion. Maybe that was the reason the Gestapo was chasing him now, or maybe not – in either case he wasn't going to stick around to find out.

As he rounded the back of the hotel, he ran full speed into the arms of another man, who pitched backwards at the force of the collision and crashed to the ground, wheezing like a deflated balloon. He should have known there would be two of them!

Erich leapt to his feet, crossed the darkened courtyard, and vaulted over the gate into an alley. He was almost to the corner when he heard a man behind him shout, "Halt! Gestapo."

He looked back to see the blue suit in pursuit, waving a gun. Erich dashed across the street, nearly colliding with an oncoming truck. The driver slammed on the brakes. The vehicle's tires screeched, then it fishtailed and overturned, sending bushels of potatoes scurrying down the street and into the alley. Erich's pursuer emerged from the alley just in time to see the potatoes rushing toward him like thousands of legless lemmings looking for a cliff to plunge over. As Erich rounded the next corner, he caught a glimpse of the man's expression: mouth and eyes flung wide open in total disbelief. The man stumbled and skidded and skipped over the potatoes, like an ice skater out of control on a frozen pond, before crashing to the ground.

Erich raced along the sidewalk, his legs pounding frantically over the cobblestones. A handful of children playing soccer in the street gaped at him. A dog in a fenced yard barked at him for the length of the fence. Two old women yelped as he pushed past them.

He saw a taxi, hailed it and jumped into the back seat, panting frantically. "Brandenburg Gate. Step on it."

They drove for ten minutes. Erich used the time to collect his thoughts and catch his breath. Then he pounded on the driver's seat. "Stop here. Let me out."

The driver pulled over. "But the Brandenburg Gate's still ten minutes away."

Erich was already out of the car. The meter said eight marks, thirty. He handed the driver a ten. "Keep the change."

The taxi disappeared around a corner. Erich waited five minutes, then hailed another cab. "Opera Square, *bitte*."

The sun had dipped below the horizon and it was getting late. *Better get off the streets and find a place to spend the night.*

Erich sat in the cab until they came to a quiet, secluded neighborhood. "Driver, pull over."

"Sir, we're not even close to Opera Square."

"I changed my mind," Erich said, hoping the driver wouldn't be suspicious of his erratic behavior.

The driver shook his head and guided the car to the curb. "Thirteen marks exactly."

Erich paid and got out.

He walked along, studying the row houses on either side of the street, the residents beginning to pull their shades down for the night. He finally found what he was looking for: a sign in a window with the words, *Zimmer Frei*. He looked up and down the street. No one in sight. He opened the gate and slipped inside. In the dim light he saw a handful of fruit trees next to a pond full of carp.

He pressed the illuminated doorbell button. Keys jangled in the door lock. The door opened half a meter. A man thrust his head into the door opening and shone a flashlight in Erich's face. "*Ja, bitte.*"

A welcome blast of warm air streamed through the door and wafted over Erich. He nodded at the vacancy sign. "*Guten Abend.* Do you still have a room free?"

"Yes," the man said matter-of-factly, opening the door wider. "Otherwise I would have removed the sign from the window."

"I need a room for the night."

"Well, come in then. No sense standing here with the door gaping open trying to heat the front yard."

Once Erich was inside, the man closed the door and locked it. In the light of the flashlight he saw an older gentleman with a red, splotchy complexion and a few strands of white hair combed back over the top of his head. Small eyes squinted behind rimless spectacles.

The man held out his hand. "The room is five marks a night. In advance."

Erich dug a five-mark coin out of his pocket and paid.

His host started up the stairs with Erich on his heels, but then stopped abruptly and turned around. "Back down the stairs, please."

Erich's face turned as white as a sheet of paper. Oh, no. What was this all about? He backed down, preparing to run for the front door and disappear into the night. Except the man had locked it!

"I'm so forgetful," the man said. "I'll need to see your papers. Government regulations, you know."

Which false documents should he show the man? Konrad had made him two sets of identity papers – one identified him as a corporal in the Germany army, and the other as a disabled accountant with a heart condition.

Erich handed the man his military ID.

The old man studied the papers. "Oh, you're in the Wehrmacht. Home on leave, are you?"

"Just for a couple of weeks."

"Why aren't you staying with relatives?"

"I'm an orphan. My father died in the Great War. My mother passed away last year."

"You don't seem to have much luggage. Why is that?"

Please stop asking so many questions! "I left my duffel bag in a locker at the train station." He pointed to the bag over his shoulder. "I have everything I need for tonight in here."

The man nodded. "Uh huh." He returned Erich's papers and started up the stairs again. "And you're serving the Führer on the Russian Front?"

"Yes, how did you know?"

"Just a guess. How are things going in Russia?" The man stopped on the stairs and turned toward Erich. "I hear rumors that things are not progressing well over there."

"Don't believe everything you hear." Especially the part about the German Army holding its own against the Russians.

At the top of the stairs the man turned left and led Erich down a cold hallway, stopping at a room halfway down. He pulled a key ring from his pocket and removed one of the keys, handing it to Erich. "Check-out time is eleven," he said, and shuffled away.

Erich opened the door and flipped the light switch by the door. A lamp next to the window came on. He locked the door behind him. The room was musty and dank, with high ceilings. He went to the window and turned on the radiator, then looked out at the courtyard below. It had started to rain, and water was streaming down the windowpane. In the window's reflection a gaunt, tired-looking man stared back at him. Would Nessa even recognize him now? The rain pouring over his image made it look as if he were weeping.

Then his eyes flew open. *I must be losing my mind.* He moved quickly to the door and flipped off the lights. Nighttime meant bombers, which meant extinguishing all lights. All he needed was to have someone report seeing a light in his room. In the darkness he moved carefully across the room and sat on the bed.

Despite his close call with the Gestapo earlier that evening, he was more determined than ever to continue the work of getting those at risk out of Germany. If that meant continuing to go out in public and putting himself in harm's way, so be it.

He took off his coat and threw it on a chair by the bed. He removed the rest of his clothes, then climbed into bed. The pillow felt cold on his face.

The next morning, he took three taxis, changing cabs every few minutes, before arriving home at Frau Sturm's.

December, 1944.

Life in Berlin was becoming increasingly more frenetic, with Allied bombings nearly every night. But at least the attacks were building some structure into people's lives. They got up each morning, crawled out from under the new layer of rubble caused by the previous night's bombing, and then went on with their day.

And, as the war dragged on, the Gestapo became increasingly more paranoid and unpredictable, racing through the streets at breakneck speed before screeching to a halt in front of this house or that business to haul away supposed offenders for "interviews" from which they seldom returned.

Shoppers ventured out to buy only what they needed, before scurrying back to the imagined safety of their homes.

The Volk had believed they were following a leader who would lead them to the Promised Land. Now, almost everyone realized that Germany had boarded a train that was racing toward destruction, and it was too late to pull the emergency cord.

Nussbaum was no longer among the half a dozen U-Boats that Frau Sturm harbored. After two near misses with the Gestapo, Frau Kleist had spirited him off to the safety of Lisbon.

One evening, as dusk crept across Berlin, Erich and Konrad were making their way home after picking up printing supplies.

"What's the definition of cowardice?" Konrad asked.

Where had that question come from? "Is this another one of your jokes?" Erich asked.

"Yes, actually. Cowardice is volunteering for the Russian Front to escape the air raids in Berlin." He laughed.

Erich gave his friend a courtesy laugh and shook his head. "I'll miss you and your dumb jokes when I'm in America."

"Maybe I'll come with you – help you keep your sense of humor."

At that moment the air raid siren sounded.

They looked at one another. "Should we ignore it?" Konrad asked. "Planes fly over Berlin all the time. It's probably just a false alarm."

"I'm not taking the chance. Come on."

They quickened their pace. "Between the air raid sirens and the all-clear signals, I never know whether I'm coming or going," Konrad panted. He nudged Erich. "Did you hear the one about Hitler and Goebbels?"

"Save your jokes until after the war. Hurry up, we're almost there."

The first series of explosions were close by. They broke into a dead run, the bombs seeming closer with each step. After two hundred meters they rounded the corner into their alley, nearly skidding to the ground on a pile of unraked leaves. Thirty seconds later they crashed through Frau Sturm's side door and dashed down the stairs into the basement. A small candle illuminated a group of frightened faces.

"Thank God you made it," Frau Sturm breathed.

"Where's Walter?" Erich worried. "I don't see him here."

"He's probably still downtown," Konrad said. "Remember, he likes to do his looting during the air raids, when everyone else is in the bomb shelters. That way he can 'shop' at his leisure."

"What if he gets picked up by the Gestapo while he's shopping?" asked a man in a dark corner of the room.

"The Gestapo doesn't have a death wish," Konrad said. "They would never troll for looters in the middle of an air raid."

The detonations marched closer. They were now perhaps two streets away.

"I don't understand why they have to bomb civilians," the man in the corner moaned. "We're not soldiers."

"Isn't it obvious?" another man grumbled. "Every soldier was once a civilian. Get rid of the civilians and the soldiers stop coming."

"Should we pray that the bombers destroy the Nazis or that the Nazis shoot down the bombers before they destroy us?" Konrad quipped.

The others ignored him, apparently in no mood for humor.

"We're going to die tonight," a man behind Erich wailed. Erich recognized Guenther's voice.

He said the same thing during every air raid. One of these nights he was going to be right. Erich covered his ears to block out the roar of the explosions. They were living from one air raid to the next. *Just survive this one. This hell can't go on much longer. The war will be over before you know it.* At least that's what he kept telling himself.

The bombs were impacting very near, the house groaning and swaying with each explosion. Then a shell landed next to the house, tearing a great hole in the earth, and shattering the windows, sending dirt, dust, and glass whistling through the basement, as the building's foundation shifted and cracked.

"God save us!" screamed Frau Sturm.

Then one of the U-Boats panicked and jumped to his feet. "I have to get out of here!" he shrieked. He bolted up the basement stairs to the door and began to unlatch it.

"Stay here!" Erich screamed at the man. He and some of the other men rushed up the stairs to restrain him. At that moment another bomb detonated next to the house. The concussion blew the door inward and sent the men sprawling down the stairs onto the basement floor.

Flashlight beams searched the darkness of the basement.

"This one didn't make it," a voice said.

"Any identification?"

"It's a she. And yes. Gabrielle Sturm."

"Check those three over there."

"They're dead also. This one's ID says Roland Bauer. There's also a Rudolf Wildetaube.

The third one has no identification."

"Write down their names and order a truck to take them to the morgue," said the search and rescue warden. He pointed to a corner. "How about that one?"

"He's just a boy. Barely conscious, but still alive. Hey son, what's your name?"

"Konrad... Konrad."

"He's pretty banged up," the rescue worker said to his boss. "I'm not sure he even knows where he is." He put his hand on Konrad's shoulder. "Lie still. We're going to get you out of here."

"One more dead one over here," the other man said. "He's a mess. His face is gone. Let's see ... here's his ID. Erich Frank."

"Erich's dead?" Konrad asked, groaning. He tried to raise himself to one elbow, but fell back, unconscious.

CHAPTER TWENTY-FOUR

January, 1945.

"How's Erich doing?" Greta asked. She had waited impatiently while Nessa finished reading the letter.

"I wish it were better news. Freezing weather, bombing raids and food shortages. I wish he would leave Germany," she said miserably. She'd read that the bombers had nearly destroyed Germany's infrastructure. Surely the trains were no longer running, so there was no way to transport Jewish refugees out of the country anymore.

"The fact that he's survived this long is promising," Franz said, trying to encourage the women.

Nessa was glad that Erich's letters were still arriving, but she couldn't help thinking that things in Germany would probably get much worse before they got better. According to the newspapers, the Americans would soon cross the Rhine and the Russians were very near the eastern outskirts of Berlin. How was Erich going to survive all that?

The front door flew open and Karl stepped into the living room, banging the door shut behind him. Everything about Karl commanded attention. Vice-president of a prestigious steel firm in Pittsburgh, he was a man who took charge, a man used to giving orders and having them obeyed.

"I'm home," he announced.

Greta rushed from the couch to hug him. "Welcome home, my son. Three weeks is too long to be gone."

"Mutti, I'm sorry. I just couldn't get away before now."

Franz was right behind his wife, extending his right hand to his son. "How's the job going, Karl?"

"Busy. We can barely keep up with our military orders." His gaze moved to Nessa, who was returning Erich's letter to its envelope. "Another letter from Erich?" he asked, with a nearly imperceptible taint of jealousy. "How's my little brother doing?"

"Fine." She met his gaze, then looked away. Those eyes, so much like Erich's – every time she looked into Karl's eyes, she saw Erich. Every time Karl looked at her, he seemed to drink up her image.

"We should have never let him stay behind," Greta said. "We should have insisted he come with us."

Once again guilt settled over Nessa like a heavy cape. It was her fault Erich hadn't left Germany with his parents. She could only pray he survived and made it to America. If he died, how could she ever make amends to the family who'd taken her in?

"Erich may be home sooner than you think," Karl hinted.

Nessa's eyes flew open. "What do you mean?"

"My reserve unit has been called up. We have orders for Germany. With any luck I'll be able to personally rescue my little brother from those Nazis."

She was fond of Karl, but his constant bravado angered her. And why did he always have to refer to Erich as "my little brother?" "He'd never leave Germany before the war was over," Nessa said. "Erich's work ..."

Karl had apparently heard the words "Erich's work" one time

too many. "What about *my* work?" he spat. Who's the one who brings money home every week? Who's the one who spends weeks away from home working sixteen-hour days in Pittsburgh? Who's the one ..." Karl broke off. "Oh, forget it," he growled, walking out of the room and into the den, where he dropped onto a loveseat by the window.

The others looked at one another in embarrassment.

Nessa hadn't seen Karl lose control like that since the scene he had made at the USO dance two years earlier. She went into the den, sat down next to him, and laid her hand on his arm. She sensed the tenseness in his body evaporate as soon as she touched him. "Karl, I'm sorry. I didn't mean to offend you. It's just that I love Erich and I miss him so much."

"You talk of him as if he were a saint," Karl crabbed disgustedly.

"I know he's not."

Karl took her hand. "There's someone here in America who loves you, too, Nessa."

Nessa withdrew her hand. The moment she had feared for so long had arrived. For two years she'd known that someday Karl would express his feelings for her in no uncertain terms. He was used to getting what he wanted, and it was clear that he wanted her.

"I'm very fond of you, but I'm engaged to Erich."

"He won't be able to offer you what I can. If you marry me, you'll have security for life."

Love is more precious than material security. "I do appreciate your offer, Karl, but put yourself in my shoes. If I were engaged to you, would you want me to entertain other offers?"

He remained silent, refusing to answer.

She left him sitting at the window, staring out at the Appalachian foothills.

~

February, 1945.

"Nessa," Greta called, looking out the kitchen window, "there's the postman. Didn't you have a letter to send to Erich?"

Nessa stuffed her letter into an envelope and sealed it, then grabbed a stamp. "I just finished it." She raced out the front door and met the postman coming up the walk. "Mr. Murdock, I have a letter for you." She licked the stamp and put it on the envelope.

Murdock, smiling, took it. "Another letter to Portugal, eh? That's a coincidence. I have one here for you, postmarked Lisbon."

Nessa squealed. "It's from Erich! Finally!" She snatched it from the postman's hand. "Thank you, Mr. Murdock! Thank you!"

Scarcely aware of Murdock leaving, she ripped open the letter as she made her way to the front porch steps, calling, "Greta, a letter from Erich!"

"At last," Greta called from inside the house. "I'll be there in a minute. I just need to put this strudel in the oven."

The warmth of the early spring sun felt good as Nessa unfolded the stationery. But the handwriting wasn't Erich's.

Dear Nessa,

I'm so sorry to have to relay bad news. A few nights ago, Erich died in an air raid. Our dear Frau Sturm was also killed. I'm writing you from a field hospital here in Berlin. I'm sorry to say that there will be no grave for us to visit. They buried him in a mass grave, outside the city. Again, I'm so sorry.

Your friend,

Konrad Spielhagen

Nessa threw her hands over her face and the letter fluttered to the ground. She was barely aware of Greta's approaching footsteps or her asking, "And what does my son have to say?" followed by the rustling of paper and then the sharp keening.

April, 1945.

Fog invaded Berlin, skulking through the streets and alleyways, nestling onto the Spree. In happier times lovers had sat on the banks of the river holding hands and watching the water slip past on its way to the North Sea. They had watched the moon dance across the waves, and the stars glisten in the gently swirling water. Like a sacred love potion, they had drunk in the sight of moonlight on the water, thanking heaven that they had found one another.

In these times lovers raised their fists toward heaven, cursing the Allied airmen who dropped bombs on Berlin, bombs that forever separated lovers and families. Nearly an entire generation of German lovers and loved ones now lay crushed and frozen beneath the ruins of Berlin and upon the battlefields of Russia and France.

And at a field hospital, which consisted of a collection of tents huddled by the River Spree, screams of agony had replaced lovers' vows.

"At least we may not be bombed tonight," Doctor Krause said to his colleague, Doctor Vogel, as he flipped back the flap of a tent whose interior was illuminated by a kerosene lamp. "They probably won't be able to find Berlin in this fog."

"They'll find us all right," Vogel countered. "They just won't be able to pinpoint specific targets."

Krause went to Erich's cot and patted him on the thigh. "How's that leg doing today?" The doctor's smock was caked with blood from dozens of operations and amputations.

Erich started to get to his feet, but Krause pressed him back down. "No, no, try to lie still. You've suffered a bad hyperextension. Your leg is healing nicely, but we still need to keep you here a few more days."

Erich didn't remember how he ended up in the field hospital. He did remember running home to Frau Sturm's when the bombing had started, and cowering in the basement with the others, convinced he had only a few minutes to live. The last thing he remembered was one of the U-Boats running up the basement steps, trying to get out of the building. After that everything was a blank.

"This one's gone," Vogel said, examining the man in the cot next to Erich. His pulled the sheet over the dead man's head and blood began seeping through the fabric. The doctor removed his eyeglasses and chewed on the earpiece. "Just as well, poor man, with both arms and one leg gone."

Krause scribbled on a pad of paper. "I'll send for the orderlies to get him out of here."

There was a scream from another tent, then a voice pleaded, "Doctor! Help me! Doctor!"

Krause nodded at Erich. "We'll be back later to check on you. Try to get some rest."

And how much rest did they think he could get in a place like this?

Once the physicians left, Erich groaned to a sitting position. Every joint in his body screamed in pain. He stood and tested the strength in his leg. A little pain, but not much. He walked around his cot. The leg seemed strong enough.

He went to the coat stand and threw on his hat and coat, leaving the cane they'd given him behind. His leg felt surprisingly good. He didn't think he'd need the cane. Besides, it would only draw attention to him.

But he did need to find Konrad, to head west toward the American lines. The Americans would surely take him to America – and to Nessa.

In a cabinet he found some food and a flashlight, then stepped outside. The darkness was laden with the stench of iodine, urine, and excrement. He walked for about a hundred meters and stumbled upon a bridge that had somehow escaped the bombing.

He crossed the bridge to the other side of the river and looked around. It was no use. It was dark and foggy, and he had no idea where he was. He decided to find a place to sleep for the night. In the morning he could orient himself and find his way back to Frau Sturm's house and Konrad.

He moved slowly along the street, passing a jewelry store, its slumbering display windows devoid of merchandise. The door to a butcher shop stood open, empty meat hooks dangling from the ceiling. He went inside and found a storeroom and a meat locker. Both rooms were cold and tiled from floor to ceiling. He couldn't sleep there.

He explored several other abandoned stores and businesses. All of them were roofless ruins, so he moved on.

After a few more blocks he came to a bulky building with a large, wide staircase leading up to double doors. He aimed the flashlight above the door. The words "Adolf Hitler *Schule*" were chiseled above the lintel. He climbed the stairs and pulled on the door handles. Locked. The long, vertical window next to the doors was shattered. With his good leg he kicked out the loose glass hanging in the frame and climbed through. In the hallway he crunched over broken glass, books, and chalk.

He found a classroom and ducked inside. His flashlight revealed dozens of chairs piled in a corner. A map of the world hung diagonally on a wall, supported only by a single thumbtack. He checked the front wall of the room. The portrait of the Führer, which hung in every German schoolroom, was missing. Taken as a souvenir? Or for target practice?

In another corner of the room, a dirty mattress beckoned. Erich sat down on it, pulled a dinner roll and a sausage from his coat pocket, brushing off the pocket lint. As he ate, he scanned the area around the mattress with the flashlight. Hundreds of textbooks lay piled on the floor, caked in dust. He picked up a fifth-year textbook and opened it. "Germany awake!" he read. "The Führer points the way to freedom ... Only an armed Volk can be free ... Traitors, mostly Jews, are intent on destroying the German Volk."

Such rubbish! Erich threw the book across the room and lay back on the mattress. He'd sleep until dawn and then try to find his way home.

∼

Morning light was streaming through the windows when Erich woke to the sound of boots crunching on broken glass in the hallway outside the classroom. Moments later a soldier came through the door. "*Was machen Sie da?*" he yelled. "*Aufstehen!*"

Erich lurched to a sitting position and squinted at the man.

"*Aufstehen,*" the soldier bellowed again, leveling his rifle at Erich's head.

He struggled to his feet, his pulse drumming wildly in his ears. "Don't shoot," he begged, raising his hands above his head. "I'm unarmed."

"Get out your identification."

Erich wasn't about to say that he had lent his ID to Christian, one of the other U-Boats, the day before the bombing in Frau Sturm's neighborhood. "I lost it," he said.

"Keep your hands up and turn around. I'm going to search you." Erich obeyed and the soldier rifled through his coat, stuffing two rolls and a sausage from Erich's pockets into his own. Then he motioned with his rifle toward the classroom door. "Move."

The soldier hurried him along the hallway with the muzzle of his rifle.

"Climb through that window next to the door. That's how you got in here, isn't it?"

Erich didn't answer. He clambered through the broken window and stood on the landing next to the front doors. The fog had lifted; daylight revealed rubble, ruins, and corpses scattered in the street.

A dozen soldiers stood at the corner guarding a group of German civilians.

The soldier stabbed the end of his rifle into Erich's back, then pointed his weapon toward the civilians. "Move over there with them. You just got volunteered for the *Volkssturm*." The *Volkssturm,* "the people's storm," was a civilian militia group – Germany's last-ditch effort at a heroic defense of the Fatherland against invading armies. This ragtag army consisted of pubescent boys, old men, and disabled soldiers. And now Erich was a member.

"I need everyone's attention," the old man barked with sharp impatience. The murmuring stopped. Fifty men and boys huddled on the ground in a forest clearing east of Berlin, behind the dirt wall that separated their trenches from the Russian lines. Some wore civilian clothes, others work clothes, and still others shabby, faded uniforms from the last war.

"My name is Kohl and I am your commanding officer," the man continued. He wore a captain's uniform from the Great War, which was littered with medals. An antique pistol was in a holster at his side. "Germany has entrusted you men of the *Volkssturm* with the final defense of the Reich against the Bolshevik hordes who have invaded our homeland."

Niemeyer, a man of perhaps sixty sitting next to Erich, grunted and whispered, "I'm sure the enemy will turn and flee back to Mother Russia when they see what's left of Germany's invincible military machine – old men and young boys."

"You," Kohl screamed, pointing at Niemeyer, "shut up and pay attention. You're not in the pub with your drinking buddies. Germany's fate is in your hands – all of our hands."

Behind Kohl, to the east, Erich heard the thunder of mortars and artillery. The Russians seemed to be closer than an hour ago.

Kohl clasped his hands behind his back and began to pace in front of the shoddy ranks of Germany's last hope. "Men, many of you will die in defense of our Fatherland." Kohl stopped pacing and glowered into the ranks. "Choose a valiant death for the Führer. Believe me, you do *not* want to fall into the hands of the Russians."

Niemeyer nudged Erich and spoke in a low, sarcastic voice. "Be proud, my young friend. The Führer has personally chosen you to die for Germany."

Erich stared numbly at the back of the man sitting in front of him. The growl of the mortars and artillery in the east continued. He chewed nervously at the inside of his cheek, breaking the skin, and tasting blood.

Kohl looked at the men for a few more moments, and then yelled, "*Weggetreten.*"

Grateful to be dismissed, Erich climbed into the trench with the rest of his platoon. The explosions in the distance had stopped, leaving in their wake a frightening, eerie calm.

Erich leaned against the wall of the trench, and then slid to a sitting position in the dirt.

"The only Russian word I know besides *nyet* is *tovaritch*," Niemeyer said to Erich. "That's the word for comrade." He pointed toward the top of the trench. "When they come over that wall, throw down your weapon and yell *tovaritch* as loud as you can."

"That's when you'll learn another Russian word," the young man on the other side of Erich said, brushing a clump of mud from his tattered *Wehrmacht* uniform. He sat on an ammo box eating beans out of a can.

"What's that, Behler?" Niemeyer asked.

"*Dasvidaniya.* It means 'goodbye.' That's the last thing Ivan will say to you before blowing your head off." He laughed, but no one joined in.

Behler stood up with a wince and limped over to the water

barrel to get a drink. When he returned, he plopped down next to Erich, removed his helmet, and threw it in the dirt. Germany's Imperial Eagle stood proudly on Behler's belt buckle, surrounded by the words, *Gott mit uns*. God is with us? Erich thought. Surely God hadn't taken sides in this war.

Behler fumbled in his uniform pocket and pulled out a bent cigarette and a wooden match. He swiped the match on his helmet, lit his cigarette and tossed the match into the mud. He took a puff, then pulled a small strand of tobacco from the tip of his tongue.

"I'm surprised you're still with us," Erich said, pointing at the holes in Behler's uniform coat.

Behler slipped his hand under the coat and poked his forefinger through a hole over his heart. That hole and two others below it were ringed in red. "This coat belonged to my best friend. I wear it in memory of him." He wiggled his finger in the hole. "Last winter at Stalingrad he took three bullets in the chest. I saw him go down just before I was hit in the leg." He rapped his knuckles on his calf, creating a hollow sound. "It's wooden. The bullet tore my calf apart. They cut my leg off below the knee." He knocked on his leg again and chuckled. "Knock on wood for luck, they say." The smile disappeared from his lips and he shook his head. "Stalingrad wasn't a lucky time for me or for my friend. I still remember his last words: 'I gladly die for my Führer.'" Behler lowered his voice and spat into the dirt. "What a waste." He stabbed out his cigarette on the ground. "And now, as you can see, even one-legged men have the honor of defending Hitler's Germany in its last hours."

Niemeyer pointed at two boys, each perhaps sixteen, who were waiting in the breakfast line. "They've even summoned the Hitler Youth to help push back the Russians."

"For me, the Hitler Youth wasn't much different than the army," Behler mused. "Except in the army the stakes are higher, of course. But you still had to carry out the same stupid orders, stand at attention while some moron with bad breath screamed in your face, hold your tongue unless spoken to." He turned to Erich. "How was your time in the Hitler Youth?"

"I never joined."

Behler's eyes widened. "How in the world did you manage that?"

"I thought Hitler was full of crap and I refused to join." Of course, after it became known that he had Jewish heritage, no one was interested in his membership.

Behler leaned in toward Erich. "It appears you were right about Hitler. But I can't believe they didn't bully you into joining."

"I was in my share of fights because of it," Erich admitted, holding up scarred knuckles. "All of my friends joined up."

"Sadly, most of us joined up as well," Behler lamented. "We did what was expected of us. *Kadavergehorsam*, you know."

The total, blind obedience of cadavers. What a perfect way to describe the Nazi mindset.

Behler began to sing:

"We will continue to march, even if everything crashes down around our ears,

"For today the nation hears us, and tomorrow the entire world."

"And now the entire world really *is* crashing down around our ears," Niemeyer complained.

Behler tossed Niemeyer a can of beans. "Here, eat these, old man. Things always look better on a full stomach." He turned back to Erich. "The Nazis used that song in the Hitler Youth to prepare us for war. Of course, the war games we played then didn't involve killing. In war that's the main goal."

"I don't think I could kill anyone," Erich said, examining his rifle.

"You do what you have to do to survive. Just remember, even if you refuse to participate in the killing, you will still die, but not so gloriously." Behler put his forefinger to his temple. "Your superiors will shoot you in the head."

Erich ran his finger along the blade of the bayonet attached to his rifle. Was this how he would spend his last few moments on earth – shooting and stabbing as many Russians as he could before they killed him? Before the war they hanged you for killing a man. Now they awarded you the Iron Cross if you killed enough of them.

It seemed his entire life had been couched in violence. As boys, after the Great War, he and his friends had taken to the streets in mock battles using stick rifles, imagining they were killing Germany's enemies. Then real battles erupted on Berlin's streets with real bullets and real blood – Nazis fighting against communists. He remembered crawling under his bed and clamping his hands over his ears to block out the sound of gunfire outside. Years later came Hitler's war against the Jews. After that, his war against Russia. And now Russia had invaded Germany, laying waste to everything in her path.

Erich felt adrift in a sea of hopelessness, abandoned and rejected by his homeland and by God. He felt like the lost sheep in the parable. But instead of coming to look for him, God had stayed with the ninety-nine.

He prayed Nessa had moved on with her life. In a few hours, or maybe in just a few minutes, he'd be dead, and she'd never know what happened to him nor why he never returned to her.

Erich woke in the middle of the night. He sat up and looked around to see Kohl crouching next to him, smoking.

"Go back to sleep. Ivan's sleeping. So should you."

Erich lay back down and fell asleep. In his dreams he and Nessa walked in the woodlands surrounding Cambridge. Autumn had donned her coat of many colors and above them sunlight filtered through the trees in hues of saffron-yellow, tawny-brown, and rusty-red. Robins sang and the scent of rain hung in the breeze. Then stillness descended over the forest. The wind paused and the birds held their breath. Above the forest canopy of sycamore, poplar and oak, black clouds moved in, swirling and billowing. A streak of molten silver darted out of the clouds and across the sky, on its heels a rolling boom of thunder. Suddenly lightning was striking all around them. They dove to the ground, clawing desperately into the forest floor.

Erich awoke and jumped to his feet. It was just before dawn and a hurricane of mortar and artillery rounds was exploding all around him, gouging huge craters in the earth.

"Get down, get down, you *Dummkopf,*" Kohl screamed, knocking him to the ground.

Erich curled into the earth, pressing his helmet onto his head.

After about an hour the artillery attack stopped. All quiet on the eastern front.

Erich stood up and peered over the top of the trench. The sun was edging over the horizon, illuminating the smoke that still hung over the battlefield from the Russian artillery barrage.

"They're probably just reloading," Niemeyer said. "In a few minutes they'll start up again."

At that moment two boys next to him leapt to their feet, eyes wide with terror, and scampered out of the trench toward the forest behind the German lines. Kohl screamed at them to stop, but they were beyond following orders. The old man pulled out his pistol, took aim, and shot them in the back. Their hands reached toward the sky, then they sprawled into the mud, arms outstretched, lying motionless.

Erich stared numbly at the boys, then over at Kohl. The old man met his gaze, waving his gun in the direction of the dead boys. "Cowardice is contagious," he said, his voice void of emotion.

They had just finished with lunch when Erich heard a battle cry rising up from a thousand throats. He peered over the top of the trench to see what looked like a million Russian soldiers flooding the plain to the east, racing toward them.

"Fire! Fire!" Kohl screamed, waving his pistol over his head. "Kill them! Kill them!"

Erich began firing into the crowd, knowing that Kohl would shoot him in the head if he didn't, but he couldn't tell if he hit anyone. To his right and to his left his comrades also pumped rifle rounds into the enemy ranks. Russian soldiers grabbed at their wounds, then pitched to the ground, tripping the men running behind them. Then the German machine guns started up, tearing bloody holes in the faces and torsos of the enemy soldiers.

After the machine gunners had mowed down hundreds of Russians, the enemy retreated, the only sounds coming from the battlefield the cries of wounded and dying Russian soldiers.

A few minutes later, the German machine guns started up again. The men jumped to their feet.

"Relax," Kohl commanded, pointing over the trench. "They're just finishing off the wounded Russians on the battlefield."

The men plopped back into the mud. Two orderlies arrived and took away the bodies of the boys Kohl had gunned down earlier. The old man lit a cigarette and watched them, his face expressionless.

Erich watched, too, numb in spirit. "My grandfather fought in the Great War," he said, speaking to no one in particular. "When he talked about the horrors of war, I would just nod politely. I had no conception of what he had gone through."

"Now you have," Kohl grunted.

Erich looked toward the eastern horizon. "Now I have."

In the distance he heard the roar of diesel engines.

"Hear that?" Behler asked. Ivan's moving into position, getting ready to resume blowing us to pieces."

Niemeyer removed his helmet and dropped it at his feet, closing his eyes. "I'm going to try to get some sleep before they get here." He yawned, stretching his arms over his head. "If I'm lucky they'll kill me while I'm napping, and I'll get to sleep forever."

Erich pulled off his helmet as well. He shivered. His feet were wet and numb in his boots. He drew his legs up against his chest, propped his face against his knees and closed his eyes.

~

Erich hadn't slept long before the morning sun washed away the last traces of night. He peeked over the top of the trench, stunned. The Russian bodies that had littered the battlefield the previous afternoon had disappeared during the night, as if they had come back to life and wandered away.

"Just after dawn," Kohl told Erich, "dozens of unarmed Russians showed up on the battlefield with white flags. We let them collect their dead. Rules of war, you know. They'd do the same for us."

A trace of humanity. Still, Erich didn't find it comforting.

"Yes, my young friend," Niemeyer said, laying a hand on Erich's shoulder, "Ivan has cleared the battlefield so he can attack us unimpeded. I think we're going to die today."

The numbness in Erich's feet spread to the rest of his body. He opened his mouth to speak but was cut off by machine gun fire from the Russian lines raking across the top of the trench.

"Return fire," Kohl screamed, pointing to his left. "Take out that Russian machine gun nest in those trees."

The men fired toward the machine gun nest, but this action only helped the Russians pinpoint their location. Machine gun rounds from other enemy machine gun nests began spattering across the top of their trench.

Next to Erich, Behler suddenly jerked up onto the tips of his toes and fell backwards. Erich dropped his rifle and knelt at his side. Blood pulsated from a wound in his comrade's neck. Erich pulled a bandage from his field bag, pressing it hard against Behler's wound. No use. Blood flowed through the bandage, making his hand warm and sticky.

From the other side of the trench he heard the roar of a thousand Russian voices. Ivan was attacking again.

Behler convulsed and vomited blood. Erich removed the bandage for an instant to reposition it. The bullet had pulverized the side of Behler's neck. He drew a wheezing breath and stated the obvious – "I'm dying," – spraying blood onto Erich's face.

And then the wounded man's eyes widened. He choked a few times, and was gone.

Erich was still staring into Behler's dead eyes when Kohl screamed, "Retreat, retreat, retreat!"

Erich grabbed his rifle and ran for his life.

CHAPTER TWENTY-FIVE

A storm descended on Cambridge, sending downtown shoppers fleeing for shelter. The wind invaded the newsstand across the street from Kennedy's Bakery and absconded with several newspapers, sending them swirling into the sky. A claw of lightning scratched across the sky, followed by the boom of thunder.

"April showers bring May flowers," Nessa said, as Mr. Kennedy delivered three cups of coffee and three plates of cherry pie to her and her friends. Paul and Annie, now officially engaged, had been dying to show off Annie's new ring. Annie was a rather plain woman, but today her smile was as bright as the diamond sparkling on her finger.

Nessa's attempt to change the subject had failed.

"Nessa, you should at least consider Karl's offer," Paul said.

Nessa poured a little cream into her coffee and began stirring. "It's only been ten weeks since we got the news about Erich. It's too soon."

Paul cut off a piece of pie with his fork. "Maybe. But give it some thought. You don't have to agree to marry Karl right away, but at some point you have to move on."

Nessa frowned. Ever since Paul and Annie had fallen in love, he'd become Cambridge's biggest advocate for marriage. That was all well and good for him and Annie. They were in love. But she didn't want to marry simply for the sake of getting married. How could she pledge herself to one man when her heart belonged to another?

"Ever since I left Germany people have been trying to talk me out of loving Erich," she muttered.

"Nobody's trying to talk you out of anything," Paul objected. "We know you loved him. Erich was your first love. But isn't there room in your heart for someone else as well?"

Nessa didn't answer. She still tensed every time someone used the words "Erich" and "was" in the same sentence.

"You could do a lot worse," Annie pointed out. "I've known Karl since he came here from Germany. Yes, he wants what he wants, but he has a good heart. He'll make a good husband and father."

"I'm happy for you two, but I just don't think I'm ever going to find your kind of happiness."

She'd settle for contentment, being able to go one day without crying. Try as she might to look on the bright side, she couldn't seem to find it. No wonder. She knew her heart was a fertile breeding ground for bitterness.

She'd prayed so hard for Erich's safety, but all her prayers had been in vain. And now she'd lost so much – her parents, her home, her old life. It seemed her grudges against God were piling up.

She opened the heart-shaped locket with Erich's picture that she always wore around her neck, and her throat tightened. *Oh, Erich.* Did he suffer in his last moments? She bit her lip and pushed the thought away. This was how she wanted to remember him – with a smile on his face, not bleeding and groaning in agony under the wreckage of a collapsed building in Berlin.

Annie laid her hand on Nessa's. "Nessa, don't torture yourself. Paul's right. You have to move on."

"I can't," she said. "I've lost too much."

"This isn't a perfect world, Nessa," Paul said sternly. "We've all lost people we love. I lost my best friend to the war. I lost my leg.

But life is about finding as well." He smiled at Annie and squeezed her hand. "Maybe instead of dwelling on what you've lost, it's time you started seeing what you can find."

Two days after Erich's unit had fled from the Russians, they waited in Berlin for Ivan to arrive there, the rumbling and thunder from the eastern horizon moving steadily toward them.

It was dawn. The rising sun accented the ruins around them in reds and yellows.

"In a day or two Ivan will flood into Berlin, my young friend," Niemeyer told Erich. They huddled in trenches whose crowns were lined with old mattresses for protection.

"And then he'll kill us all," a stumpy little man added, pulling his cap deeper over his face. Helmut Fackel had joined them from another *Volkssturm* unit whose numbers had been decimated to a mere handful. The words *Deutsche Reichsbahn* were embroidered across the front of his cap. "Civilians shouldn't have to do battle. I'm a railway worker, not a soldier." He spit on the ground. "And here I am crawling around in the mud like a dung beetle."

"Pay no attention to Fackel," Niemeyer told Erich. "He's a bit of a pessimist."

"I am not," Fackel countered. "I'm a realist. The Russians have bullied and tortured and raped their way across Germany. When they get to Berlin, there'll be no sense trying to surrender – they'll shoot us anyway just for the fun of it."

"They can't all be that merciless," Niemeyer replied.

"I'm not going to surrender to find out." Fackel patted his rifle. "I'm going down fighting."

Niemeyer pulled a white flag from his backpack. "As soon as I see Ivan, I'm waving this at him."

"That'll look nice riddled with bullets and soaked in your blood," Fackel taunted. "We'll bury you in it."

Erich turned his head to watch the Spree crawl by. It was dark and oily, clogged with pieces of furniture, suitcases, even a few corpses – the hopes, dreams and future of Germany drifting by in the filth.

Across the river stood an abandoned apartment house. The building's façade had been torn away, exposing the interiors of the apartments. It looked like a gigantic dollhouse. Living rooms with furniture arranged in comfy groupings awaited an evening with good friends. A dirty cream-colored living room carpet dangled down grotesquely, swaying in the breeze like a huge surrender flag. Bedrooms beckoned, with beds ready to be snuggled into. A bathtub tempted Erich to come and enjoy a cozy soak. We've been thrown back to the Stone Age, Erich thought.

A group of refugees rushed past the apartment building. A man lugged a brown leather suitcase and dragged a skittish mongrel on a leash behind him. Why hadn't that man been scooped up by the *Volkssturm*? A woman with two girls in tow followed him. One of the girls clutched a doll to her chest. She stumbled over a cinder block, dropping her doll. She began to cry, reaching out to where the doll lay, but the woman paid no attention, pulling her on through the rubble. On their heels a decrepit old man, wearing a winter coat and hat, hobbled on crutches, trying to keep up.

"The Russians will be here soon, my young friend," Niemeyer said for the tenth time in two days. The old man propped his rifle upright in front of him and studied it. "Does anyone here like leftovers?" No one answered his question. "Well, that's what we're fighting with. Look at these rifles. When were they made? Three hundred years ago during the Thirty Years' War? And they expect us to hold Ivan back with weapons like these?"

~

The sun had not yet risen on the following day when Kohl made his way through the ranks. "Wake up. The Russians have entered the city. Be ready."

Wake up? None of us slept a wink. Erich peered over the top of the trench to see ragged groups of refugees fleeing past them, heading west.

Then it began again. Mortar rounds crashing into the ruins nearby, converting the existing rubble into smaller pieces of rubble. After a few minutes the shelling was replaced by the rat-ta-tat-tat of small arms fire in the distance. *Street fighting.*

After that came the whine of a mortar shell followed by a flash of light a few meters to his right and a deafening explosion. A huge mound of earth lurched toward them, bringing blood and body parts with it. Then everything went black.

When he regained consciousness, Erich found himself on his back, buried in dirt from the chest down. He drew a breath to speak, but choked, his mouth full of dirt. He looked up to see Kohl racing around screaming orders.

But something was very wrong. Kohl's mouth was moving, but Erich couldn't hear his voice. He slapped his hands hard against his ears. Then again. No use. He was deaf. He pulled himself out of the dirt and scrambled to his feet, spitting the dirt out of his mouth.

He screamed in anguish until his throat burned in pain, but he couldn't hear his own screaming.

Kohl, shrieking silent screams, seized Erich's arm and dragged him over to a mound of earth with a foot protruding from it. They dug at the mound by hand, uncovering a dark blue cap emblazoned with the words *Deutsche Reichsbahn*. Under the cap they found the face of Fackel, his lifeless eyes wide open and full of dirt. He would no longer have to worry about going down fighting.

～

Over the next few hours, Erich's hearing gradually returned. His comrades' conversations at first sounded like mumbling, then like voices echoing in a subway tunnel. Kohl's curses and insults were the first sounds he could discern clearly. How often he had wanted to shoot the man. And now he was so thankful to be able to hear again that he wanted to hug him.

"The Russians are only a few streets away," Kohl yelled. "Get ready to defend the lives of your mothers and sisters and wives."

Russian rifle and machine gun fire tore into the mattresses on the top of the trenches and Erich spotted Russian troops zigzagging through the rubble in their direction.

"Shoot them. Shoot them. Kill them!" Kohl screamed.

A few men took aim and fired. "What's wrong with the rest of you cowards?" Kohl shrieked. "Kill them, kill ..."

Erich turned to see why Kohl had stopped in mid-sentence. Niemeyer stood over him. He had clubbed Kohl in the head with the butt of his rifle. Then he threw down his weapon, ran to his field pack and removed his white flag, waving it at the Russians. "*Tovaritch! Tovaritch!*"

As the Russian troops swarmed their position, Erich and his comrades dropped their weapons, raising their arms in surrender. The Russians bullied their captives into groups of about ten, and then marched them away. Niemeyer ended up in a different group and Erich never saw him again.

After a hundred meters, the soldiers ordered Erich's group to stop, throwing several field shovels at their feet and gesturing with their rifles at the ground. The message was clear – they were going to dig their own graves.

When they had finished the grave, a Russian major brandished his gun and barked something in Russian at his men. Erich stared at the major and then at the three guards. Another Russian, a lieutenant, Erich thought, translated into broken German. "He say, climb in hole and stand side by side."

Before they could obey, a howl made Erich jump. An old man,

teetering on the edge of the pit had turned around to face the Russians, raising his hands. "I was never a Nazi," he wailed. "Please don't shoot me. I have a wife, children, grandchildren."

"You all Nazis!" the lieutenant screamed. He stepped closer to the old man. "You invade, kill Russian wives and children – five years."

"But they forced me to join the *Volkssturm*," the man wept, falling to his knees. "The Nazis said they would kill me if I didn't fight."

The lieutenant leveled his revolver at the old man's face. "Now Hitler kaput. Now we kill you."

The sound of the detonation sent Erich to his knees. The old man's head jerked back at a sickening angle, spurting blood, and his body plummeted absurdly onto his back into the hole.

Two more old men standing at the edge of the pit had also been startled off balance and had tumbled into the hole as well. The lieutenant gunned them down as they struggled to get out.

Then he waved his revolver at the rest of the captives. "All you get in hole now," he commanded.

Erich stood in the line trembling. In a moment, the Russians would shoot them and then cover them with dirt. If Berlin were ever rebuilt, they would rebuild it right over their corpses.

A few streets away he heard gunfire. Probably other *Volkssturm* units fighting the Russians. Or other Russian firing squads.

The sun had almost dipped below the horizon and darkness began engulfing the city. Maybe he should make a break for it. If he could just slip into those shadows over there, maybe he could get away before his captors could get a shot off.

But it was too late. The major said something to his lieutenant and the lieutenant repeated it to one of the guards, who snapped a fresh cartridge into his machine gun. Erich clenched his fists, preparing himself for the end. *Goodbye, Nessa.*

The man with the machine gun leveled it at the prisoners and began firing from left to right. Just as the man to his left fell,

Erich flinched and jerked his head to the right and felt a bullet sting his left cheek and graze his ear. As he tumbled backward, the man to his right shrieked in agony and fell on top of him. Erich held his breath and remained motionless, although the side of his face felt as if someone had extinguished a burning cigarette on his skin.

In the near darkness he heard footsteps shuffle away. A motor started and the Russians left the killing grounds, apparently planning to return when it was daylight to fill in the grave.

Erich slipped his hand into his pocket, removing his handkerchief. He pressed it hard against his face and played dead for the next hour, thanking God for his good fortune, praying that the Russians hadn't left a guard behind to finish off anyone who had survived.

Then he crawled out of the tangle of bodies. He still heard gunfire and explosions in the distance, but not a sound nearby. He searched the pockets of his fallen comrades for anything that might prove useful. He found some matches as well as an apple. Then he inched out of the pit and fled toward the faint rays of light in the western sky, stumbling through ruins and rubble, determined to reach the American lines. Behind him he heard the Russians moving steadily west through Berlin, shelling the city before them as they went.

After a few kilometers he found an abandoned two-story home that seemed intact. He lit one of his precious matches and slipped into the basement, crawling over furniture into a far corner. Through a basement window he saw the moon rising through clear skies. All the better for enemy bombers.

But what seemed at first to have been an abandoned neighborhood was now alive with the crunching of footsteps and the murmur of voices. Erich crept over to a window. In the moonlight he saw men and women throwing things from the windows of an apartment building to people standing on the street below. A mantle clock thrown from a second story window missed a man's outstretched hands, crashing to the street, and exploding into a thousand pieces.

"Can't you catch, you idiot?" the man in the window hissed. "Are you trying to wake the entire neighborhood?"

"Wake the whole neighborhood?" the man on the street replied. "No one lives here anymore. Throw the stuff *to* me, not over my head."

Refugees with bundles and suitcases moved past the looters, disappearing into the darkness. Erich returned to his corner of the basement and sat down. Overcome by exhaustion, he tucked his thighs against his chest, leaned his forehead on his knees and drifted into uneasy dreams.

He awoke the next morning to pain and hunger. He left the basement and walked to the front door of the house. The ever-present Russian Army rumbled in the east, but he was too tired and hungry to care. In a bathroom cabinet he found bandages, aspirin, and iodine. He washed his wound with some schnapps he found in the kitchen and examined it in the bathroom mirror. There was a horizontal crease along his cheek and part of his earlobe was gone. It was ugly and crusted with dried blood, but had stopped bleeding. He dressed it, then sat in the corner of the kitchen and feasted on some stale dinner rolls that he found in the pantry.

At dusk he moved west, figuring it was safer to travel at night. The sound of the Russian artillery was louder now. He made his way through the sea of rubble, sometimes crawling over the remains of buildings that had been blown off their foundations and blocked the roadway.

After a few hundred meters he found an oasis in a desert of ruins – a small two-story house, old and tilting to the right, stood wedged between two apartment buildings. It was mostly intact, except for a hole in the roof. The front door stood open, a sure sign that the owners had left in a hurry.

In the living room he lit a match. A pendulum clock hung next to the door, its weights drooping to the floor. On the wall opposite the front door hung a portrait of Kaiser Wilhelm. The former leader of Germany wore a sky-blue uniform with a large gold, glimmering star on his chest. Against another wall stood a couch. A cabinet behind it contained dishes and crockery. Nothing had been overturned or ransacked, which probably meant the owners had only recently fled.

Erich found a candle and lit it. He left the living room and passed through a small hallway that led to a bedroom. A clothes cabinet stood against a wall, its doors open. In it he found a pair of gray trousers and a shirt, exchanging them for what he was wearing. He fingered a winter coat. It was moth-eaten, but still an improvement over his muddy, bloody uniform coat.

On the nightstand next to the bed stood a framed picture of a girl in her white confirmation dress. He picked up the photograph. She had dark hair and full lips. She held a bouquet of flowers and a hymnal and beamed into the camera as if she hadn't a care in the world. Why hadn't the family taken the picture with them?

The photo reminded him of the confirmation picture of Nessa that hung in the living room of her home. He fell onto the bed, held the picture to his chest and wept.

Erich slept until the sun woke him. He was still clutching the picture. He got up. The leg that had been injured at Frau Sturm's during the bombing still smarted, but felt much better, despite what he had been through the past days. He made his way to the kitchen where he found a shelf laden with home-canned food. Beans, carrots, plums and pears – a Garden of Eden in jars! God had blessed him with manna in the wilderness!

He took a seat at the kitchen table and popped open a jar of pears and one of beans. As he ate, he thought of breakfast at home before the war. He picked up the jar of beans and laughed. His mother would have never served beans for breakfast. At home the table was spread with a red and white tablecloth, laden with Brötchen and raspberry jam, dark bread and honey, together with sliced meats and sausage, boiled eggs and fruit, hot milk, and coffee. His mother would sing while preparing the meal, the canary in the living room joining in.

What time was it in America right now? he wondered. Was his family gathered around a table enjoying a meal? Did they talk of him? Were they praying for him? Perhaps, after such a long silence, they thought he was dead.

He finished his breakfast and left the kitchen, stepping into a large courtyard. He sat down on the ground and leaned against the courtyard wall, staring up at the sky. He still heard the din of the advancing Russians, but couldn't tell whether they had moved any closer. To look at the sky one would think peace ruled the world.

"Heaven knows no war," he murmured. Had he heard that saying somewhere or had he just made it up? He didn't know. He closed his eyes, absorbing the rays of the sun on his face, breathing calmly for the first time in days, soaking in the comforting warmth. Within a few minutes he fell asleep.

Even though he hadn't wanted to linger, the much-needed rest did him good, and when he awoke, he explored the rest of the house. He followed a narrow staircase to the second story. He stepped into a bedroom and gasped. A pale, bearded man stood against a wall, eyes open in terror, mouth agape. Erich stumbled back. The man stumbled back. Erich thrust his head forward to get a better look at the man. The stranger did the same.

Erich pointed at the man. "Who are you?" The man in the full-length mirror pointed back at him. He approached the image in the glass and stared in disbelief. His face, beard and hair were filthy with dried mud. Good Lord, is that me?

Then he heard movement downstairs. When he moved to hide, the floor creaked beneath his feet, so he froze in place.

"Is someone up there?" a man's voice called from the first floor.

Erich didn't answer. Was it the Gestapo? The police? The Russians? But none of those people would bother asking questions, he realized. They'd just charge up the stairs and shoot him.

"I know you're up there," the man downstairs called. "I mean you no harm."

"Who are you?" Erich called down.

"Trust me, I won't hurt you."

It had to be a trick. Erich looked for a way out of the bedroom besides the stairs. The only possibility was the window. He could jump to the street below, but he'd probably break both legs in the process. He looked up and saw a hole in the roof. He could crawl through that hole and ...

"I'm coming up," the man downstairs announced, beginning a slow, creaky ascent of the stairs.

Erich looked around for something to use as a weapon. He spotted a lamp and ripped the cord from the wall and held the lamp above his head, ready to attack. He backed up, banging into the mirror. He heart was beating so violently, he was sure it was going break a rib. Where could be hide? he wondered. Behind the bedroom door! He lunged forward and ducked behind it.

He heard the man stop at the top of the stairs. Then he saw a gun come through the doorway at the end of a hand. This man meant no harm and yet he had a gun? The stranger stepped into the bedroom and Erich brought the lamp down hard on the arm. The man dropped the weapon and it tumbled in Erich's direction. He snatched it and pointed it at the intruder.

The man raised his arms. He was smallish, in his mid-twenties, and wore a dingy cap and a full beard. "Listen, I only carry the gun for protection," he said. "I wasn't going to hurt you, I promise." He stepped closer. "What in the world happened to your face? Did someone shoot you?"

"Yes," Erich said, waving the gun at him. "Now don't come any closer."

The trespasser looked Erich over. "Hey, are you Jewish?"

Was this a trap? "Of course not."

"The beard. Your coloring. You look Jewish."

"I haven't shaved or bathed in weeks. That's mud on my face."

The man took another step toward him. Erich pointed the weapon at the stranger's head. "That's close enough. I mean it."

"Your eyes are blue, but that doesn't mean anything. I have cousins with blue eyes and they're as Jewish as Abraham." He put his hand over his mouth as though he had revealed a secret better kept hidden. "Oh, no," he mumbled behind his cupped hand.

Erich's eyes widened. He waved the gun toward the man. "*You are* Jewish, aren't you?"

The stranger folded his arms across his chest. He gave an embarrassed laugh, then unfolded his arms, dropping them to his side. "Looks like I can't keep a secret. My parents were Russian Jews."

Erich lowered his weapon. "You were almost right about me being Jewish. I'm a *Mischling*."

"Don't let the Nazis hear you say that a *Mischling* is someone who is *almost* Jewish," the man quipped. "To them, just a few drops of Jewish blood makes you completely Jewish." He smiled, reaching out his hand. "My name is Isaak, Isaak Aleksandrovich."

Erich took his hand. "Erich Reinhold. I'm trying to reach the American lines before the Russians overrun this area."

"So am I. I don't suppose you have anything to eat. I'm starved."

"Follow me."

Erich led the stranger down the stairs and to the kitchen to show him his find.

Isaak stopped in his tracks and stared in disbelief. "Blessed be the God of Isra'el."

Erich smiled. *Indeed.*

Isaak opened a jar of carrots. "I never really cared for carrots," he quipped while chewing, "but beggars can't be choosers." He looked at Erich and then down at himself. "Although I've seen beggars who look better than we do."

Erich laughed. "Do you have family?"

"I doubt it. When I came home from an errand two years ago, I found my parents' apartment empty. A neighbor told me that they had been picked up by the Gestapo. I never saw them again." He shook his head. "I've been a U-Boat ever since."

"So have I," Erich said.

"Are you an orphan, too?"

"No, my family's in America."

Isaak stopped chewing. "Why on earth didn't you go with them?"

"My fiancée and I stayed behind to work in the underground. But she's in America now as well."

"Love makes you do crazy things, doesn't it?"

Erich's thoughts raced away to be with Nessa. He clenched his jaw, momentarily overcome by the sadness of separation. "Yes, it certainly does," he managed.

Erich and his new companion left their refuge that afternoon instead of waiting until dusk. The gunfire and shelling in the east had grown louder and it seemed there was no time to lose – if the Russians caught up to them, they'd have to face a firing squad.

They had walked for an hour when they heard the roar of airplane engines behind them and machine gun fire ahead of them. Russian fighter planes. He had seen them circling overhead earlier in the day – now they were picking off the refugees who were on the road that led west.

"We should have waited until dark to leave," Erich said, as one of the planes swooped around in their direction.

"We need to take cover," Isaak yelled. "Over there." Isaak sprinted toward an apartment building, with Erich on his heels.

They zigzagged through the rubble, swerving around abandoned furniture and vehicles, all the while pursued by bullets from the plane, throwing up dust and dirt all around them. Just before they reached the building a row of bullets worked its way along the ground ahead of Erich and up Isaak's back. His friend threw his arms up, staggered a few steps and fell onto his face near the building. Erich caught up to him, grabbed his arms and dragged him to a broken basement window. He jumped inside, then pulled Isaak in after him.

They lay in a corner on the damp floor while the Russian plane continued to strafe the building, sending machine gun rounds through the basement window and ricocheting off the walls.

"It's no use," Isaak said, coughing up blood onto his beard. "They know we're here." He coughed up more blood. "I'm dying. Leave me and save yourself."

"I'm not leaving you," Erich said sternly. He removed his cap and pressed it over a wound that had gone through Isaak's back and exited through his chest.

Then a deafening explosion shook the building, sending debris and dust raining onto them from the first floor.

"They're shooting missiles at us," Isaak gasped. He expelled more blood and laughed. "Killing mice with missiles."

"Lie still. You need to save your strength."

Another explosion rocked the building and Erich leaned over Isaak to protect him from falling debris.

Then all was silent. "Maybe they're gone," Erich said, raising his head. He looked at his friend, who stared at the ceiling. Isaak was the one who was gone.

Late May, 1945.

Katydids chirped at one another, filling the air with their shrill songs. The sun glared off the roof of the barn, intensifying an already hot, humid morning.

Nessa sat on the front porch swing, clinging to a tissue moist with tears and staring toward the Appalachians, praying that it was all a big mistake, wishing Erich would step out of the forests that covered those mountains to take her into his arms, kiss her, and give her a reason to go on living. Wishing somewhere another woman named Nessa, and not her, was trying to figure out what to put into the vacuum left behind by her loss.

Then shame set in. How could she be so selfish as to wish her misery on someone else? To prefer someone else to suffer in her place?

The front door swung open and Karl stepped out onto the porch, joining her on the swing.

"Nessa, I feel like you've been putting me off." Karl always got right to the point. "It's been almost two months since I asked you. Surely you've had enough time to think about it."

She tensed. "Yes, I have, but ..."

He interrupted her. "I know it's hard losing someone you love. I lost Erich, too. But he's not coming back. Don't you think it's time to move on?"

She scowled at him. "No, I don't. It's only been four months since we got the news."

That silenced him, but only for a moment.

"Nessa, dear, I'm not trying to pressure you. But you know my unit's leaving for Germany in a few days. I'll be gone for months. I'm not asking you to marry me this instant, but I would like an answer, something I can hang on to while I'm far away from those I love."

Nessa frowned. "It seems to me you've spent a great deal of time far away from those you love."

"That was my parents' decision. They encouraged me to come to America to make a new life for myself. It's a good thing I did. I've been able to help all of you." And he had. His job had brought in much needed income for the family. "Please don't make me feel guilty for still being alive," he added.

"Please don't make me feel guilty for not feeling alive," she replied.

Mr. Taylor, their elderly neighbor, shuffled past the front gate. He smiled and waved. "Good morning, you two."

Karl nodded and returned their neighbor's wave.

"Good morning, Mr. Taylor," Nessa managed. How different life was in America than in Berlin. Everything was so stable here, the people so happy. Could she eventually be happy? She wasn't sure.

"Nessa," Karl urged.

"I just can't believe he's dead." She laid a hand over her heart. "Surely I'd know it here if he was."

"What about the rest of us? Wouldn't we know? Wouldn't my mother?"

She had no answer for that, so he continued. "If I had the power to bring him back to you, I would. But I don't. Nobody does and nobody can. He's gone and you can't go back to when he was alive. The only way you can go is forward, Nessa. Let me help you do that."

She laid her hand on his. "Give me until tomorrow. I promise I'll have an answer for you then."

Tomorrow came.

A storm thundered across the plateau, rumbling above the forests, sending sparks of lightning earthward. Nessa sat on the living room couch rereading a letter from Erich. Greta entered the room and took a seat next to her.

"Nessa," she said, putting an arm around her, "you really must move on with your life. Erich would want you to."

"I know he would. It's just that he's the only man I've ever loved." How would she ever be able to cut the cord that connected her with his memory?

"I realize that. And I understand how you must miss him. There isn't a day goes by that I don't mourn the loss of my son. I don't think I'll ever get over it. But I've lived my life. You still have yours to live."

"It's not worth living without Erich," Nessa sobbed, tears stinging her eyes. Sometimes it seemed so unfair that he was gone while she was left here to struggle on without him.

Greta pointed through the window to the roses blooming in the flowerbed. "Every year winter comes and kills the blooms, but they come back every spring. Life goes on, Nessa dear. That's how it's meant to be. We can't change that."

Life could have gone on beautifully if Erich had left Germany with her. "If only ..." Nessa whispered.

Greta laid a hand on her arm and cut her off. "Don't say it. We have no 'if onlys.' We just have what we have."

Greta was right. Nessa knew that. But it was small comfort. She had believed Erich would come to her, but he hadn't. She did have Karl, but what if she agreed to marry him and *he* never came back from Germany?

"Karl has asked you to marry him. He deserves an answer."

Why does everyone keep telling me that? "I don't love him."

"No, not the way you loved Erich. That was the love of youth, full of passion and dreams. But love can take many forms. It can start small and grow."

Could she find a small amount of love for Karl? He was often arrogant, but he was also hardworking and responsible. He cared for his family.

"Erich's gone, but I still have another son, and I'd like to see him happy," Greta continued. "I'd like to see you happy as well – and settled into a happy marriage."

Nessa watched the storm as it moved south, away from Cambridge. "I told Karl I'd give him an answer today."

Later that afternoon, her answer came. "Yes." But "yes" delayed for six months. "I still need time to heal."

Karl slipped his arm around her. "I understand. I don't mind waiting until I get back to set a date for the wedding."

He leaned forward, wanting her lips. She offered him her cheek.

He sighed in resignation. "I'll make you happy. I promise."

Nessa forced a smile even though she was already half regretting her decision. Poor Karl. What kind of wife would she be if she were still mourning Erich? Erich had possessed everything that Karl didn't: Tenderness. Modesty. A sense of humor.

But maybe marrying Karl was for the best. She would officially be part of the Reinhold family. She'd have security and a measure of happiness. As Greta had said, love took many forms. Maybe in time she'd find a way to love Karl.

She was kidding herself. Deep down she knew it.

A few weeks later First Lieutenant Karl Reinhold sped along the Schlierbacher Landstrasse east of Heidelberg, on his way to a meeting in Mannheim. On his right the Neckar River flowed lazily westward as it pressed towards its confluence with the Rhine a few kilometers away.

He eased his jeep into one curve after another as the road mimicked each bend in the river. The sun, nearly on the western horizon, was often blinding. He had just passed Dilsberg and was leaning into a sharp right-hand curve when a truck approaching from the opposite direction appeared out of the sun's glare and crossed over into his lane. He reacted instantly, swerving sharply to the right, his overcompensation taking him off the road and into the river.

Weeks afterwards his body washed up downstream.

CHAPTER TWENTY-SIX

June, 1945.

The war was over, but Berlin, like much of Germany, lay in ruins. The Volk were exhausted. Neighbor no longer denounced neighbor. No one in Germany could remember having been a Nazi.

So many Germans now boasted about how they had helped German Jews that one had to ask how anything dreadful could have possibly happened to God's chosen people during the previous twelve years.

In Germany, the chain of command had been broken. Gone were those who demanded submission and obedience, a concept that had been drummed into every German from the cradle. Now the Führer, the architect of Germany's brief rise and utter ruin, was dead, and the Nazis had vanished from the stage as if they had been shooed away by an invisible magician.

Berlin's infrastructure was nearly nonexistent. No electrical power, no postal service, practically no communications services. No newspapers or radio stations. Few trains running.

Nussbaum had returned from Lisbon to what was left of Berlin and on this sunny day sat with Konrad at an outdoor table at Café

Nola. A small band played as several of the guests danced on the sidewalk.

"At least we don't have to hide in the back of the café anymore, wondering who might come through the front door to arrest us," Nussbaum rejoiced.

"I just wish Erich was sitting here with us," Konrad lamented. "I really feel for Nessa. I got a letter from her a few months after Erich died. She sounded miserable and didn't have the slightest idea what the future held for her. Of course, neither do we."

"I miss Erich, as well," Nussbaum said and sighed. "But he won't be back. The rest of us must simply move on and do what we can to survive. Be thankful you have this job here at the café," Nussbaum added. "Already you have a way to pay your bills."

Konrad nodded. "I am grateful." He looked at his watch. "Speaking of paying bills, my break is over." He got up and made his way to the table where a young couple had just sat down.

The band struck up the latest hit in Berlin, a foxtrot. A band member stepped forward and began to sing:

"My heart is full of sadness, as through the streets I pass,
But what's the use of fretting, the past is in the past,
And in spite of all that's happened, I still believe in Berlin.
Berlin is bouncing back."

"Finally, peace," Nussbaum said to himself, watching the band play on.

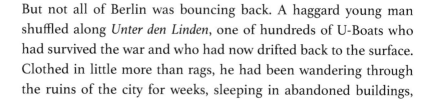

But not all of Berlin was bouncing back. A haggard young man shuffled along *Unter den Linden*, one of hundreds of U-Boats who had survived the war and who had now drifted back to the surface. Clothed in little more than rags, he had been wandering through the ruins of the city for weeks, sleeping in abandoned buildings, foraging for food.

He came to a display window in a shop that had somehow

survived the bombs. He studied his reflection. He looked like an escapee from a death camp: emaciated, filthy tatters for clothing, mismatched shoes, no socks, disheveled hair and beard. Erich was staring at a man he didn't recognize.

As he moved along a young woman crossed his path and the scent of roses wafted in his direction. He had a vague recollection of walking along this same street ages ago with Nessa. She had always smelled of roses. All he smelled these days was the stench of Berlin burning and smoldering, and of bodies rotting under the rubble.

But the city buzzed all around him. A horse-drawn cart rattled past over the cobblestones, a dozen turnips rolling around in the bed. Armies of gaunt women in shoddy dresses scavenged through the ruins, trying to cobble back together the scattered pieces of Berlin. They collected bricks and cinder blocks, sorted them, then removed the mortar. Perhaps, they hoped, Berlin could someday be puzzled back together again. And if they were lucky, they would be able to cobble back together what was left of their families and their lives.

Erich stopped and watched the women for a while. Where were all the men?

Stupid question – millions of them lay dead in Russia and France and Poland.

An old woman shuffled past him in a filthy dress, a soiled head-scarf tied under her chin. A pair of oversized, tattered slippers augmented her wardrobe. Like precious jewels, she carried a handful of potatoes in her apron. Erich's stomach growled. Where had she gotten those potatoes? He moved on, hoping to find something for his own aching belly.

He finally did cross paths with some men, all of them old, who were dragging the crushed remains of a fellow Berliner out of a bombed-out home. Two others squatted, hands wet with blood, next to an emaciated dead horse that lay in the street. The animal stared toward the sky while the men carved steaks from its flanks.

For several more days he stumbled through what remained of

Berlin, helping wherever he could, while his fellow Berliners buried their dead and dug out from under the rubble. As he watched the city start to piece itself together again, he tried to figure out how he was going to piece his own life together.

Then one afternoon he found himself standing in front of Café Nola. At last something familiar – although the front of the building was now pockmarked with bullet holes. He really didn't understand how he had managed to stumble upon it, for he had great difficulty finding his way around in what was left of Berlin. The city that he grown up in had been blown to pieces and few of the landmarks that had existed before the war had survived.

He peered through the front door for a long time, then slipped inside. The café was doing a brisk business. Obviously, not everyone was having to pick through the ruins to find something to eat. He shuffled to the back of the café and took a seat at an empty table. He knew that he would be shooed away as soon as the waiter discovered that he had no money, but for a moment this was a place to sit to try to remember something of who he had been.

At the next table a couple in shabby clothing stood up. "Waiter," the man called, lifting his hand to draw the man's attention.

Konrad came to their table to do their bidding. Good Lord, it really was Konrad!

Erich tried to speak, but emotion choked his speech.

"We'd like to pay," said the customer.

"Certainly," Konrad said, making a slight bow. He lowered his voice. "I'm sorry about the limited menu – most of our food comes from the black market, you know. How was the strudel?"

"Very good. Excellent."

"That will be two marks thirty, please."

The man paid, put on his hat, and he and his wife walked past Erich on their way out of the café.

Konrad turned and made his way to Erich's table. "Yes, sir, what can I get ...?" He stared at Erich as though he were seeing a ghost. "Erich?"

Another voice called from behind them. "Did you say 'Erich,' Konrad? Who are you talking to?"

A large, bald man stepped out of the shadows. It was Nussbaum. "Erich, it is you!" He rushed across the room and grabbed him, lifting him from his chair and embracing him in a bear hug. After a few seconds he released him and held him at arm's length. "When I returned from Palestine a few weeks ago, I never thought I'd run into a dead man."

Konrad was shaking his head in disbelief. He took Erich's hand, apparently to ascertain that his old friend was indeed warm and alive. "Herr Nussbaum's right. You're supposed to be dead. You died in that bombing raid. How in the world ...?"

Erich smiled a weak smile at Konrad. "The day before that air raid I lent my ID and ration card to Christian and forgot to get them back in the panic of the air raid. I remember seeing him duck into Frau Sturm's basement just before we did."

"So that's what happened," Konrad said. "The rescue workers found your ID on Christian's body, thinking it was you." He moved his hand to Erich's shoulder. "Erich, I'm sorry to say that Frau Sturm died in that air raid as well."

"I'm so sorry to hear that," he said, shaking his head. "I'll miss her."

"The other sad thing I must tell you is that after we thought you had been killed, I wrote Nessa and gave her the bad news."

"Nessa thinks I'm dead?" Erich fell back onto his chair in sick panic. "Dear God!" He reached out and grabbed Nussbaum's arm. "I have to get a message to her!"

"Sadly, you won't find a working telegraph in all of Berlin," Nussbaum told him. "The telephone system is in shambles and it will take months before postal services are up and running again in Berlin."

He'd already waited too long. Years too long. He looked from one friend to the other. "There must be something we can do. You must still have *some* connections. I have to get to America."

Konrad shrugged and looked at Nussbaum, whose expression was noncommittal. "I'm not sure that will be possible for some time. Everyone wants to get to America these days." Nussbaum put his hand on Konrad's shoulder. "Let's contact Frau Kleist and see what she can do for us."

"I'll send a courier to her house right away," Konrad said. He turned to Erich. "Just remember, my friend, this could take quite a while and there are no guarantees."

Erich's shoulders sagged. "I understand. No guarantees."

Nussbaum pressed Erich onto a chair. "Now we're going to get you something to eat and then you're going to tell us the story of what happened to you and how you managed to come back from the dead."

Food. How Erich ached for a real meal after wandering the streets for weeks, struggling to survive, eating garbage and drinking out of mud puddles. But that ache was nothing compared to the sharp need he now felt to get to America, to reunite with Nessa and his family.

After Erich finished his meal, he told his story. How he had found himself in a field hospital after the bombing raid and how he walked away from it one night. He described his time fighting in the *Volkssturm*, waging war against the advancing Red Army and how he managed to survive that firing squad with only a scarred face. And how his friend, Isaak, died in his arms. Erich then talked of wandering the streets of Berlin in search of anything to eat.

"I don't know how long I did that," he finished. "I spent most of my time combing through the rubble of demolished buildings looking for food or something to trade for food. One day I found three packs of cigarettes in the ruins of a store. I traded them for a loaf of bread and a few carrots. I can't remember the last time I slept in a bed."

"That's all over now, my friend," Konrad assured him. "I have a small apartment – you can stay with me. Soon you'll be strong enough to work again. As a matter of fact, we need an errand boy here at the café. I think I can get you the job."

~

Time seemed to move in slow motion while Erich waited for the hope of getting to America to possibly turn into reality. Meanwhile he contrived desperate plots to get to Nessa, like stowing away on a ship bound for New York. Or sneaking aboard a military plane on its way to anywhere in America.

He even went to the American embassy in Berlin and asked if they could get a message to Nessa. "You'll have to take that matter up with the U.S. Army Headquarters in Zehlendorf," the man at the desk told him. Erich made his way there, only to discover that thousands of other Germans displaced by the war were also attempted to contact relatives in America and that it would be many months before his request could be processed.

July was on the horizon and summer temperatures combined with the stench of bodies rotting under the rubble and raw sewage collecting on the streets made life in Berlin that much more miserable.

One humid evening Erich returned to Café Nola from running errands to find Konrad waiting for him on the sidewalk. "I've got some great news," his friend said excitedly.

"What is it?"

"Start working on your English."

"Do what?"

"You're going to America."

Suddenly the burden that had been weighing Erich down for what seemed a lifetime, melted into nothing. He dropped onto a chair and wept. "What? How?"

"It turns out Frau Kleist has connections with the American authorities in Berlin. She got you an American visa."

"That's impossible," he said, brushing away the tears, "I don't even have a passport."

Konrad reached into his pocket and produced a German passport. "What does this look like?"

Erich took it and shook his head. "Konrad, I can't use a forged passport."

"It's real! Not forged, real!"

"There's just one problem."

"Getting to America?"

"Exactly."

"Don't you suppose the woman who got you a passport could also find a way to get you to America?"

Erich sat speechless. Could it be this easy? After everything he'd gone through, it didn't seem possible.

Konrad reached into his pocket again. "Here are your travel documents and your visa. You leave in a few days. The trains are still unreliable, so we've arranged for a car to take to Amsterdam. From there you'll sail to New York."

"Thank you, my friend!" Erich sobbed, taking Konrad's hand.

"May God be with you." Konrad leaned over and embraced him.

Surely God was already with him. God had given him a chance to find Nessa and to make a new beginning in a new country. God hadn't abandoned him after all. The lost sheep had been found.

July, 1945.

Erich had said goodbye to Konrad and Nussbaum and Frau Kleist. He had said goodbye to Germany, the land of his youth, the land that had nurtured his family for generations. Soon he would be in America, the country he hoped would nurture many new generations of Reinholds.

CHAPTER TWENTY-SEVEN

The telephone rang at the Reinholds and Marianne Schulz rushed to answer it. It had to be her son-in-law, Franz, with an update on their return trip to Cambridge with Karl's body. Marianne and her husband were minding the Reinholds home and livestock while they were away. "Hello Franz?"

There was a brief silence on the line. Then a voice spoke in German. "Mama, is that you? It's Erich."

Marianne closed her eyes at the shock of hearing a voice in her native language. "*Who* is this?" she demanded.

"It's me, Erich. Erich Reinhold. Oma, is that you?"

"Is this some kind of sick joke?" she snapped. "My grandson Erich is dead!"

Her husband, Rolf, hurried over and took the receiver from his wife's hand, putting it to his ear, while Marianne dropped in shock onto a nearby chair. "Hello, this is Rolf Schulz. Who is this? What's this all about?"

"Opa, it's Erich, your grandson."

"My grandson is dead," Rolf said. "My wife just told you that. I'm going to call the police if ..."

"No, Opa, there was a mistake. I'm alive. I'm at the train station here in town."

"What? Here in Cambridge?" Rolf raked his hand through his wispy hair in disbelief. His shout startled his wife out of her daze.

"Mama, Erich's alive! It's a miracle!" He turned his attention to Erich. "Where have you been all this time? Why didn't you let us know sooner that you were alive?" Tears spilled down Rolf's face. His grandson had come back from the dead.

"That's a long story. I did try to call from New York, but the long-distance operator said the phones in Cambridge were out of service. So I sent a telegram. Did you get it?"

"A telegram?"

"Yes. You never got it?"

"We had a terrible storm two days ago that knocked out both the telephone and telegraph lines. They just fixed the phone lines this morning. The telegraph lines are still down."

"Opa, can I talk to Nessa?"

"I'm sorry, Erich. She went to New York with your parents."

"New York? What on earth are they doing there?"

"They're picking up Karl."

"Karl? Why? Is he working in New York now?"

"Erich, Karl was killed in Germany."

Erich gasped, and then nearly shouted into the receiver. "What do you mean killed in Germany? What was he doing there?"

"He joined the Army Reserve last year. His unit was called up and sent to Heidelberg. A few weeks ago, his jeep skidded off the road into a river. He was killed."

Erich was too stunned to speak.

"I'm so sorry, Erich. This war has taken a great toll on our family. It was a great shock losing both you and Karl in the same year. You can't imagine what it did to your parents, to all of us." He paused to collect himself. "But this is wonderful news, a miracle. Nessa and your parents will be so excited to see you."

"When will they be home?"

"Tomorrow at noon. They were able to phone us with their

arrival time just before the lines went down. Listen, Erich, wait right there. We'll be there in a few minutes to fetch you."

~

Erich stood near the tracks, watching workers unload cargo from the train that had just arrived. Bulging canvas sacks full of mail and boxes of every size and shape from Montgomery Ward and Sears and Roebuck began to fill the platform, while men and women and children swarmed around the boxes like locusts in an attempt to spot their own shipment.

Erich heard someone call his name. He turned to see an older couple moving quickly toward him and he rushed to embrace them. "Oma, Opa, it's so good to see you again."

His grandparents wept as they hugged him. After a few moments, his grandmother pulled back and held him at arm's length. "Let's have a look at you. Except for the hair, you look just like your brother. But you're so skinny, Erich, dear. Too skinny. What happened to my pudgy little six-year-old? And how did you get that nasty scar on your face?"

Before Erich could answer, Rolf interjected, "He's just come through the war in Germany, Marianne. It's a miracle he's alive at all."

"We'll soon fill you full of good food," Marianne said, leading Erich toward the car. "I've prepared *Rolladen* and *Spätzle* for dinner. They were your favorites, remember? You'll have meat on your bones in no time."

They were barely to the car when Erich asked, "How's Nessa doing?"

His grandparents exchanged uncomfortable glances. "She's doing fine. She's adjusted well."

"That's good."

Marianne cleared her throat, then reached into the back seat and took his hand. "Yes, but there's more to it than that. Erich, we might as well tell you the truth. You're going to find out anyway. Nessa and your brother were engaged."

"What?" The news hit Erich like a bomb blast. Granted, Nessa had thought he was dead, but she sure hadn't waited long to replace him.

"We all urged her to move on with her life," Rolf said, "but her heart wasn't in it. Anyone could see that."

But she did move on. Still, he couldn't blame her. How could anyone expect her to wait for a dead man to return?

Nessa ignored the scenery that slid past her window as the train neared Cambridge. She was barely aware of Greta sitting stoically next to her, holding her hand. Nessa had already endured so many losses, and now Karl was lying a few feet behind her in the baggage car, waiting to be laid in a grave in the Old City Cemetery. She'd loved her parents deeply. She'd loved Erich desperately. She had hoped that one day she would grow to love Karl. Now all of them were gone. So many loved ones had vanished in such a short space of time.

A few days earlier she had stood by a ship in New York Harbor while workers unloaded Karl's casket. One word kept etching through her mind: Why? But no answer came.

The conductor, announcing their approach to Cambridge, interrupted Nessa's thoughts. As they passed over a bridge, she watched Wills Creek, brown and sluggish, meander by. Two minutes later Union Depot came into sight. In a few minutes Karl would be unloaded from the train like so much cargo. And after that she would help Greta arrange the funeral. After that they would lay Karl to rest. And after that?

At 11:45 that morning Erich and his grandparents were driving along Wheeling Avenue when they heard a train whistle sound. On their left the train rumbled past them in the direction of Union Depot.

Marianne checked her watch. "That has to be their train."

Erich slid across the back seat and rolled down the window and looked over at the train, studying the faces in the windows, hoping to catch a glimpse of Nessa or his parents. After so many years it felt strange to be so close to them.

But Erich's efforts were in vain. The train was too far away, the images too blurred. It moved ahead of them and soon all he could see was the caboose swaying back and forth.

By the time they pulled into the parking lot, passengers were disembarking while a small crew of men offloaded freight. Before Rolf could bring the vehicle to a full stop, Erich had his door open.

"Go ahead," his grandfather said. "We'll catch up with you."

Erich scarcely heard him. He dashed from the car and ran around the station house and onto the platform.

And then he saw Nessa, looking older, to be sure, and disturbingly worn and sad. She was dressed in black and standing with his parents – heads together, deep in discussion – at the end of the platform. Behind them stood a wooden casket draped in an American flag.

Erich stopped a few feet from them, joy and mourning wrestling within him.

After their conversation, his parents left Nessa and went into the station house, probably to sign for Karl's body, Erich surmised. Nessa watched them go, then laid her hand on the casket and bowed her head.

In prayer? Or was she mourning poor Karl? Had she fallen in love with him after all?

"Karl, I'm sorry," Nessa said. She was sorry for so many things. Sorry that two good men had died, leaving their parents with no hope for the future, no happy family gatherings, no weddings, no grandchildren. She was sorry she hadn't married Karl before he left. If she had, maybe there would have been a baby on the way, someone to carry on the family name. She was sorry for herself. She'd lost not only the man she had ever loved, but also the man she'd hoped to come to love.

At least the family had a son to bury this time. But with Erich ...

"Oh, Erich," she sobbed, dropping her hand from the casket.

"Nessa ..."

That voice. Was it the voice of a ghost? But even a ghost would be better than this horrible void.

She spun around and gasped, her heart pounding wildly. "Erich?" She had to be dreaming. "Dear God, you're alive!"

He moved closer. "I kept my promise," he said simply. "I returned to you. I made it to America."

She fell into his arms. "It really is you," she wept, barely able to breathe. "We thought you were dead."

"Believe me, I thought so, too, many times. I've been as close to hell as a man can get on this earth, but I'm here now. Please tell me you still want me."

"I've never stopped wanting you," she said, and kissed him.

With those words the awful memories of the past were swept away so new ones could be made. At last they would have their safe harbor.

AUTHOR'S NOTE

This is not a novel about submarines during World War II, but it is a book about U-Boats.

It is a love story, but also a story about Jews in Berlin who disappeared underground, submerging illegally below the surface of everyday life – people who came to be known as U-Boats.

In the wake of Nazi race laws in 1935, many Germans were reclassified as Jews. These people were proud of their Jewish heritage, but their reclassification meant they were undesirables and therefore in danger of deportation and death.

Many U-Boats spent the entire war living underground, rarely coming to the surface, but others looked more Aryan than even the average German and, although they were illegals, they were able to hide in plain sight using false identification papers and forged ration cards. They were visible, but their identities were invisible.

This is also the story about two young U-Boats who chose to stay in Germany and help other U-Boats escape the Nazi dragnet, two people who could have escaped Germany anytime they wished, but felt it more important to stay and help rescue others from imprisonment and death.

. . .

THE GERMAN TERMS used in this novel are translated in the glossary at the end of the book.

GERMAN TERMS USED

Translation of German terms used in the novel

Abendessen. Evening meal.

Arbeit macht frei. Work makes you free.

Aufstehen. Get up.

Bin gleich wieder da. (I'll) be right back.

Bitte. Please.

Blöder Hund. Stupid dog.

Brötchen. Bread roll.

Darf ich bitten? May I have this dance?

Das ist das Ende Deutschlands. This is the end of Germany.

Deutsche Reichsbahn. German Imperial Railway.

Deutsches Jungvolk. Boys' division of Hitler Youth.

(Es) freut mich. Glad to meet you.

Feldpost. Military mail.

Für Elise. For Elise (by Beethoven).

Gasthof zur Eiche. Inn at the Oak Tree.

Gott mit uns. God with us.

Guten Tag. Good day.

Habt Erbarmen! Have mercy!

Hat keinen Sinn. It's no use.

Hausverbot. Ban on entering a house.

Ich heisse ... My name is ...

Herr Wachtmeister. Officer (policeman).

Hey da, was machen Sie bloss? Hey there, what are you doing?

Hilf mir. Help me.

Hilfe bitte. Help, please.

Juden nicht erwünscht. Jews not welcome.

Juden raus. Throw the Jews out.

Kadavergehorsam. Following orders without thinking.

Kaffee. Coffee.

Lauter. Louder.

Mein Herr. Sir.

Meine Damen und Herren. Ladies and gentlemen.

Mein Kampf. My struggle.

Mittagessen. Midday meal.

Na, na, dann kommen Sie nur. Well, come on, let's do this.

Natürlich. Of course.

Post für Sie. A letter for you.

Rache ist doch süss, nicht wahr? Revenge is sweet, isn't it?

Rouladen and Spätzle. Rouladen and dumplings.

Ruhe bewahren. Stay calm.

Scherben bringen Glück. Broken glass brings good fortune.

Schlachtensee. A lake on the outskirts of Berlin.

Sofort aufmachen! Open up. Now!

Stehenbleiben ihr Juden oder ich schiesse!

Stand still, you Jews or I'll shoot!

Stillgestanden! Augen geradeaus! Stand still! Eyes straight ahead!

Verfixt und zugenäht! Damn it all!

Was machen Sie da? What are you doing?

Weggetreten! Dismissed!

Willkommen. Welcome.

Woran denkst du? What are you thinking about?

Zu Befehl, Herr Oberst! At your command, colonel!

"THE WALL BETWEEN US" BY
GERHARDT ROBERTS

A Cold War Historical Romance

IN COMMUNIST EAST GERMANY, Pastor Klaus Hirt has lost faith in the government and is not afraid to say so. But following his wife's dementia and painful death, he suffers a crisis of faith. All he has left is his anger against God and the government that has betrayed his people.

Stasi Agent Wilfrid Berg is intrigued when he finds himself in possession of a Bible thrown from a train into the snow. This sends him on a quest to discover the owner. He gets more than he bargains for when he meets Klaus Hirt's daughter.

In a country that rewards free speech with punishment and imprisonment, both men embark on a journey that will change their lives.

(Available on Amazon as a paperback or Kindle book.)

ABOUT GERHARDT ROBERTS

Gerhardt Roberts is a Professor of German who grew up in Germany and served as a German language linguist with the Army Security Agency. He is an expert on German history and he and his wife make frequent trips to Germany, where they lived when first married. He enjoys discussing all things German and can be contacted at the email address below.

DERSELTENERABE@GMAIL.COM

PLEASE VISIT Professor Roberts's website at: www.gerhardtroberts.weebly.com

Made in the USA
Middletown, DE
10 February 2022

60353044R00217